THE SCHOOL PSYCHOLOGY INTERNSHIP

Dr. Newman has used his many years of experience working with interns and field supervisors to create this comprehensive guide to the school psychology internship. The second edition of this text includes updated research and tools, including a new job interview video, and new templates for developing a cover letter, CV, and remediation plan. Expanded content includes brand new chapters focused on applying for doctoral internships through the APPIC Match process, and successfully transitioning from the internship into the early career.

Students and internship supervisors alike will find this easy-to-use guide helpful in alleviating anxiety around common internship concerns. Emphasis is placed on the idea that the internship year is a dynamic and formative experience, not a static event, and that interns and supervisors both must be proactive planners, coordinators, and shapers of the experience. Interns and supervisors will find this guide to be a critical support for planning and enacting a high-quality school psychology internship.

Daniel S. Newman, PhD, NCSP, is an associate professor in the school psychology program at the University of Cincinnati. His teaching and research focus on school consultation, clinical supervision, and professional issues in school psychology.

THE SCHOOL PSYCHOLOGY INTERNSHIP

A Guide for Interns and Supervisors

Second Edition

Daniel S. Newman, PhD

Routledge
Taylor & Francis Group

NEW YORK AND LONDON

First published 2020
by Routledge
52 Vanderbilt Avenue, New York, NY 10017

and by Routledge
2 Park Square, Milton Park, Abingdon, Oxon, OX14 4RN

Routledge is an imprint of the Taylor & Francis Group, an informa business

First edition published by Routledge 2012

Library of Congress Cataloguing in Publication Data
A catalog record for this book has been requested

ISBN: 978-1-138-23208-2 (hbk)
ISBN: 978-1-138-23209-9 (pbk)
ISBN: 978-1-315-31349-8 (ebk)

Typeset in Bembo
by Swales & Willis Ltd, Exeter, Devon, UK

Dedication

To Yael, Elan, and Galia: You inspire me to grow in new ways each and every day.

CONTENTS

FOREWORD

The Capstone Internship Experience: Shaping a Career as a School Psychologist

Mark E. Swerdlik, PhD, ABPP

ILLINOIS STATE UNIVERSITY

Not too long ago I visited with my former supervisor, Jim Mooney. In 1976, he served as Director of Diagnostic Services during the first year of my tenure as a school psychologist. We were collaborating on an article about the history of school psychology in Illinois, to be published in our state school psychology association newsletter. Being retired for many years, my former supervisor reflected on his career as a school psychologist spanning four decades. He noted that he had written a letter in 1954 to the then Illinois Director of Special Education, applying for what was described as "at least a year of supervised clinical practice in the individual examination of children of school age." Jim was accepted as the second trainee to what would in the next decade be referred to as a "school psychology internship." Thus, his career in school psychology was launched. Jim also commented on the enormous impact the supervision he received on his internship had on his development as a school psychologist. If you are a current or prospective intern supervisor, perhaps you have similar sentiments about your internship. As I reflect on both my master's and doctoral level school psychology internships, both school-based, I recognize the significant impact my supervisors had on shaping me as a professional school psychologist. If you are a current or prospective intern reading this book, my hope is that your internship experience will be as rewarding to you as it was for the many of us in our field who have practiced before you.

In addition to the potential for the significant impact the capstone internship experience can have on one's professional knowledge and skills, the reality is that completion of an internship is required for certification and/or licensure as a school psychologist in all fifty states. APA and NASP have developed internship standards, which have been adopted by state boards of education and professional psychology licensing boards, to satisfy requirements for school-based and/or independent practice. The *NASP Blueprint for Training and Practice* series has also had a significant impact on school psychology training and practice and subsequent development of the *NASP Model for Comprehensive and Integrative School Psychological Services*, also referred to as the NASP Practice Model. The authors of *NASP Blueprint III*, as compared to *Blueprint I and II*, recognize that competence in school psychology knowledge and skills is a developmental process. The *NASP Blueprint III* authors conceptualize trainees as demonstrating novice levels of competence prior to beginning their internship. The internship is viewed as a formative process of skill development with the expectation that after the capstone internship the trainee will be competent for entry-level practice as a school psychologist. Being an expert in any of the eight practice domains is not expected until after five to ten years of professional practice. Further, expert status is only expected in a limited number of domains. The *Blueprint III* also stresses the need to develop "rich" internship sites, both in terms of breadth and depth, that offer opportunities to build expanded competencies in all of the eight domains of practice. However, despite the requirements and guidelines offered by these documents, no two internships will provide the same experience. Individual internships will require interns, field, and university supervisors to collaborate to build the most diverse and enriching experience possible.

Since my former supervisor completed his internship in the 1950s, there has existed only a limited research base related to best practices in the administration of and supervision during the school psychology internship and the roles and responsibilities of all of the "players," including the intern, field, and university supervisors. *The School Psychology Internship: A Guide for Interns and Supervisors, Second Edition* (hereafter, the *Guide*) represents a significant contribution in applying the relevant literature from clinical, counseling, and organizational psychology to the school psychology internship to identify best practices during a school psychology internship. Dr. Newman views school psychology as a field experiencing perpetual change and the internship as part of the ecology of the system that serves as the setting for the non-doctoral or doctoral-level internship. Newman also stresses throughout the *Guide* that the habits of professional learning practiced and established during the internship year carry over into the intern's early career.

For many decades, surveys on job satisfaction of school psychologists have suggested that the quality of the supervision school psychologists receive in their professional lives, including their internship, is one of the most important correlates of career satisfaction or dissatisfaction. Further, these surveys relate that in practice most field supervisors, and many university supervisors, have not received any formal training in supervision. The *Guide*'s "keystone" chapter focuses on supervision during the internship and includes an up-to-date review of supervision models, frameworks, and techniques of effective supervision to help field and university intern supervisors structure supervision during all phases of the internship.

Dr. Newman brings to this *Guide* his years of experience working with interns and field supervisors in his role as his university's internship supervisor and instructor of their required internship seminar. The *Guide* is organized around "big ideas" and provides a thorough review of the relevant literature, integrating numerous examples presented through illustrative vignettes to reinforce effective practices.

The internship is addressed through all of its stages and phases with implications for both interns and their supervisors using a developmental perspective. After an introductory first chapter, the *Guide* begins with a chapter new to the second edition focusing on the Association of Psychology Postdoctoral and Internship Centers (APPIC) Match process for doctoral-level intern applicants. This chapter includes guidance for training program faculty regarding how they can best support applicants, timelines, and suggestions for APPIC application preparation, how to facilitate successful matching with an excellent internship site, and steps to take if the match is not successful. This chapter is followed by a discussion of topics important to consider early in the internship experience including a focus on developing and using an internship plan to both guide the internship, and its use for formative and summative evaluation. Additional topics addressed are entry into the internship setting/system, changes that occur in the intern and the supervisory relationship as the internship progresses through the year, and termination issues to consider with clients, colleagues, and supervisors. This second edition also includes a new chapter on navigating entry of the intern into their early career phase. The chapter is based on a framework of "First year, learn the job; second year, do the job; third year, change the job" with Newman presenting relevant considerations for each of these first three years of practice including distinct characteristics, needs, challenges, and an emphasis on the importance of supervision and mentoring in promoting a successful transition from trainee to early career professional. Throughout the *Guide*, the development of the school psychology intern's professional skills is considered from the perspective of an integrated process rather than a series of isolated skills.

Newman recognizes that a successful internship experience is based on several critical "building blocks." These "blocks" include developing a positive supervisory experience to reduce anxiety on the part of both supervisor and intern; engaging in ongoing communication and collaboration with all parties to the internship; and facilitating interns to be actively involved in advocating for a productive internship experience. As there are limited opportunities to receive clinical supervision beyond the internship in many work settings, a major goal of any internship should include the development of the intern's ability to self-supervise. The promotion of self-evaluation throughout the internship is a critical component of self-supervision. The *Guide* stresses that interns should be self-advocates, including serving as active planners, coordinators, and shapers of their internship experience.

The *Guide* also addresses a number of the often-neglected topics in the school psychology literature. Such topics include differentiating a doctoral from a non-doctoral level school-based internship and the often ambiguous relationship between the university and the field site, including how they both impact each other. Newman expands on the idea that non-doctoral and doctoral internships should have similar breadth but doctoral internships have the potential for greater depth because of the more extensive on-campus coursework and varied practical experiences the intern brings to the internship. Practical strategies are also provided for building mutually beneficial relationships between university preparation programs and internship sites. Throughout the *Guide* the importance of collaboration is stressed. Practical strategies to promote collaboration among interns and their supervisors, interns and their work colleagues and fellow interns, university and field supervisors, and within university preparation programs are discussed.

Newman also addresses in the *Guide* the important topic of the frequently occurring divergence between training and practice, such as the expanded role advocated by training programs versus a more limited role encountered in some internship settings. Related to the common school-based setting for school psychology internships, the *Guide* explores the complexities of school systems and draws on organizational psychology and communication sciences literature to highlight "best practices" on how to effectively impact entry of the intern into a school-based placement.

APA, as part of their revised Standards for Accreditation for doctoral programs and internships in Health Service Psychology, which includes school psychology, has now identified engaging in self-reflection regarding one's personal and professional functioning in order to maintain and improve their well-being as a Profession-Wide Competency under the category of Professional Values and Attitudes. Dr. Newman emphasizes self-care throughout the *Guide* including addressing the issue of burnout, particularly among young professionals, and practices that can be learned on the internship to prevent it from occurring in the future. The critical role of modeling, by both the field and university supervisor, is emphasized throughout the *Guide* from the perspective of promoting not only professional skills related to direct and indirect service roles but also restorative/self-care to prevent burnout.

Particularly for interns, the *Guide* includes a discussion of the next steps in their career path, including transitioning to the first year of professional practice, with practical strategies for the job search, application and interview process. Newman stresses throughout the *Guide* habits of professional practice that will ensure not only a successful internship but also early career success. For university internship supervisors, Newman provides a useful guide to structure their internship seminar, which is a component of many university preparation programs. University supervisors will also find the *Guide* helpful in providing topics to discuss with field supervisors during site visits and helpful points to consider when reviewing proposals and approving internship sites, supervisors, and plans.

As I read the *Guide*, I was impressed with how Newman actively engages his reader through critical thinking questions and case examples. Through engaging in novel perspective taking, Dr. Newman challenges experienced intern supervisors to offer a dynamic versus static internship experience based on the needs of each individual intern.

No matter what your role – intern, field or university supervisor, reading the *Guide* will assist you in the process of learning ways to insure a successful capstone professional training experience. You will gain knowledge and strategies to ensure you have as professionally satisfying an experience as my former supervisor Jim and I had as interns over four decades ago and during our careers as internship supervisors. I assure you, the rewards in completing such an internship will last a lifetime.

PREFACE

If you are reading this book, then the chances are you play a role in the school psychology internship year. Regardless of your role or your prior experiences, you are probably wondering how exactly the year will turn out. I do not presume to have a crystal ball containing the answer to this question. However, I do believe the internship year has an increased likelihood of being successful when interns, field supervisors, and university supervisors (a) *purposefully* prepare for the year and (b) engage in ongoing communication and collaboration. The necessity of these actions is more evident than the processes by which they are accomplished. Therefore, one purpose of this text is to provide interns and supervisors with things they can do (i.e., actions) to promote a high-quality internship experience.

In addition to clarifying important actions for interns and supervisors, the second purpose of this book is to demystify what tends to be a mysterious and often anxiety-provoking process for school psychology trainees. Anxiety is a typical experience for interns. In my opinion, and based upon my own experiences as an intern and a university internship supervisor, anxiety is often the product of unclear expectations. Clarifying the expectations of supervisors and interns can increase feelings of preparedness for all and significantly decrease this anxiety. By reading this text, I hope that prospective interns, current interns, and those supervisors who work with interns achieve increased clarity regarding (a) what to do during the internship year, (b) how to do it, and (c) expectations from the earliest days of the internship through the end of the year.

Big Ideas

As in the first edition of this text, several big ideas are incorporated and elaborated upon, woven throughout each section and chapter, much like the themes of a symphony.

- The school psychology internship year is a dynamic and formative experience, not a static event.
- The development of an intern's professional skills should be treated as an integrated process, not a series of isolated activities.
- Supervision is a critical component of the internship year, but supervision processes need increased clarity for interns, site supervisors, and university supervisors to be maximally effective.
- Interns should be proactive planners, coordinators, and shapers of the internship experience.

One additional big idea has been added to this book's second edition:

- Habits of professional learning are practiced and established during the internship year and carry over into the early career.

If these big ideas are used to inform the actions of interns and supervisors, the internship year will be a meaningful experience for all those involved.

The Text

Structure

The book consists of 12 chapters divided into four sections: (1) pre-internship considerations; (2) getting oriented, (3) clarifying roles, developing relationships, and (4) moving beyond the internship. Each section focuses on different facets of the internship year and contains chapters that integrate the big ideas of the section and overall book. The appendices supplement the text's content with a variety of tools to support interns and supervisors.

New to this Edition

The second edition of this text has been significantly updated. The book contains two brand new chapters. Chapter 2, co-authored by Tai Collins, Renee Hawkins, and Meredith Murphy, focuses on how doctoral interns can best navigate the Association of Psychology Postdoctoral and Internship Centers (APPIC) Match process and how training programs can best support applicants. To the best of my knowledge, this is the first chapter in any text to cover this process with a focus on school psychology trainees. Another new chapter, Chapter 12, is focused on the transition from the internship to early career practice.

In addition to the two new chapters, all chapters and appendices have been updated in this edition of the text. Since the publication of the first edition, a number of key guidelines, conceptual articles, and research studies have emerged with relevance to school psychology internship training and supervision. The book synthesizes the most up-to-date literature and resources to support interns and their supervisors. Finally, in addition to drawing from my own experiences, I have consulted with other school psychology trainers, field supervisors, and prospective, current, and former school psychology interns to verify the pertinence and pragmatism of the book's content.

Section I: Pre-internship Considerations

The first section of the book (Chapters 1 and 2) covers critical issues to consider prior to entering the internship. Important concepts and terminology utilized throughout the book are defined in Chapter 1. The second chapter, which is targeted for school psychology doctoral students and the university faculty that support them, demystifies the APPIC application and Match process.

Section II: Getting Oriented

The second section of the book (Chapters 3 and 4) addresses issues important to consider during the first few weeks of the internship experience. The section is intended to orient interns, and their supervisors, as they begin the internship year. Concepts and terminology vital to internship success are defined. A key component in this section is establishing a dynamic internship plan, which provides a formative roadmap to structure the internship year. The section concludes with strategies to help interns successfully enter the internship site.

Section III: Clarifying Roles, Developing Relationships

The third section of this book (Chapters 5 to 9) moves beyond introductory concepts, vocabulary, and entering the internship site to describe the role of the school psychology intern and the critical relationships that are developed over the course of the internship year. One goal of this section is to empower interns and supervisors to clarify the expectations of the intern, a key to successful internship navigation. A second goal is to clarify the expectations for interns and supervisors within the internship supervision process. A third goal is to describe how to build relationships through effective communication and collaboration. Relationship-building is a critical skill as interns are interactive professionals who work with teachers, administrators, children, parents, and supervisors.

Section IV: Moving beyond the Internship

Finally, the fourth section of the text (Chapters 10 to 12) focuses on concluding the internship year and transitioning into the first year of professional practice as a school psychologist. Job search, application, and interview processes are described to help interns be competitive candidates for open positions. Concluding the year is considered from professional (e.g., concluding cases, transitioning case information), personal (e.g., saying goodbye to students, staff, and supervisors), and administrative (e.g., completing university-based requirements) perspectives. Chapter 12 explores challenges and opportunities in transitioning from the internship experience to the first year of professional practice.

How to Use this Book

The text is intended to be useful for several audiences, including prospective and current interns at the non-doctoral and doctoral levels, internship field supervisors, other individuals from the school district contributing to internship supervision, and university supervisors.

Non-doctoral and Doctoral Internships

School psychology is unique compared to other psychology disciplines because, in most states, school psychologists can practice at the non-doctoral level (e.g., with degrees such as Masters of Education, Education Specialist, and others) as well as the doctoral level. The majority of non-doctoral school psychology programs are structured based on a specialist level of training as recognized by the National Association of School Psychologists (NASP, 2010c) including sixty hours of graduate training (Rossen, Politikos, & Prus, 2018). Approximately 75% of school psychologists in the United States are trained at a non-doctoral level and only 25% at the doctoral level (Rossen et al., 2018; Walcott & Hyson, 2018). The intent of this book is to provide information that is applicable and useful for school psychology interns at both levels of training.

Although the big ideas of the text are universally relevant, distinctions between interns at different levels of training are recognized when implications are salient. Some distinctions between non-doctoral and doctoral interns include:

- number of years of coursework and practicum prior to the internship (e.g., in general, non-doctoral interns are in their third year of their school psychology program and doctoral interns are in their fifth);
- length of the internship (e.g., the length of internship is frequently 1,200 plus hours for non-doctoral interns versus 1,500 plus hours for doctoral);
- internship selection options (e.g., internships are typically obtained by applying directly to schools or districts, but doctoral-level interns have the option or are sometimes required by their training programs to pursue internships through APPIC, approved by the American Psychological Association [APA]);
- exposure to research prior to and during the internship (e.g., doctoral programs often require more intensive research experiences than non-doctoral programs; some doctoral interns may work on a doctoral dissertation while on the internship);
- post-internship options (e.g., doctoral interns may have a wider selection of options such as post-doctoral or faculty positions).

Prospective doctoral-level interns will hopefully find attention to the APPIC Match process in Chapter 2 provides helpful support for a complex process that is under-described in the literature. *Current* doctoral interns will find sections exploring issues such as applying and interviewing for academic positions (Chapter 10) to be pertinent. Additionally, the exploration of early career issues specific to doctoral-level school psychologists is highlighted in Chapters 11 and 12, including considerations for obtaining post-doctoral licensure hours in pursuit of becoming a licensed psychologist.

Prospective Interns

For school psychology trainees who are not yet on their internships this book offers a sneak preview of what is to come; future interns can develop a clear picture of the internship year. In addition, prospective interns may apply ideas from this text to practicum or other field-based experiences that take place prior to the internship. For example, topics such as developing goals and a plan (Chapter 3), site entry (Chapter 4), proactivity (Chapter 6), supervision (Chapter 7), and self-care (Chapter 9) are broadly applicable.

Interns

Current school psychology interns are the primary audience for this book. To get the most out of this text, interns should first preview the chapters before reading the book in depth from beginning to end. Although the book starts prior to the internship, moves towards its beginning, and eventually its closure, particular topic areas may be relevant early in the year but are not detailed until later in the book. For example, internship supervision is covered in depth in Chapter 7 even though it is immediately relevant during the internship year and the job process is explored in Chapter 10 although interns should begin searching for jobs in the middle of the year. Second, if possible, supervisors should utilize this book concurrently with interns. Even if supervisors do not purchase the text, interns are encouraged to share with their supervisors any ideas they find striking or believe would promote a high-quality internship experience. Proposing and discussing ideas and actions with one's supervisor is part of being a proactive intern (Chapter 6). A third suggestion is for interns to take the time to work through the various critical thinking questions and case examples integrated within the chapters; these activities are designed to enhance the learning experience.

Primary Field Supervisors

This text serves several pragmatic purposes for primary field supervisors – the school psychologist(s) responsible for the daily functioning of the intern at the internship site. Included in the book are guidelines on how to create an internship plan (Chapter 3), actions to help successfully integrate interns into the internship site (Chapters 4 and 5), and best practices in internship supervision (Chapter 7). The text also provides an opportunity for supervisors to engage in novel perspective taking. In other words, supervisors may develop new ways to think about the school psychology internship year. For example, the internship year is illustrated as a dynamic whole rather than a single isolated event, or a series of isolated activities to be accomplished. In a *dynamic internship*, supervisors collaborate with each other as well as with the intern to formatively adapt supervision processes and training activities to be responsive to the intern's developing goals, skills, and needs. In contrast, in a *static internship*, training and supervision are provided as they always have been regardless of the intern's goals, strengths, needs, or formative development of professional skills.

Thinking critically about whether the internship being offered is dynamic may be a new consideration for many supervisors. Engaging in novel perspective-taking challenges supervisors to check their assumptions, beliefs, and actions. While reading this text, supervisors are also encouraged to revisit their own internship experiences, reflect on what experiences were most helpful, and consider how they might apply these lessons learned to the interns they are supervising.

Other Field Supervisors

Primary field supervisors are not the only supervisors that work with school psychology interns. Other field supervisors, such as heads of psychological service units, resource psychologists, and administrative supervisors, are also contributors to the internship year. The text can help field supervisors to work with each other, and with the intern, to achieve shared perspectives, vocabulary, and expectations regarding the internship year. For example, the text may spark ideas and discussion about big ideas underlying the internship, how to develop a dynamic and formative internship plan, and how to best coordinate a structure for internship supervision.

University Supervisors

Many school psychology training programs provide an internship seminar led by a university supervisor – a designated faculty member who works with the program's interns. The structure of internship seminars likely differs from program to program, but may include exposure to professional content knowledge as well as opportunities for supervision (from the university supervisor and from peers). University internship supervisors may find this text to be a useful guidebook for internship seminars. For instance, even though internship seminars are frequently shaped by supervision of trainees' content knowledge needs (e.g., What is the best research-based intervention to deal with this particular problem?), the book provides an overview of *processes* that in many ways anchor the internship year (e.g., see aforementioned big ideas). In addition, the book offers a means for university supervisors to collaborate with field supervisors by considering entry into the internship, discussing various topics when conducting site visits, reviewing the internship contract, developing the internship plan, and considering the structure of internship supervision. University supervisors will also benefit from various resources in the text's appendices.

ACKNOWLEDGEMENTS

First and foremost, I would like to thank my wife Yael for her support and patience as I worked on both editions of this text. Thank you to the many students and colleagues that I acknowledged in the first edition of the text who provided feedback, resources, and case examples that continue to form the core of the book. Additionally, thank you to the students at the University of Cincinnati who supported the development of job interview examples in this edition: Bryn Endres, Hannah McIntire, Christa Newman, Megan Scott, and Julia Villarreal.

I would also like to thank those whom I have collaborated with in the area of school psychology training and supervision in school psychology, as our work together has informed this text, especially Tracy Cruise, Meaghan Guiney, Karen Monahan, Arlene Silva, Dennis Simon, and Mark Swerdlik. Thank you also to my wonderful colleagues at the University of Cincinnati who continuously inspire my development as a graduate educator and supervisor: Tai Collins, Janet Graden, Renee Hawkins, and Julie Morrison.

Thank you to all the individuals at Routledge who supported the writing of the first edition of this text and those who have encouraged and supported the development of the second edition, including Amanda Devine. In addition, much gratitude to Daniel Schwartz, who has been an invaluable support for my work with Routledge.

Thank you to all of the supervisors who supported me during my own school psychology practicum experiences and internship and helped me understand what makes for an optimal supervision experience. Finally, I wish to acknowledge the many interns that I have supervised over the past several years, as well as the supervisors I have worked with in the field throughout Illinois and Ohio. My own professional development and learning has hinged on our collaboration.

CONTRIBUTORS

Tai A. Collins, PhD
Associate Professor, School Psychology Program
College of Education, Criminal Justice, and Human Services
University of Cincinnati
Cincinnati, OH, USA

Renee O. Hawkins, PhD
Professor and Program Coordinator, School Psychology Program
College of Education, Criminal Justice, and Human Services
University of Cincinnati
Cincinnati, OH, USA

J. Meredith Murphy, MEd
Advanced Doctoral Trainee
College of Education, Criminal Justice, and Human Services
University of Cincinnati
Cincinnati, OH, USA

SECTION I
Pre-Internship Considerations

1
INTRODUCTION

The internship year marks the culmination of school psychology training. It has been described as a "capstone experience" (Hebert & Patterson, 2010, p. 55), "a rite of passage" (Hoff, 2006) and "the most important single experience in school psychology training programs" (Alessi, Lascurettes-Alessi, & Leys, 1981, p. 468). Surprisingly, few resources exist to support interns or their supervisors through a year considered so vital to school psychology training. This book is intended to offer increased clarity on the school psychology internship process from start to finish and to provide interns and supervisors with things they can do to promote a high-quality internship experience.

The chapter begins by defining the school psychology internship, with consideration given to documents that guide training such as the National Association of School Psychologists (NASP) *Standards for Graduate Preparation of School Psychologists* (2010d), *Best Practice Guidelines for School Psychology Intern Field Supervision and Mentoring* (NASP, 2014a), *Best Practice Guidelines for School Psychology Internships* (NASP, 2014b), *School Psychology: A Blueprint for Training and Practice III* (Ysseldyke et al., 2006), and the *NASP Practice Model* (NASP, 2010a). Next, other key concepts and terminology central to the internship are introduced and described. Once clearly defined, the internship is considered within the context of the evolving of field of school psychology. The chapter concludes with critical thinking questions for interns, field supervisors, and university supervisors to consider as the internship year begins.

Defining the School Psychology Internship

Since the turn of the nineteenth century, student completion of field-based experiences has been considered an essential component of school psychology training

(Fagan, 2010). Historically, the terms *practicum* and *internship* were not distinguished in definition or in practice; however, contemporary school psychology training programs do discern between practicum and internship experiences.

How Do Practica and Internships Differ?

In most school psychology training programs, distinctions between practica and internships are informed by the *Standards for Graduate Preparation of School Psychologists* (NASP, 2010d). According to these Standards, practica are defined as:

> Activities . . . completed as part of separate courses focusing on distinct skills or as part of a more extensive practicum field experience that covers a range of skills. Candidate skill and competency development, rather than delivery of professional services, is a primary purpose of practica.
>
> *(p. 7)*

The document also specifies that practica "are distinct from, precede, and prepare candidates for the school psychology internship" (p. 7).

The subsequent internship in school psychology is defined as "a supervised, culminating, comprehensive field experience that is completed prior to the awarding of the degree or other institutional documentation of completion of the specialist or doctoral level program" (NASP, 2010d, p. 7). The internship is intended to provide interns the "opportunity to integrate and apply professional knowledge and skills acquired in program coursework and practica, as well as to acquire enhanced competencies consistent with the school psychology program's goals and objectives" (NASP, 2010d, p. 7). In short, at the end of practicum experiences, it is expected that trainees will be prepared to embark on their internship year; following completion of the internship, they are expected to have attained the skills to practice professionally as entry-level school psychologists.

Internship Standards and Guidelines

In addition to distinguishing between and defining practicum and internship experiences in school psychology, the NASP (2010d) *Standards for Graduate Preparation of School Psychologists* specify five broad standards that should be included as part of the school psychology internship. The NASP standards that are specific to the internship are listed in Table 1.1, including a truncated summary of the elemental components composing each. The NASP's *Best Practice Guidelines for School Psychology Internships* (NASP, 2014b) and *Best Practice Guidelines for School Psychology Intern Field Supervision and Mentoring* (NASP, 2014a) reiterate the standards, and add a few guidelines consistent with expectations for the profession. Each of these documents is available, open access, on

NASP's website. In short, foundational components of the internship include a contract between the intern and his or her internship site, sufficient depth and breadth of experiences, collaboration amongst contributors to the internship year, and supervision with formative and summative evaluation. These documents offer helpful starting points for interns and supervisors to structure the internship year and provide universal expectations for school psychology interns across the country.

TABLE 1.1 NASP Standards for Graduate Preparation of School Psychologists Describing the Internship

Standard	Standard Wording	Abridged Details
3.2	The school psychology program requires a comprehensive, supervised, and carefully evaluated internship in school psychology.	• Completed for academic credit • Includes breadth, quality, attainment of competencies, and integration/application of school psychology domains • Results in direct, measurable, and positive impact on children, families, schools, and others • Includes formative and summative evaluations completed by program faculty and field-based supervisors to ensure attainment of professional competencies
3.3	The school psychology program requires that the internship be completed for a sufficient time period and in appropriate settings to achieve program objectives.	• Minimum of 1,200 (specialist) or 1,500 (doctoral) clock hours • Minimum of 600 hours in a school setting • Minimum of one academic year (full-time) or two consecutive years (half-time) • Settings are relevant to training program objectives for candidate competencies and allow direct oversight by the training program
3.4	The school psychology program requires that each intern receive appropriate and regularly scheduled field-based supervision.	• Field supervision provided from a school psychologist with appropriate state school psychologist credential • Average of at least two hours of field-based supervision per week • Field-based supervision provided on at least a weekly, individual, face-to face basis, focused on attainment of competencies

(continued)

TABLE 1.1 *(continued)*

Standard	Standard Wording	Abridged Details
3.5	The school psychology internship represents a collaboration between the school psychology program and internship placement agency consistent with program goals and assures attainment of competencies by interns.	• Completion of a written plan specifying collaborative responsibilities of the training program and internship site • Formative and summative performance-based evaluation of intern by program faculty and field-based supervisors • Appropriate support for the internship by the placement agency, including (a) internship as a learning experience for a school psychology trainee; (b) a written, detailed agreement; (c) expense reimbursement, a safe and secure work environment, adequate office space, and support services for the intern consistent with that afforded agency school psychologists; and (d) ongoing professional development
3.6	The school psychology program employs a systematic, valid process in which program faculty ensure that interns, during their culminating internship experience, demonstrate competencies to begin effective practice as school psychologists.	• Integration of domains of knowledge and application of professional skills for delivering a comprehensive range of services • Effective service delivery evidenced by direct, measurable, positive impact on children, families, schools, and others

Note. Adapted from *Standards for the Graduate Preparation of School Psychologists* (pp. 7–9) by the National Association of School Psychologists, 2010d, Bethesda, MD: Author.

School psychology: A Blueprint for Training and Practice III

In addition to NASP standards and guidelines, a series of documents called the NASP *Blueprints for Training and Practice* (Ysseldyke et al., 2006; Ysseldyke et al., 1997; Ysseldyke, Reynolds, & Weinberg, 1984) have largely influenced training and practice in the field of school psychology. In fact, the *Blueprints* have shaped the composition of standards, shifting the focus from specific course content towards domains of practice around which content is organized (Fagan, 2010; Ysseldyke, Burns, & Rosenfield, 2009). Lest we forget that interns are in fact school psychologists in training and not yet full-time practitioners, *School*

Psychology: A Blueprint for Training and Practice III (subsequently referred to as *Blueprint III;* Ysseldyke et al., 2006) treats the internship as a formative process of skill development and is a reminder of the competencies we expect interns to build during the internship year.

The Model

The model from *Blueprint III* (Ysseldyke et al., 2006) is depicted in Figure 1.1. As described by its authors, training and practice in school psychology is informed by eight integrated domains of competence, four foundational and four functional. These competencies are built upon knowledge bases in psychology and education, and the application of the scientific method to school psychology service delivery. As illustrated in Figure 1, school psychologists' services are delivered using a three-tiered model (multitiered models of service delivery are defined later in this chapter) with the intention of building the capacity of systems and improving the competencies of all students. The *Blueprint III* model is intended to inform the training trainees receive prior to the internship as well as the paradigm of practice they will encounter and contribute to as interns and, eventually, practitioners. Indeed, the *Blueprint III* is conceptually linked to the NASP *Practice Model* (NASP, 2010a), which is NASP's official policy intended to inform school psychologist practitioners' comprehensive service delivery (Armistead & Smallwood, 2014). The reader is referred to the *Blueprint III* document (Ysseldyke et al., 2006) and the NASP *Practice Model* (2010a) for fuller descriptions of domains and more in-depth overviews of each of these models.

Levels of Development

Unlike previous *Blueprint* documents, *Blueprint III* (Ysseldyke et al., 2006) recognizes that competence in school psychology knowledge and practice emerges over time. The developmental frame of *Blueprint III* has several implications for interns and internship sites. As explained by Ysseldyke et al. (2006):

> As training programs prepare their students for expanded roles, appropriate internships must be available to support novice practitioners. Given the anticipated capacity of training programs to build skills relevant to the new domains at the "novice" level during the coursework phase, internship sites will need to provide enriched experiences to assist trainees to develop these competencies by the conclusion of their internships. Developing standards for internships and supporting schools with innovative service delivery systems to become rich internship sites that meet those standards are critical goals.
>
> *(p. 21)*

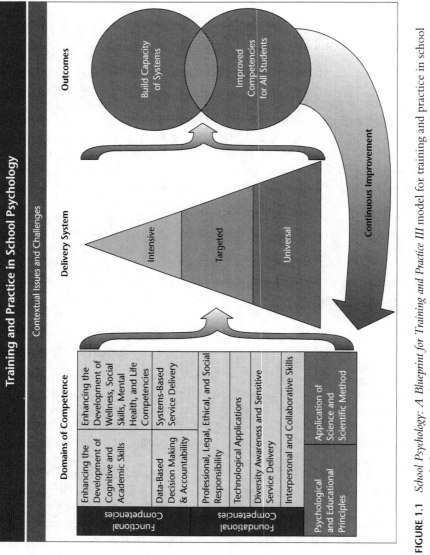

FIGURE 1.1 *School Psychology: A Blueprint for Training and Practice III* model for training and practice in school psychology. Copyright by the National Association of School Psychologists, Bethesda, MD. Reprinted with permission of the publisher. www.nasponline.org

The concepts of developmentally appropriate training and supervision, including defining terms such as novice and expert, are revisited in greater depth at the end of the chapter.

Every Internship Is Different

NASP training standards (NASP, 2010d), internship best practice guidelines (NASP, 2014a, 2014b), and the *Blueprint III* (Ysseldyke et al., 2006) jointly provide a map of several necessary components of the internship year. However, each internship experience will have differentiated aspects influenced by a multitude of factors. First, interns differ from one another in the breadth and depth of training they received in the various areas of school psychology practice prior to the internship. Therefore, it is vital for interns and supervisors to carefully consider the intern's unique strengths and needs prior to beginning the internship year and during its early stages (Hebert & Patterson, 2010; Sullivan, Svenkerud, & Conoley, 2014).

Second, district and school sites differ from one another on applied opportunities that may be available to interns. For example, while one intern may spend some of the internship working in a school with students with severe and profound special needs, another intern may not have this opportunity but be exposed to a different unique experience, perhaps the rolling out of a system-wide initiative such as a Positive Behavioral Interventions and Supports (PBIS) program.

Third, given the variety of school psychologist roles, site supervisors may prioritize different areas of their practice. Even though interns ideally participate in a breadth of activities, it is expected that each intern will be exposed to one or more areas of practice in more depth than others in part based on supervisor interests and functions. Related, a supervisor's priorities may be informed by state-, district-, or school-wide level initiatives. For instance, a district may be beginning to apply a multi-tiered service delivery system and implementing scientifically-based instruction and interventions prior to making special education eligibility decisions. In such a scenario, the intern would learn about the school psychologist's shifting role with respect to special education decision making and also the process of system-level change.

To summarize, there are innumerable dynamics that compose one intern's internship experience. Therefore, despite the delineation of standards and guidelines from NASP, it is unlikely that any two internships are exactly the same. Given the array of possibilities, it is important for interns and their supervisors to work collaboratively to consider internship expectations and flexibly structure a successful internship year. As you read this text, it is hoped that you begin to view the internship as an organic and dynamic process to be collaboratively shaped, rather than a list of static guidelines or isolated standards.

Frameworks of Development

For school psychology interns, the internship year is a learning process that is developmental in nature. In this book, two stage-based models – a model of adult learning principles utilized in the field of education (Joyce & Showers, 1980, 2002) and a developmental approach to supervision (e.g., Harvey & Struzziero, 2008; McNeill & Stoltenberg, 2016; Simon & Swerdlik, 2017; Stoltenberg, 2005) – provide frameworks that encapsulate interns' learning processes during the internship year. These two models, plus the role of supervision across the stages, are summarized in Table 1.2. The discussion of frameworks of development that follows is theoretically based but the concepts are included in the book for pragmatic purposes. To explain, the development of clinical skills can be seen as a nebulous process resulting in many questions regarding internship training and supervision. For example, how do we know an intern has made developmental progress in a given area of clinical skills? Which activities are most appropriate for the intern to be involved in at a given point in the year? How does the role of the supervisor change as the intern's skills develop?

TABLE 1.2 Convergence of Stage-Based Models of Learning, Development and Supervision

Adult Learning Outcomes (Joyce & Showers, 1980, 2002)	Developmental Levels of Supervision (Harvey & Struzziero, 2008; Stoltenberg, 2005)	Supervision Statuses (Knoff, 1986)
Awareness: Realize the importance of particular content and home in to learn more.	Novice or Beginner: No prior training or experience in the field. Focus on own behaviors, high levels of mixed emotions, and high levels of motivation. Need high levels of supervisory support.	Practicum: Supervision provided primarily by university faculty; may be supplemented in field.
Conceptual/ Organized Knowledge: Organize chunked information into larger concepts.	Advanced Beginner: Shift focus from self toward the client. Practice with more independence and less anxiety than novices. Have limited conceptual understanding, so need continued support in supervision, but with less structure and more autonomy.	Internship: Supervision provided primarily from external (i.e., field-based), peer, and administrative supervisors; may be supplemented by university faculty/staff.

Principles and Skills: Become aware of content and use skills in real or simulated situations.

Competent: Focus on the client and self are both enhanced. Increased levels of reflection, confidence, and autonomous practice. May be the final stage of development for some practitioners. Can structure supervision sessions themselves based on needs.

Entry: Same as internship, without supervision from university faculty/staff.

Application/Problem Solving: Integrate concepts, principles, and skills into applied practice.

Proficient: Both reflection and integration of skills are at higher levels. Recognize nuances and patterns of situations, and think about long-term consequences. Supervision helps maintain subjectivity, reduce resistance, and upgrade skills.

Independence: One may simultaneously supervise and be supervised. Peer supervision may be present.

Expert: Ability to handle complex and changing situations. No longer reliant on rules or guidelines. Practice with intuitive automaticity. Supervision with same purposes as in proficiency, but may act as metasupervisor.

Metasupervision: One supervises a supervisor.

With a developmental framework in mind, an intern's skill growth can be more clearly monitored by the intern and intern supervisors and interns can better advocate for their own needs. Further, supervisors can respond to intern needs with developmentally appropriate supervision techniques such as increasing or decreasing the amount of scaffolding provided to the intern during various activities and supervision sessions. For example, an intern with limited knowledge and applied experience in the area of group counseling may begin the year observing the internship supervisor facilitating a group, take a more active co-facilitator role in the middle of the year, and take responsibility for being the primary group leader by year's end. Related, the supervisor may encourage the intern to take a more autonomous role in identifying his or her own needs for supervision as the intern's skills develop. In the sections that follow, theoretical foundations of frameworks of development are summarized and a case vignette is provided to illustrate the importance of taking developmental level into consideration during internship training.

Adult Learning Outcomes

Joyce and Showers (1980, 2002) described professional development learning outcomes for adult learners such as teachers and other education professionals. According to the authors, a first outcome is the learner's development of initial knowledge or awareness of theories, practices, or other content. Next, adult learners establish a greater understanding of their own attitudes toward themselves, those they work with, and the content they are learning; accordingly, content knowledge is better organized than their initial levels of awareness. Once understanding of self and others as well as organization of knowledge increase, adult learners acquire skills and begin to apply them in action. The final developmental outcome for adult learners is the "transfer of training and 'executive control'" (Joyce & Showers, 2002, p. 71). In other words, skills are internalized by the learner in such a way that they can be applied appropriately, consistently, and with increasing automaticity in real-life situations.

Levels of Development

Also demonstrated in Table 1.2, learning outcomes described by Joyce and Showers (1980, 2002) converge with Harvey and Struzziero's (2008) developmental model of supervision for school psychologists. The Harvey and Struzziero model is largely informed by the prominent Integrated Developmental Model (IDM) of supervision (Stoltenberg, 2005; McNeill & Stoltenberg, 2016; Stoltenberg & Delworth, 1987) and an additional developmental model by Benner (1984). With integration of skills, knowledge, and qualitative changes in thinking over time, school psychology supervisees move through the levels of novice or beginner, advanced beginner, competent, proficient, and expert (Harvey & Struzziero, 2008). At each stage, supervisees should be met with developmentally appropriate supervision. Hallmarks of the developmental stages are summarized in Table 1.2. It should be noted that the definitions of each stage are consistent with the use of the terms "novice," "competent," and "expert" in the NASP *Blueprint III* (Ysseldyke et al., 2006).

On the far right side of Table 1.2, various supervision statuses have been adapted from the work of Knoff (1986), including practicum, internship, entry, independence, and metasupervision. This demonstrates the relevance of supervision at every stage of school psychologists' career, irrespective of developmental level of clinical skills (Harvey & Struzziero, 2008; Knoff, 1986; NASP, 2018). In this book, supervision processes are emphasized as central to the school psychology internship experience.

Developmental Trajectory Prior to and During the Internship

General developmental expectations for non-doctoral school psychology trainees from the first year in their program through the internship year are delineated in Table 1.3. Developmental levels are aligned with learning outcomes (Joyce & Showers, 1980, 2002), as well as with developmental benchmarks building towards the capstone internship experience. Table 1.3 is constructed based on the assertion that interns will develop competence over the course of the internship year (Ysseldyke et al., 2006). Working inductively, it can be assumed that most trainees begin their first year of graduate study with beginner skills in most clinical areas (e.g., foundational and functional competencies designated by *Blueprint III*, or NASP domains designated in the NASP Standards). Theoretically by their second year, trainees move from beginner to advanced

TABLE 1.3 Three Years in the Making: Developmental Steps Towards a Successful Non-Doctoral School Psychology Internship

Year in Program	Developmental Level	Learning Outcomes	Internship-related Developmental Benchmarks
1	Beginner	Awareness To Organized Knowledge	• Awareness of field of school psychology including assessment, consultation, and counseling. • Early practicum experiences. • Supervision primarily from university, but coordinated with site(s).
2	Beginner to Advanced Beginner	Organized Knowledge to Skill Acquisition	• Develop applied skills in assessment, consultation, and counseling. • More extensive practicum experiences. • Supervision primarily from university, more involvement from site than Year 1. • Self-reflection regarding specific areas of interest and need is used to inform internship decisions.
3	Advanced Beginner to Early Competence	Skill Acquisition to Skill Application	• Self-reflection regarding goals for the internship year based on areas of interest and need. • Begin internship. • Develop initial internship plan and goals for the year. • Plan and goals are formatively shaped based on development of skills. • Supervision primarily from site, but coordinated with university.

beginner developmental levels in many clinical areas of practice, acquiring skills to be applied during field-based experiences. By the end of the internship year, trainees should move from advanced beginner levels to achieve early levels of competence and be ready to successfully enter the field as first-year school psychologists. Although Table 1.3 focuses on non-doctoral interns, over the course of years four (advanced practica) and five (doctoral-level internship), doctoral-level interns presumably could develop competence and perhaps even proficiency in conjunction with applied and well-supported learning opportunities. Such development is consistent with the discussion of depth of knowledge and skill in Chapter 8.

The reader is encouraged to think of developmental levels as domain specific rather than an overall collection of clinical skills (Simon & Swerdlik, 2017). As noted by Harvey and Struzziero (2008), "All school psychologists are beginners when they enter situations in which they have no previous experience, either in terms of the population with which they are working or with regard to the procedures and/or tools used" (p. 41). For example, an intern who is applying Cognitive Behavioral Therapy (CBT) for the first time is developmentally a beginner in that area despite being in the third year of training. Further, some school psychology trainees may enter the program with more advanced skills in some domains. For instance, an incoming trainee who worked as a teacher for several years may have prior knowledge and competence in several relevant clinical skill areas. It is also possible that there are developmental differences between non-doctoral- and doctoral-level trainees during the internship year and beyond, especially given differences between hours of coursework and amount of time spent in the field. However, little to no research yet exists to confirm developmental differences between non-doctoral and doctoral trainees at commencement or conclusion of the school psychology internship (Miller, DeOrnellas, & Maricle, 2010). Further, research on expertise suggests the number of hours of training is less relevant than the training experiences themselves in determining the development of applied skills (e.g., Ericsson & Pool, 2016).

VIGNETTE 1.1 **DAVID, REBA, AND DEVELOPMENTAL LEVEL**

A contrast between two specialist-level interns in the same school psychology program, David and Reba, demonstrates the applicability of frameworks of development to the internship year. David and Reba both briefly learned about the NASP school crisis prevention and intervention model called PREPaRE (Brock et al., 2016) during a second-year course on mental health interventions. As part of Reba's practicum experience at a high school she participated on her school's crisis team, including taking part in a three day PREPaRE training workshop. Later in the year, a venerated teacher at the high school died unexpectedly, greatly affecting the school community. Reba participated in the crisis response including attending the crisis team's planning and debriefing meetings, observing her supervisor counseling students and debriefing with classrooms during the crisis, and providing direct triage counseling for a few students.

Although David had developed awareness of crisis response through coursework, he had not yet developed a deep level of understanding regarding the process of crisis prevention and response, acquired skills, or applied them in a real-life circumstance. He would fall in the novice or beginner level with regard to crisis skills. On the other hand, Reba has learned about crisis prevention and intervention in some depth, and is on the verge of independent application of skills. Reba can be considered to be at an advanced beginner level of skills in this clinical domain entering the internship and would likely move into competence with some more opportunities for applied practice. Given distinctions in their skills entering the internship year, training and supervision regarding crisis management should be distinguished for David and Reba. For example, David would benefit from gaining additional content knowledge and engaging in simulated practice of skills such as crisis counseling prior to engaging in an actual crisis response.

Supervision

A consideration of skill development during training is inexorably linked to processes of supervision. Supervision is a critical component of the school psychology internship for many reasons, perhaps most striking being that the internship is the last opportunity for students to learn and apply skills with a safety net before entering the field (Sullivan et al., 2014).

Defining Supervision

Supervision in school psychology is defined by McIntosh and Phelps (2000) as "an interpersonal interaction between two or more individuals for the purpose of sharing knowledge, assessing professional competencies, and providing objective feedback with the terminal goals of developing new competencies, facilitating effective delivery of psychological services, and maintaining professional competencies" (pp. 33-34). This definition is inclusive of supervision structures other than hierarchical supervisor-supervisee dyads (e.g., group supervision, peer supervision) and settings other than schools (e.g., university-based settings). Further, the authors highlighted the inherent complexity of supervision given the variety of potential settings (e.g., university; field; postdoctoral), the assortment of contexts for supervision within each setting (e.g., amount of formality; level of depth; subject matter discussed; amount of teaching involved), and the number of individuals who may act in the role of supervisor (e.g., faculty members; practitioners; advanced graduate students; classroom peers). The complexity of supervision is likely confusing to interns and at worst may be experienced as overwhelming. Therefore, it is essential that supervisors achieve clarity on their approaches to supervision and how responsibilities are divided amongst the various internship supervisors and that they are able to communicate these expectations to interns.

Models of Supervision

The supervisor's theoretical orientation and model of supervision contribute to the construction of supervision. There are numerous supervision models represented in the psychology supervision literature. Bernard and Goodyear (2019) suggested that major categories of psychology supervision models include (a) those rooted in psychotherapy, (b) developmental models, and (c) process-oriented models, with supervisors often practicing across these categories. Although much has been written about theoretical models of supervision, research does not yet point to one model as superior to others (Kaufman, 2010a). Further, most models are based in literature outside of the field of school psychology. Simon, Swerdlik, Cruise, Huber, and Newman (2014) and Simon and Swerdlik (2017) have recently developed the first school psychology specific model of supervision, the Developmental, Ecological, and Problem Solving (DEP) model. Consistent with contemporary approaches and the focus of this text on school psychology, developmental models, including the DEP model, are the primary supervision models applied throughout this text and are explored in greater depth in Chapter 7.

Types of Supervisors

School psychology interns are often supported by several supervisors at the same time, including a Local Education Agency (LEA) or administrative supervisor, the primary site or professional supervisor, the internship supervisor or coordinator, the university supervisor, and peer supervisors (Hebert & Patterson, 2010). The LEA supervisor is often responsible for supervising several professionals at once and plays a role in helping the intern successfully enter into the district or school and learn policies and procedures. An example of an LEA supervisor may be the head of the psychological services unit of the district. A second type of supervisor, the professional or internship site supervisor (sometimes also called the field supervisor), "monitors best practice and ethics," "is responsible for the [intern's] day-to-day functioning . . . and has ultimate responsibility for clients under the intern's care" (Hebert & Patterson, 2010, p. 59). Many interns have more than one professional supervisor but one is often designated by the LEA supervisor as the primary supervisor.

Some school psychology internships are organized by a third type of supervisor, an internship coordinator, who is accountable for managing and coordinating the internship curriculum, coordinating the supervision provided to interns, and troubleshooting through any difficulties that arise. For APPIC internships, highly sought-after internships accredited by the APA that facilitate licensure eligibility in most states, the internship coordinator may also be responsible for making sure the internship experiences are consistent with APA expectations (Hebert & Patterson, 2010). The APPIC Match process is described further in Chapter 2. A fourth type of supervisor during the internship year is the university supervisor, a designated faculty member from the trainee's school psychology program who monitors the internship experience to make sure it is consistent with training program goals. The university supervisor evaluates the intern's skill development as appropriate for entry to the profession, conducts site visits (in person, via video conference, or other means), and provides ongoing feedback to trainees. Some university supervisors facilitate ongoing university-based seminars to support interns' continuing professional development and to provide in-person supervision to those interns completing the internship locally.

In addition to the aforementioned supervision processes, interns may also be engaged in peer supervision. Peer supervision can take place in internship settings (e.g., all of the interns in one district) and/or university settings (e.g., all of the interns from one training program) and can be conducted in a small or large group format. Peer supervision differs from the types of supervision provided by other supervisors because it is non-hierarchical. However, Hebert and Patterson (2010) stressed that supervisors from the internship site and/or university should (a) provide clear expectations and guidelines for peer supervision; (b) ask interns to develop ground rules, establish a peer supervision schedule, and document how the supervision time was spent; and (c) utilize a specific process for problem solving through concerns. It is important for supervisors to encourage interns to engage in a peer supervision process that is formal, strategic, and purposeful because the process is modeling the primary type of supervision the interns will likely engage in once they enter the field (Hebert & Patterson, 2010).

Timelines, Roles, and Responsibilities

With so many individuals simultaneously contributing to the internship year, it is helpful to delineate roles and responsibilities. The internship year is divided chronologically in Table 1.4, with the roles and responsibilities of prospective interns, current interns, primary field supervisors, and university supervisors designated. Prospective interns are engaged in coursework and practicum experiences throughout the year and should begin considering potential internship sites as early as the fall. The internship search, application, and interview process will be in full gear by the winter, culminating in a decision in the early spring.

For current interns, the summer prior to the internship provides an opportunity to consider one's own skills, and to decipher goals for the year to come. Early in the year, interns should collaborate with their field and university supervisors to develop an internship plan related to strengths and needs. Consistent with developmental frameworks and the consideration of the internship as dynamic and formative,

TABLE 1.4 Roles and Responsibilities of Prospective Interns, Current Interns, and Supervisors throughout the Internship Year

Timing	Prospective Intern	Intern	Primary Field Supervisor	University Supervisors
Summer prior to Internship	—	• Self-reflection regarding strengths and needs.* • Broad-based goal setting for year to come.	• Consider opportunities available to incoming intern(s). • Introduce intern(s) to school staff, and include intern(s) in new staff orientation, if possible.	• Encourage interns' self-reflection and goal setting.* • Professional development conference for interns and intern supervisors.*
August to November	• Attend fall state association conference, if possible. • Consider potential internship sites. • Continue to develop content knowledge in coursework.* • Complete practica and other field-based experiences.*	• Enter the internship site (see Chapter 4). • Identify unique opportunities at site. • Collaborate with supervisors to develop dynamic internship plan that addresses strengths and needs (see Chapter 3). • Use evaluation and discussion to inform internship activities.* • Attend fall state association conference, if possible. • Complete state credentialing exam, if applicable (see Chapter 11). • Complete the School Psychologist Praxis Exam (5402) per NCSP credentialing requirements (see Chapter 11).	• Facilitate site entry (see Chapter 4). • Discuss dynamic internship plan with intern, and university supervisor (see Chapter 3). • Formative evaluation: discuss intern's developmental points of entry, including strengths and needs (see Chapter 7). • Use evaluation and discussion to inform activities.* • Attend fall state association conference, if possible.	• Initial site visit: Discuss internship contract and dynamic plan; clarify expectations of intern and supervisors. • Attend fall state association conference, if possible.

December to March	• Attend NASP conference, if possible. • Internship search, application, and interview process.	• Attend NASP conference, if possible. • Search, apply, and interview for jobs (see Chapter 10).* • Complete graduation audit.	• Attend NASP conference, if possible. • Complete formative evaluations: discuss intern's ongoing development including goals, strengths, needs, and internship plan.	• Attend NASP conference, if possible. • Distribute/collect/analyze formative, midyear evaluations. • Second site visit: discuss formative evaluation and intern growth including goals, strengths, needs, and internship plan.
April to June	• Attend spring state association conference, if possible. • Finalize internship decision.	• Attend spring state association conference, if possible. • Finalize job decision. • Attain signatures on state and national certification/licensure documents from site and university supervisors (see Chapter 11).	• Attend spring state association conference, if possible. • Complete summative evaluations: discuss closure, transitions in professional practice and options for support.	• Attend spring state association conference, if possible. • Distribute/collect/analyze summative evaluations. • Final site visits: Discuss closure, transitions into professional practice and continued needs/options for support. • Assure completion of internship and graduation requirements. • Sign state and national certification documents.

Note. *Indicates a yearlong, ongoing process.

interns' goals and the internship plan should be periodically revisited with supervisors to inform activities. Also in the fall, or perhaps even earlier depending on state requirements, interns should take any exams required for eventual credentialing as a school psychologist. Some states require interns to pass a state-specific licensure exam, and others accept a passing score on the School Psychologist Praxis Exam (5402), which is one requirement for the Nationally Certified School Psychologist (NCSP) credential (see Chapter 11). Interns should begin the job search process during the winter, ideally securing a position during the spring.

The responsibilities of the primary field supervisor and the university supervisor are consistent with earlier descriptions regarding types of internship supervisors. University internship supervisors may consider providing professional learning opportunities for supervisors and interns prior to or at the beginning of the internship year and, if possible, at other times throughout the year. For example, school psychology educators in states such as Illinois and Massachusetts host supervision institutes for practicum and internship supervisors.

The interrelated nature of responsibilities in Table 1.4 intentionally underscores the importance of collaboration between field and university supervisors, and supervisors and interns. For example, attendance at local and national conferences is included to highlight the value of ongoing professional learning and networking for interns, practitioners, and university educators. Further, all parties are involved in ongoing evaluation processes and the development of a dynamic internship plan. The intention of Table 1.4 is to provide a timeline of benchmarks for various parties to consider before the year begins rather than to provide a comprehensive list of every role and responsibility. Of course, given the wide differentiation in the structure between internships, there may be facets that are more or less relevant to an individual's experience.

Critical Thinking

A final key concept to be explored in this introductory chapter is critical thinking. The phrase "critical thinking" frequently appears in both popular and academic education literature but its definition is not always clarified. In this text, critical thinking refers to "a unique kind of purposeful thinking . . . [that] involves the careful examination and evaluation of beliefs and actions in order to arrive at well-reasoned decisions" (Gambrill, 2012, p. 11). Characteristics of critical thinking include: (a) identifying and questioning our beliefs and assumptions; (b) attending "to the process of reasoning (how we think), not just the product"; (c) considering "questions from different points of view"; and (d) contemplating "the possible consequences of different beliefs or actions" (Gambrill, 2012, p. 11).

In a field that increasingly requires the application of a problem-solving model, data-based decision-making and evidence-based practice, the need for school psychology practitioners to engage in critical thinking is greater than ever before. As described by Gambrill (2012):

Critical thinking, evidence-based practice, and scientific reasoning are closely related. All use reasoning for a purpose (i.e., to solve problems), relying on standards such as clarity, relevance, and accuracy. All regard criticism (self-correction) as essential to forward understanding; all encourage us to challenge our assumptions, consider well-argued opposing views, and check our reasoning for errors.

(p. 12)

Critical thinking skills can be learned. The internship year provides an excellent opportunity for interns to learn, develop and practice the critical thinking skills they will later employ as practitioners.

Interns learn critical thinking by making mistakes and planning for better decision making in the future. For example, early in my internship year a first-grade teacher asked me to work with three boys she said were disruptive in her class. I knew the students from having spent time in the classroom, enjoyed my interactions with them, and eagerly began meeting with them once a week to work on "social skills." After meeting with my site supervisor, I realized there was a lack of clarity on the nature of the problem(s) that necessitated the group (e.g., what was meant by "social skills"?). Further, the teacher was in her first year and had challenges with classroom management that may have inadvertently created some of the students' behavioral problems. I used my mistake as an opportunity to formally consult with the teacher. We discussed the use of classroom management strategies, which she increasingly employed as the year went on. The group, which the students enjoyed, was used as a behavioral incentive and its curriculum tied directly to classroom expectations. The students' behavior improved, as did the teacher's classroom management skills.

Trial and error is not the only way to learn critical thinking skills. For interns that have supervisors that apply critical thinking in their clinical practice (hopefully the majority!), observing supervisor decision making can be an excellent learning tool. In supervision sessions, the supervisory dyad can process how and why certain decisions (either the supervisor's or the intern's) were made, what the intern might do similarly or differently in the future, and how decisions are linked to evidence-based practices (Bernard & Goodyear, 2019).

At the end of each chapter of this book, critical thinking questions are presented to interns, field supervisors, and university supervisors. Consistent with the aforementioned definition of critical thinking, these questions are intended to encourage readers to question their own assumptions and beliefs, attend to the process of decision making, engage in perspective taking, and consider the consequences of their beliefs and actions.

Internship in an Evolving Field

The school psychology internship is embedded within the context of a changing field. For most practitioners the traditional "refer-test-place" role is no longer the preferred method of practice. School psychologists increasingly favor alternative and expanded roles and functions (Bahr et al., 2017; Ysseldyke & Reschly, 2014). Broader roles for school psychologists include moving away from a medical model paradigm towards an ecological framework of service delivery (Sheridan & Gutkin, 2000; Gutkin, 2012); applying an experimental/problem solving model of practice rather than a correlational model (Merrell, Ervin, & Peacock, 2012; Ysseldyke & Reschly, 2014); and utilizing a multitiered service delivery system of early intervening services as a preventative tool (Jimerson, Burns, & VanDerHeyden, 2016; Walker & Shinn, 2010; Ysseldyke et al., 2006). Examples of alternative practices include data-based decision making at the individual student *and* system levels (Ysseldyke et al., 2006), implementation of direct interventions (e.g., counseling), indirect interventions (e.g., consultation), and conducting of research (Hosp & Reschly, 2002; Ysseldyke & Reschly, 2014).

Multitiered Systems of Support and Response to Intervention

Consistent with the ongoing paradigm shift in the field of school psychology, schools are increasingly incorporating multitiered models of service delivery, also called multitiered systems of support (MTSS), that include scientifically-based interventions of varying intensity at each tier. Interventions are matched according to student needs as indicated by universal screening and progress monitoring data (Jimerson et al., 2016; Walker & Shinn, 2010). A multitiered service delivery system is also often times considered synonymous with what has become known as Response to Intervention (RTI). However, as described by Walker and Shinn, "RTI has become a ubiquitous term that seems to have taken on a life of its own . . . it means different things to different people" (p. 7). Although many educators view RTI as a means to special education entitlement, Walker and Shinn defined RTI as

> a means of building a more comprehensive, coordinated, and effective service delivery system that is based on the *proactive* foundational practices of (a) prevention, (b) evidence-based interventions across tiers, (c) data-based decision making, and (d) early intervention that uses universal screening rather than referral.
>
> *(p. 8)*

A three-tiered model of service delivery, consistent with the above definition and illustrated by Walker and Shinn (2010), is featured in Figure 1.2. The Figure is similar to earlier illustrations of multitiered models (e.g., Sugai, Horner, & Gresham, 2002) but is flipped to emphasize prevention and promotion of positive outcomes for all students and to deemphasize the interpretation of RTI as a special education eligibility process (Walker & Shinn, 2010). Readers are referred to Shinn and Walker (2010) and Jimerson et al. (2016) for a more in-depth consideration of MTSS, RTI, and evidence-based interventions.

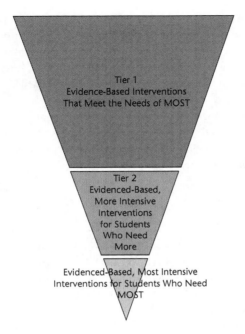

FIGURE 1.2   Three-tier model as conceptualized by Walker and Shinn (2010).
Copyright by the National Association of School Psychologists,
Bethesda, MD. Reprinted with permission of the publisher. www.
nasponline.org

Interns May Encounter Discord between Training and Practice

Because multitiered service delivery systems for early intervening services are
increasingly prevalent in schools (Jimerson et al., 2016), chances are interns will
encounter and perhaps contribute to the implementation of such a model during
the internship year. However, the reality remains that for a variety of reasons,
many school psychologists still tend to devote the majority of their time to traditional "refer-test-place" services (Ysseldyke & Reschly, 2014). Practice trends
contrast with training programs structured to be consistent with NASP training
standards (2010d) and the *Blueprint III* (Ysseldyke et al., 2006), which aim to
prepare students for practice in expanded roles. As a result, differences may exist
between emphases of interns' training programs and what is happening within
schools or districts. For example, an intern may have completed coursework that
stressed the importance of Curriculum Based Measurement (CBM) as a preventative progress monitoring tool, and even collected and analyzed CBM data on
practicum, but be based at an internship site which does not utilize CBM data
to monitor student progress. As a result of gaps between training and practice,

interns may experience feelings of surprise or dissonance as they observe their supervisors in action (Fagan & Wise, 2007; Tarquin & Truscott, 2006).

On the other hand, field supervisors may perceive interns as naïve, sheltered from the realities of school-based practice. To be extreme, interns might as well forget what they learned in the classroom because to begin the internship is to enroll in the proverbial "school of hard knocks." In actuality, most interns *will* encounter experiences that will make them think, "Wow - this is certainly different than what I learned in class!" Such realizations are consistent with moving from early levels of awareness and conceptual understanding to acquisition and application of skills in practice.

Internship as a Bridge

Although divergences between training and practice are inevitable, what makes the internship year so special is the opportunity to bridge those divides. Interns are trainees that have not yet graduated and are still embedded within their training program – especially those interns enrolled in an ongoing, university-based internship seminar. Simultaneously, interns work full time in the school psychologist role and thus are entrenched in the field. Given their hybrid identity, interns are well suited to "articulate how university and field-based trainers can work together to create congruent change" (Hughes, Kaufman, & Hoover, 2010, p. 314), thereby bridging gaps between two worlds.

Bridging Training and Practice

It is increasingly challenging for training programs to prepare students for the evolving nature of school psychology practice; building symbiotic relationships between universities and the field is central to creating and sustaining positive change (Hughes, Kaufman & Hoover, 2010). Opportunities for collaboration between universities and the field abound. For example, Hughes, Kaufman and Hoover (2010) pointed to several potential university-field partnerships, such as sharing of resources; co-documenting the implementation of interventions; co-conducting action-based research that can be presented in courses or at conferences; providing training (e.g., presentations at a school by faculty or students, or practitioners presenting in the graduate classroom); and offering professional learning opportunities (e.g., discounted graduate courses for practitioners, or faculty or student access to district or school workshops). Interns can act as liaisons between training programs and the field and encourage such collaborations.

Interns as Learners and Leaders

The hybrid identity of interns is further reflected in the fact that they can be both learners and leaders during the internship year. From the perspective of interns as learners, even individuals that begin the internship year with highly developed clinical skills should still be considered trainees engaged in a learning experience. In fact, internship guidelines for doctoral level internships from the Council of Directors of School Psychology Programs (CDSPP, 2017), NASP (2014b) *Best Practice Guidelines for School Psychology Internships*, and APA (2015b) *Standards of Accreditation for Health Service Psychology* all direct internship programs to use a title such as "intern" or "resident" to make it clear that the intern is of student status. Further, intern access to ongoing professional learning and supervision opportunities from their internship sites and training programs is considered a vital component of the internship year (NASP, 2010d; NASP, 2014a; Hughes, Kaufman, Crespi, et al., 2010).

What is sometimes forgotten is that interns can also take on leadership roles during the internship year, especially as the year progresses. For example, at the University of Cincinnati, interns with a strong background in applied behavior analysis may be able to take on more advanced or complex behavioral cases than trainees without such a focus in their training. Interns often have state of the art training, including access to the most current research, and have the potential to link their training programs with the front lines of practice in a constantly evolving field. It is important to stress that taking on leadership roles does not nullify the fact that interns are trainees. The internship supervision process should provide interns with a safety net of supervisory support during all activities. Additionally, although an intern might have highly developed skills in one or more areas, some skill areas likely need further development. As stated by Hebert and Patterson (2010), "in order to create an internship experience that supports integration of skills, internship trainers need to appreciate the range of roles typical for the school psychologist and address each" (p. 66). The internship should be treated as a dynamic experience structured to best fit the needs of individual interns; doing so calls for internship activities and supervision to be differentiated to fit with each intern's training needs.

A Bidirectional Bridge

As asserted in the NASP *Blueprint III* (Ysseldyke et al. 2006), "there is a growing need to build bridges between academic generated research and applications by practitioners" (p. 22); this includes the dissemination of evidence-based practices facilitated by research, informed by issues pertinent to the field and relevant to practitioner needs. Just as the research of trainees and faculty members can influence school psychology practice, practice should inform the content and process of training programs. When university educators communicate with field-based practitioners, training goals become more relevant to contemporary practice and students are better prepared to enter the field (Kaufman, 2010b). In short, the nature of internship training demands a collaborative process in which interns, university educators, and practitioners work together to shape the culminating experience.

From Internship into Practice

Today's interns are tomorrow's practitioners. The practice of early career school psychologists is determined by a combination of content knowledge developed during coursework and professional learning opportunities, applied experiences including practica and internships, and ongoing supervision from university and field-based supervisors throughout training. Consequently, the individuals who educate and supervise interns have a wealth of influence over the future directions of the field of school psychology. When interns and their field- and university-based supervisors treat internship training as a collaborative opportunity, the potential to build the capacity of systems and to promote positive outcomes for students is maximized.

Summary

The school psychology internship is the culminating experience of school psychology training, a chance for trainees to integrate classroom training with real world experiences. During the internship, students are supposed to attain the necessary competencies to be ready to enter the field as entry-level school psychologists. Several documents, including the NASP training standards (NASP, 2010d), *Best Practice Guidelines for School Psychology Intern Field Supervision and Mentoring* (NASP, 2014a), *Best Practice Guidelines for School Psychology Internships* (NASP, 2014b), and the *Blueprint III* (Ysseldyke et al., 2006) outline recommended features of school psychology internships. However, each internship has some unique features due to differences in interns' entry level skills, opportunities available at internship sites, site supervisors' preferred practice roles, and school- or district-level initiatives.

The school psychology internship is embedded within a field of change. Increasingly, the school psychologist role is informed by an ecological perspective that incorporates problem solving, prevention, and a multi-tiered model of service delivery to promote positive outcomes for children and systems. Accordingly, practitioners' employment of critical thinking skills is vital to effective clinical practice. Although interns may be trained for expanded roles, some internship sites have not yet caught up. In many ways, the internship can contribute to bridging gaps between training and practice. For instance, field and university supervisors can collaboratively plan the internship training program. The importance of collaboration is further demonstrated by the complex developmental process interns experience during the internship year. Collaborative dialogue between interns and their supervisors promotes training and supervision processes that are formative, dynamic, developmentally appropriate, and individualized to support the intern's goals and needs.

Critical Thinking Questions and Activities

The following are critical thinking questions for interns, field supervisors, and university supervisors to ponder immediately prior to the beginning of the internship year.

For Interns:

- What areas of school psychology practice are your areas of strength? What areas are most challenging for you?
- How will the internship year help you build upon your strengths and improve upon areas of need?
- List three broad-based goals for the internship year.

For Field Supervisors:

- What unique opportunities are available for interns at your internship site (think about both school and district levels)?
- How do available opportunities match with the intern's reported needs?
- How will you assess the intern's entry-level content knowledge and applied skills in various areas of school psychology practice?

For University Supervisors:

- How can you assist interns in thinking critically about their strengths and needs and in setting broad-based goals for the coming year?
- Do the intern's goals match the training program's goals for interns?
- In what ways can collaboration between interns, internship sites, and training programs be advanced?

2

NAVIGATING THE APPIC MATCH

Tai A. Collins, PhD
Renee O. Hawkins, PhD
J. Meredith Murphy, MEd

The doctoral internship is the culminating experience of doctoral training in school psychology (Council of Directors of School Psychology Programs [CDSPP], 2017). As the last formal training experience prior to the awarding of the doctoral degree, the doctoral internship provides students an opportunity to integrate and apply the knowledge and skills they have gained during their doctoral program through a structured and closely supervised experience. Given the importance of the doctoral internship in the overall preparation of doctoral-level school psychologists, it is crucial that trainees secure a high-quality internship placement that will allow them to develop the professional competencies recognized as integral for the practice of school psychology (American Psychological Association [APA], 2015b; National Association of School Psychologists [NASP], 2010a).

One pathway for securing a doctoral internship is through the Association of Psychology Postdoctoral and Internship Centers (APPIC) Match process (subsequently referred to as "the Match"). The Match is designed to efficiently connect prospective interns and internship programs. Although some resources are available to support the Match process for APPIC applicants at large (e.g., Williams-Nickelson, Prinstein, & Keilin, 2018), to the best of our knowledge there are no distinct resources to support doctoral-level school psychology trainees applying for internships through the APPIC process. Yet there are some unique considerations school psychology trainees should be aware of as they embark on this process. Therefore, the purpose of this chapter is to provide a resource to support doctoral-level school psychology interns in successfully applying to the Match and securing the right internship position. The chapter concludes with critical thinking questions for doctoral interns who will apply to the Match and for training program faculty who support these interns.

APPIC Match Phases

The Match consists of two phases. In Phase I, the process unfolds through the following steps: 1) prospective interns apply to internship sites using a universal application (the AAPI Online), 2) internship programs interview selected applicants, 3) applicants submit a rank ordered list of desired placements and internship programs submit a rank ordered list of preferred applicants following interviews, and 4) applicants are informed of their placement on the pre-determined Match day. After Phase I is complete, internship sites that have unfilled positions post these positions through the Match site. Unmatched applicants submit materials to these sites and another Match day is held for Phase II of the Match. For an internship program to offer placements through the Match, the site must be either accredited by the APA and/or the Canadian Psychological Association (CPA) or meet specific criteria outline by APPIC (APPIC, 2018c). The overwhelming majority of sites included in the Match in 2018 were accredited (3,383 APA or CPA accredited positions offered out of 3,906 total positions offered; APPIC, 2018a). Programs that are not accredited must go through an application process to demonstrate that they meet the APPIC criteria. Once approved by APPIC, programs are reviewed every three years (APPIC, 2018c).

Why Participate in the Match?

Although the Match process is competitive and can be stressful for graduate students, there are several reasons why a school psychology doctoral trainee may choose to participate. First, the Match includes a large number of diverse internship opportunities. In 2018, 3,906 internship positions were offered in the Match (APPIC, 2018a). Internship programs participating in the Match include placements in schools, hospitals, community agencies, and private clinics. Unique training experiences may be available through APPIC internships that are not accessible to doctoral trainees outside of the Match.

Second, given that all APPIC internships are either accredited or have met APPIC standards to be included in the Match, there are some quality assurances offered by securing an internship via the Match. Internship programs are held accountable to APA, CPA, and APPIC, and must report to these organizations on the training experiences and outcomes for interns, such as data on graduation, licensure, and post-internship employment. Accreditation status may be of particular importance for trainees interested in becoming licensed. Although, currently, no states require completion of an accredited internship for licensure, most states require that the internship meet certain criteria (APPIC, 2018d). Completing an accredited internship can increase the likelihood that the internship meets state licensing requirements. In addition, many posted open faculty positions in APA-accredited doctoral programs seek faculty who are licensed or are license-eligible.

Another benefit of seeking and attaining an internship through the Match is the opportunity to interface with doctoral trainees from other training programs nationally. Completing an internship along with other interns with diverse previous training experiences can expand trainees' learning and further their professional growth. Doctoral graduates quickly learn that they are joining a small professional community of school psychologists. Making connections outside of their own doctoral training program can end up serving trainees well as their careers take off.

Next, some APPIC sites that offer internship programs also offer post-doctoral training opportunities. Post-doctoral experiences provide trainees with the opportunity to continue to receive highly supervised training, hone and specialize their skills, and often accrue hours toward licensure. Seeking a post-doctoral fellowship may be the next step for many doctoral graduates post-internship, and there may benefits to continuing in the same placement if opportunities are available, such as familiarity with the setting, and building on professional relationships established during the internship year. Related, some sites have strong national reputations that can set the stage for the next steps in trainees' careers due to the specialized training and research opportunities offered from well-respected leaders in the field.

Finally, some school psychology doctoral programs *require* students to participate in the Match for the reasons described above, along with others. According to APA's Standards of Accreditation (SoA; 2015b), doctoral students are "expected to apply for, and to the extent possible, complete internship training programs that are either APA- or CPA-accredited" (p. 13). Under APA's SoA, it is permissible for students to complete an internship that is not accredited but the doctoral training program must be able to provide evidence that the internship is appropriate. Certainly, if students can obtain an APA-accredited internship through the Match, there is less of a burden on the training program to find an appropriate, high quality internship option and to demonstrate that the internship is essentially equivalent to an APA-accredited internship. Further, although doctoral training programs may see the benefits to obtaining a national internship through the Match for their trainees, the trainees may not be as eager to take on the expense and stress of going through the Match process if given another option. Requiring students to at least enter the Match may give them the nudge they need to explore new, exciting possibilities.

Some doctoral programs may not be able to identify appropriate internship alternatives for trainees outside of the Match. Generally, school psychology programs have collaborative partnerships with numerous school and community settings to provide appropriate practicum experiences but there are different requirements for the school psychology internship that are not as easy to meet if a program is trying to create a local internship opportunity for a doctoral-level intern. For example, a challenge for school psychology doctoral programs is the limited number of school-based practitioners maintaining a license through the state board of psychology, as this license is typically not required for practice in the schools. Most school-based school psychologists are solely credentialed by the department of education, which is appropriate for their role but does not meet the requirements for supervising a doctoral-level school psychology intern in most cases.

Early Steps in Trainees' Graduate Career to Prepare for the Match

Long before it is time to prepare the APPIC internship application, there are steps trainees can take to make themselves competitive internship applicants and successful interns. The first and most important step to take toward securing a high-quality internship through the Match is to be a dedicated and engaged doctoral student during pre-internship training. This is consistent with descriptions of interns' proactive behaviors described elsewhere in the text (e.g., Chapter 8). Throughout trainees' graduate careers, they should seek to master the knowledge provided through their graduate program curriculum and develop the professional competencies needed to be effective psychologists through practicum and other field-based experiences. Soliciting supervisory feedback to continuously improve and being an active partner with faculty and field supervisors are also important components of preparation for the internship. Graduate students should take the initiative and seek out opportunities to gain a broad range and depth of practicum and research experiences. While developing well-rounded knowledge and skills, trainees should also develop their professional goals. Doctoral trainees are often unsure of their path post-graduation. They may have interests in research, teaching, school-based practice, or practice in clinical settings, with various client populations. As such, trainees should take advantage of opportunities afforded by their doctoral training program to explore these different roles, and help them consider their options. With increasingly clear professional goals, there is an increasing chance that students will apply and match to an internship site that will help them achieve their professional goals.

Dissertation

Doctoral-level internship applicants can become more desirable to internships by having their dissertation as complete as possible prior to starting the internship. First, designing and conducting a high-quality dissertation study is a major task and trainees' ability to make timely progress toward this task completion generally reflects well on their knowledge and skills. Consistent with research (e.g., Krieshok, Lopez, Somberg, & Cantrell, 2000), internship sites may view progress on the dissertation as a predictor of success on internship. Second, internship sites are held accountable to APA and APPIC regarding outcomes for interns. Internship sites want interns to go on to graduate from their doctoral training programs in a timely manner and contribute to the field of psychology. Dissertation completion is a common barrier to degree completion for trainees and making significant progress on dissertation research prior to the internship puts them closer to the ultimate goal of graduating – a goal shared by interns, internship sites, and training programs.

In addition, internship sites would like interns who will be appropriately focused on the internship experiences. Supervisors will expect that interns' primary focus is on internship-related activities and that their time and attention are dedicated to the internship site. In most placements, interns have significant responsibilities and it can be challenging to balance these responsibilities with trying to complete a dissertation. This challenge can be exacerbated by the physical distance between the intern's training program and the internship site. In most circumstances, the intern will no longer be meeting with the dissertation chair in face-to-face meetings. There may be a decreased sense of accountability for making progress on the dissertation as the intern is focused on responsibilities as an intern and faculty are focused on the trainees they are supporting day-to-day back on campus. Although it is true that internship programs often include research as a planned internship activity, interns who have completed or are near completion of a dissertation can use this time as an opportunity to get involved in new or ongoing research projects that may be available at their internship sites. Aiming to have successfully defended a dissertation proposal and have data collected prior to the internship is a reasonably ambitious goal that can set trainees on a successful path for attaining an internship and optimizing learning experiences and opportunities on the internship. Defending the dissertation prior to internship is a stretch goal that would allow interns to focus on additional experiences and post-graduation planning while on the internship. Doctoral dissertation completion is further described in the context of closing out the internship in Chapter 11.

Peers and Faculty as Resources

Applicants can learn from those who have been involved in the Match process in previous years, including peers and faculty. Taking time to talk with graduate student peers while they are going through the application process, after the match, and once they are on internship, is a worthy endeavor. Similarly, program faculty, some of whom likely also participated in the Match, can offer guidance based on their knowledge and experience. Peers and faculty can offer invaluable insights as to which internship sites may be good potential matches based on the goals of the training program as well as the applicant's professional goals. Further, peers and faculty can help with logistical tasks such as categorizing practicum hours for the AAPI and travel planning for interviews. Peers who have most recently gone through the Match process can provide information regarding the interview process at specific sites and offer tips to help trainees prepare. From selecting potential internship sites all the way through to submitting final rankings, peers and faculty can be a significant source of information and support.

Identifying Sites

A major initial step in the Match process is selecting sites to which to apply. Based on Match statistics, APPIC reports that applying to more than 15 sites does not significantly increase the chances of getting matched (APPIC, 2018b). On average, students apply to between 13 and 14 sites (APPIC, 2018b). Considering these data on the number of applications submitted per applicant is important for planning and resource management on the applicant's part. Each application takes time and costs money, and wasting either is unproductive. Although 13 to 14 applications may seem like a lot, it is important to consider that applicants are not likely to interview at all the sites to which they apply, either because they are not invited for an interview or logistically their schedule does not permit it. Also, remember with nearly 4,000 internship positions in the Match, it may actually be challenging to get the number down to 15 or fewer sites of interest. It is never too early to start browsing the APPIC online directory of internship sites (https://membership.appic.org/directory/search). Trainees can search the directory using numerous criteria (e.g., geography, accreditation, agency type) to help narrow the search. When narrowing sites to which to apply, two major considerations should weigh heavily in applicants' decision making: 1) the match between their professional goals and the internship and 2) the match between their doctoral training and the internship placement.

As mentioned before, thinking forward to post-graduation goals is important as trainees complete their doctoral training. Having a sense of direction for the future can help trainees consider to which internship programs they will apply. Each internship program participating in the Match has a page in the APPIC directory that provides an overview of the site. The page also includes data on the post-internship employment of past interns. These data can be considered in light of applicants' professional goals as one indicator as to whether or not the site may be a good match. In addition to reviewing the information available from the APPIC directory, trainees should carefully review each internship program's website, which can provide much more information about the program and the types of activities in which interns are engaged.

Applicants should also seek internships that are an appropriate match to the training received in their doctoral program. Although it is appropriate to seek an internship that will expand upon current knowledge learned throughout the graduate program, the internship is not the time to seek training in areas in which trainees have no formal background and which are not linked to their graduate preparation. In addition to learning during the internship, interns also provide valuable services to their internship sites. Seeking placement at sites that will readily see how applicants' previous experience and training is appropriate for their site will likely increase their chances of getting an interview and ultimately matching. Faculty and peers can help provide information on each program's Match history with specific sites. To increase the likelihood of finding a successful match, prospective interns should select a large number of sites with which previous applicants had success with regard to securing interviews and matches. Also, when searching the APPIC internship directory, students can search by program type to focus on internships that accept applicants from school psychology training programs, as not all sites will be fits for school psychology trainees. Further, on the profile page for each site, applicants can see the number of interns coming from different types of training backgrounds (e.g., PhD, PsyD, counseling, school, clinical). Even though a site may indicate that it accepts students from school psychology programs, it can be valuable to look at the history of interns to get a better sense as to whether the applicant's training may be appealing to that site.

Preparing the AAPI Application

The AAPI is a standard application process completed by all applicants participating in the Match. The following sections detail the different components of the AAPI application and Table 2.1 includes a sample timeline of activities involved in preparing the application.

TABLE 2.1 AAPI Preparation Timeline

Month	Activity
July	• Access the AAPI Online.
	• Register for the Match and sign up for email alerts.
July–October	• Explore and start narrowing internship sites of interest.
	• Organize field experience hours for transfer to APPI Online.
August–September	• Update CV.
	• Request letters of recommendation.
	• Write essays.
October	• Finalize internship sites.
	• Write cover letters.
	• Prepare supplemental materials if necessary.
Late October–December	• Submit applications.
December–January	• Interviews.
January–early February	• Prepare and submit rank order list for Phase I.
February	• Phase I Match Day.
	• Apply to positions through Phase II if unmatched.
March	• Submit rank order list for Phase II.
	• Phase II Match Day.
	• Participate in Post-Match Vacancy Service if unmatched.

Curriculum Vitae

The curriculum vitae (CV) is an excellent opportunity to highlight the breadth and depth of applicants' skills and experiences throughout their training. CV development is covered in more detail in Chapter 11 of this text, with a focus on job applications. For the purpose of doctoral internship applicants, the CV should be as clear as possible regarding the applicants' unique experiences while also being concise and efficient. Applicants should take the time to carefully construct a CV that accurately portrays their experiences. Seeking feedback from peers and faculty advisors can also be helpful, as applicants may not explain experiences with sufficient detail and they may neglect to include relevant experiences.

Letters of Recommendation

Letters of recommendation are critical components of internship applications as potential internship supervisors can glean important information from previous supervisors' comments in recommendation letters. A number of considerations for applicants and reference writers are included below.

Considerations for Applicants

Three letters of recommendation are to be included in the application for each APPIC internship site; however, applicants are encouraged to think strategically about how many letters of recommendation to request and from whom they should be requested. In the event that applicants are applying to different types of internship sites (e.g., schools, clinics, hospitals), it may be appropriate to request letters from different reference writers who can speak to the applicant's skills and experiences in different settings. Applicants can then carefully select which letters would be most applicable to each internship site.

When choosing which reference writers to ask for a recommendation, applicants should request letters from individuals who are knowledgeable about the applicant's skills and experiences, enthusiastic about recommending the applicant, and able to complete the letter of recommendation in a timely manner. The Director of Clinical Training (DCT) and the applicant's dissertation chair are two examples of university faculty who are likely to be able to provide strong letters of recommendation. Applicants should also request letters from supervisors with whom they have worked extensively in school and clinical settings.

When requesting letters of recommendation, applicants should give the reference writer a considerable amount of time to complete the letter. Due to various competing responsibilities and time constraints, reference writers should be given at least a month to complete the letters. This should be feasible for applicants as application due dates are known in advance and applicants should have an organized calendar of activities that need to be completed in advance of due dates (see Table 2.1). Applicants should be sure not to submit the reference writers' names in the AAPI system until they have agreed to write a letter as it is inappropriate for reference writers to be surprised by receiving an email from the AAPI system prior to agreeing to complete a letter. Applicants should be prepared to provide a copy of their current CV and points that they would like to be emphasized as reference writers may request additional information to write a complete and detailed letter.

Considerations for Reference Writers

Reference writers should not agree to complete a letter of recommendation unless they are enthusiastic about commenting on the applicant's skills and experiences. If their perceptions of the applicant's qualifications for internship are tepid or mixed, then letter writers should decline the invitation to complete a letter. Recommendation letters should be detailed, complete, and unique to each applicant, with examples supporting the qualities described. Reference writers should also complete the letter in a timely manner, especially since applicants should give reference writers a feasible amount of time. APPIC requires that reference writers utilized the Standardized Reference Form (SRF; APPIC, 2018b), which includes prompts to discuss applicants' skills, strengths, and growth areas.

Essays

The AAPI essays provide applicants with a valuable opportunity to provide a context for their training, skills, and experiences, and describe their approach to the practice of school psychology. Four essays are required, including the personal statement, research essay, theoretical orientation, and approach to serving diverse clients. Consistent with this book's big ideas, it is critical that these essays do not read as a laundry list of experiences. Rather, they should be framed in an integrated manner demonstrating the applicant's intentionality in seeking out various experiences and the unique ways in which their experiences have shaped their development as a school psychologist.

Personal Statement

First, applicants are required to compose a personal statement, which is an opportunity to discuss unique aspects of the applicant's development that influence their practice. Applicants often describe the personal statement as the most difficult essay to write, as they struggle to make the essay unique while avoiding inappropriate disclosure of personal information. Applicants should utilize the personal statement to discuss their personal background and unique experiences that will make them stand out among a pool of qualified applicants. Applicants are also encouraged to highlight their passion for improving the outcomes of children and families. This essay should not be a chronology of experiences through undergraduate and graduate training, nor should it disclose inappropriate personal information such as the applicant's mental health diagnoses or special education classifications. The personal statement should provide enough personal information to provide a unique context to the applicant's experiences, but it should not include any information that would raise questions or potentially be viewed negatively by those reviewing the application.

Research Essay

Next, applicants are required to submit a research essay detailing their research experiences and interests. Applicants are encouraged to discuss enough details of their dissertation to make the project clear to potential supervisors, as well as discuss the status of data collection and expected completion date. It is important to discuss the "why" of the dissertation project as well (i.e., why is this an important area of study?) as this can provide an excellent opportunity for the applicant to discuss the potential applied impact of their work. It is critical to connect the applicants' research experiences to their work in schools and other settings so that internship sites can discern how these experiences might positively influence the applicants' delivery of applied psychological services.

Theoretical Orientation

Third, a theoretical orientation essay is required which is expected to provide a clear and concise summary of the applicants' model of professional practice. For example, applicants may ascribe to orientations such as school-based mental health or cognitive behavioral, and they must be able to convey how their practice is informed by theory. The applicant should discuss the themes that guide their practice, with examples of situations in which their theoretical orientation was particularly useful or relevant. Examples illustrate how the applicant applies a theoretical orientation in their practice. Rather than focusing solely on the training themes of their program, the applicant should discuss how their personal approach to serving clients and families has been influenced by their training. It is also appropriate to express the applicant's interest in working with individuals who ascribe to other theoretical orientations as potential supervisors are likely to come from a variety of training backgrounds with different orientations.

Diversity Essay

Finally, the application requires an essay on diversity, which is expected to cover applicants' range of experiences with a variety of clients and their approach to serving these children and families. It is critical that applicants avoid writing a list of experiences with culturally and linguistically diverse clients; instead, a description of relevant experiences should be integrated into an overall framework of culturally relevant service delivery. Applicants should address diversity broadly (e.g., race/ethnicity, socioeconomic status, gender identity, sexual orientation), especially with regard to addressing diversity in case conceptualization. It would be appropriate to discuss their own cultural background and how they reflect on their own culture, biases, and behaviors to better support a variety of clients. Applicants should avoid making the diversity essay bland and formulaic and truly reflect on their approach to serving clients from different backgrounds.

Supplemental Materials

According to a policy statement released by the APPIC Board of Directors (APPIC, 2012), internship sites are discouraged from requesting supplemental materials as APPIC prefers that applicants complete one universal application. The two types of supplemental materials allowed by APPIC include case summaries and deidentified psychological evaluation reports (APPIC, 2012). Applicants should thoroughly review the requested application materials for each potential internship site and build the preparation of supplemental materials into their timeline if necessary. If supplemental materials are requested, applicants should carefully choose cases that highlight a specific skill or competency unique to their doctoral training. Applicants should also deidentify any materials to ensure client confidentiality.

Experience Hours

Applicants should be prepared to submit their experience hours for each of the categories into the AAPI system. Online tools such as Time2Track© can be helpful because tracked hours can be imported directly into the AAPI system. Applicants should consult with each other, previous interns, and faculty advisors when creating decision rules regarding the classification of their experiences into the AAPI categories. Applicants are also asked to list the psychological assessments with which they are familiar, along with a corresponding number of administrations.

Cover Letters

Applicants are to write a cover letter for each internship site to which they are applying. Appendix A includes a sample APPIC cover letter. Cover letters should be addressed to the DCT for each site and should be a maximum of two pages and between 500 and 1,000 words. When writing cover letters, applicants should ensure that the letters are not solely about their own experiences and skills. Rather, applicants are encouraged to frame cover letters to be about the match between the applicant and the internship site. This requires the applicant to discuss their own skills and experiences, as well as the specific experiences and training opportunities offered at each site. Including specific information about each internship site in the cover letter demonstrates that the applicant is knowledgeable about the site and interested in the associated opportunities. It also allows the applicant to clearly articulate how the internship site will prepare them to pursue their career goals. Rather than putting the match wholly into the hands of the internship site, the applicant should clearly demonstrate how they would be a good fit in the internship placement and how their professional goals and the training goals of the site are aligned. Cover letters are a critical component of the application and they should be carefully crafted to make a strong impact.

Interviews

The process of scheduling interviews requires organization and planning. When receiving emails requesting confirmations for interviews, applicants should respond as soon as possible so that they can choose from a variety of available dates. Some internship sites publish the dates of their interviews each year, which allows applicants to anticipate when interviews may be scheduled. Applicants should anticipate having to make some tough choices, as interview dates for different sites may overlap in December and January. Internship sites may also include informal opportunities to network with the supervisors and current interns, which may also complicate travel planning. Applicants should refrain from scheduling flights until multiple interviews are booked in a week, as travel may be scheduled from one interview to another. Collaboration with peers is encouraged so that applicants can share travel expenses and provide support for each other when visiting internship sites for interviews.

During interviews, it is critical that applicants dress professionally and come to the interview prepared to make connections with the supervisors and current interns. Applicants should make a good impression on everyone at the internship site (e.g., supervisors, current interns, other staff) and remember they are always being interviewed, even during informal periods. Applicants should bring a portfolio or tablet to take notes during the interviews, and they should also record a list of site-specific questions to ask. When engaging with potential supervisors, applicants should be themselves so that they can find a true match. Applicants should also avoid selling themselves too short (i.e., lacking specificity and enthusiasm when discussing their experiences and skills) and be prepared to discuss what makes them a unique applicant. Because each interview will be time-limited, applicants should address each answer succinctly but with specificity and intentionality. Table 2.2 includes potential interview questions that applicants should be prepared to answer during an APPIC interview. Immediately after leaving each interview, applicants are encouraged to take note of their perceptions and experiences of the site so that the information from different sites is not confused when deciding how to rank potential internship sites. Applicants should also send a note (preferably via mail) thanking the internship

TABLE 2.2 Sample Interview Questions

Topic	Questions
Match with Site	• Why are you interested in this internship? • What are your goals for internship? • What skills/experiences do you have to offer our internship? • What are your future professional goals? • Where do you see yourself in 5 years? • What are your interests outside of psychology? • Tell us about yourself. • How did you become interested in psychology? How did you become interested in school psychology? • What are some of your personal/professional strengths and weaknesses? What have you done to address your weaknesses? • Tell us about any unique aspects of your doctoral training that have prepared you for internship.
Clinical Skills	• Tell us about a successful case experience and what you contributed to the success. • Tell us about a challenging case experience you have had and what you learned from the experience. • What are your clinical interests? • Describe your theoretical orientation and how you apply it to your case conceptualization. • What assessments have you done? • What further assessment training do you need? • Tell us about the process you use in determining special education eligibility. • Tell us about your counseling experience.
Research	• What is the focus of your dissertation and where are you in the process? • What are your research interests?
Supervision	• Tell us about a time when you disagreed with or had a conflict with a supervisor. • What kinds of supervision have you had and what style works well for you? • What do you want from supervision?
Diversity	• Share an example that demonstrates your respect for diversity. • How have you worked to understand the perspectives of others? • What behaviors, techniques, or decisions allow you to effectively serve diverse clients? • Describe your experiences working with children and families from diverse cultural backgrounds. • What reading/didactic experiences influence the way you think about diverse populations? • What is your approach to working with children and families from culturally and linguistically diverse backgrounds?

site for the interview. Per APPIC regulations, applicants and internships are not allowed to discuss their level of interest with each other. As such, the thank you note should not indicate the likelihood that the intern will rank the site (i.e., "This is my first choice!") or request information about the site's likelihood of ranking the intern.

Ranking

Submitting the final rank order list is often an anxiety-inducing endeavor as applicants spend a considerable amount of time debating which sites to rank and in which order to rank them. The APPIC website includes a frequently asked questions page with helpful tips for ranking internship sites (APPIC, 2016). Applicants should rank internship sites in the order of their interest in each site and refrain from considering their perceptions of their performance in the interviews or how likely the sites are to rank them. Highly preferred sites should always be ranked highest, as the likelihood of ranking at a site is not impacted by the order in which they are ranked according to the algorithm. Applicants should keep in mind that many internship sites have multiple tracks with different Match numbers that will need to be ranked separately. When considering how to rank sites, applicants should think about the big picture in terms of the unique skills and knowledge to be gained at each site, the potential for post-doctoral fellowship opportunities, and the ability to expand upon their experiences while maintaining a connection to their theoretical orientation and training themes. Seeking supervision from faculty advisors when making these high-stakes decisions is advisable.

APPIC Match Phase II

Phase II of the APPIC Match provides a standardized opportunity for internship sites and applicants to participate if Phase I does not result in a successful match. Applicants should be aware of the timeline and requirements for Phase II (APPIC, 2017). Phase II consists of an accelerated process of applications, interviews (often by phone or videoconference), and submission of a second rank order list. If an applicant is unsuccessful in Phase II, they should plan to participate in the Post-Match Vacancy Service, refer to their program handbook, and remain in contact with their faculty advisor and DCT to discuss next steps in the completion of their doctoral requirements.

Guidelines for School Psychology Programs

School psychology programs are responsible for providing the knowledge and experiences to prepare graduate students to successfully complete the doctoral internship. As such, DCTs should ensure that their program's training and experiences are consistent with APA guidelines and the expectations of internship sites. With regard to preparation for the Match, program faculty should closely advise applicants as they navigate this often confusing process. Regular meetings should be scheduled between a faculty member or members and the cohort of students applying for the internship each year. During these meetings, faculty can provide an overview and timeline of activities for the Match process and monitor trainees' progress in completing their applications. Actionable and timely feedback on applicants' CVs, cover letters, essays, and supplemental materials ensures that applicants put their best foot forward and adequately discuss their experiences and skills. Faculty can also support opportunities for within- and cross-cohort collaboration on the Match process during doctoral colloquia and other meetings. From our experience, a collaborative training program culture can mitigate some of the stress associated with the Match process, while a competitive culture is likely to exacerbate applicants' anxieties. Mock interviews can also be scheduled to provide feedback on applicants' interview presentation and how to respond to common questions that might be expected during interviews. In this manner, program faculty can provide advice and feedback to increase the likelihood of a successful internship match.

Summary

The Match process can often be intimidating for doctoral trainees, as there are a number of moving parts that require organization and execution. Trainees may also feel pressure to secure a highly coveted internship placement consistent with the history of their program, and to find the right fit for their culminating graduate training experience. The purpose of this chapter is to demystify the APPIC internship process by providing a detailed description of the process and each of the associated requirements.

Prospective interns are encouraged to utilize this chapter as a guide for their activities when navigating the Match process. Utilizing this resource early on in the graduate training program can also allow trainees to preview the process and plan ahead. Trainees should allot adequate time to perform each of the activities, such as identifying potential sites, preparing the four essays, editing their CV, and securing recommendation letters. Applicants also need to carefully consider how they will present themselves during interviews and make important decisions when ranking. Utilizing the step-by-step guidelines in this chapter should assist applicants in navigating a potentially overwhelming process.

Program faculty are also encouraged to utilize this resource when supporting trainees. Faculty should provide strong mentoring, informed by their own Match experiences and the experiences of previous trainees, to guide applicants through the Match process. Faculty are encouraged to ensure that trainees are adequately planning and completing each of the steps so that the trainees have the highest likelihood of securing a high-quality internship match.

Critical Thinking Questions and Activities

The following are critical thinking questions and activities for applicants and faculty supporting applicants:

For Applicants

- What are your career goals? How will your internship further your career goals?
- What are the non-negotiables for your internship experience?
- What are the unique aspects of your personal background (i.e., culture, experiences) and graduate training experiences that make you stand out from other applicants?
- What sources of support could you use from your program faculty, fellow applicants, and other trainees when navigating the APPIC process? How might you access these supports?
- What sources of accountability will help you to complete each of the required steps of the Match?
- How will you manage the financial aspects of interviewing across the country (e.g., flights, lodging, other travel expenses)?
- In what ways will you practice self-care when participating in the Match process?

For Faculty Supporting Applicants

- What are the unique aspects of your training program that make your trainees stand out from other applicants?
- How do your program faculty currently support applicants during the APPIC process? In which ways could the support be strengthened?
- How do your program faculty facilitate and encourage collaboration between and within cohorts regarding the Match?
- Are trainees provided feedback on their interviewing skills (e.g., via mock interviews)?
- What is the history of your program with regard to the Match? At which sites have previous trainees had success in securing interviews and internship placements? At which sites have previous trainees been less successful? How might this inform how you advise prospective interns?

SECTION II
Getting Oriented

3

THE INTERNSHIP PLAN

As a university supervisor I often work with interns and field supervisors to develop and implement a plan to organize the internship year. In my experience, I have noticed a phenomenon which I refer to as *internship plan hibernation*:

1. At the very beginning of their internship, the intern spends a significant amount of time developing a plan for the year. The result often is a comprehensive list of every activity a school psychologist may encounter in his or her role rather than a specific plan. The intern also evaluates his or her entry-level skills across domains.
2. The field supervisor(s) and intern collaboratively review the plan as well as the evaluation, and perhaps make a few minor changes.
3. I conduct a beginning of the year site visit (usually in person, sometimes by phone, or videoconference) and discuss the plan and evaluation with the field supervisor(s) and the intern.
4. The plan gets filed away.
5. A few months later I conduct a midyear site visit and we briefly discuss the plan, which may or may not peek out from the file cabinet. In most cases, we talk about what the intern is doing at the site without specific reference to the plan.
6. At the end of the year, the field supervisor completes a summative evaluation of the intern, and I conduct a final site visit where we revisit the plan and evaluation together. With rare exception, interns and supervisors report that they have not looked at the plan since the beginning of the year.

When an internship plan is used to structure the internship year (as is required by a few states, some training programs, and some internship sites), I imagine that internship plan hibernation is common. For others, an internship plan is not developed at all. A plan that is hidden away during the year or no plan at all are unsurprising considering the fast-paced and overscheduled realities of daily school psychology practice. Interns and supervisors are busy engaging in experiences, including discussing how to address real challenges during supervision, rather than deliberating about whether or not the intern has completed activities in various domains of practice.

This is not to say that an internship plan is not an important feature of the school psychology internship. On the contrary, if developed in a pragmatic way that is meaningful to interns and supervisors, the internship plan can be a critical facet of a successful internship. In this chapter, the concept of an internship plan is defined and features of an effective internship plan are described. The development and implementation of an internship plan is illustrated by a diagram and by various case examples throughout the chapter. The chapter concludes with critical thinking activities and questions for interns and supervisors.

Internship Agreement Versus Internship Plan

Before delving into a consideration of internship plan development and implementation, it is important to first distinguish an *internship plan* from what is called an *internship agreement*. An internship agreement is a written contract signed by the intern, internship site, and training program that specifies administrative and logistical details of the internship. Such a contract is required by some school psychology training programs as well as some state boards of education, and is recommended by NASP training standards (2010d) and Best Practice guidelines (NASP, 2014a, 2014b). Several items may be included in an internship agreement, including but not limited to beginning and end dates of the internship; total hours of service required; details regarding supervision (e.g., supervisor information, number of supervision hours required); information about the school and/or district sites; release time and/or reimbursement for attending professional learning activities; access to office space; and monetary compensation and other benefits. An example of an internship agreement, adapted from the state of *Illinois School Psychology Internship Manual* (2014), is provided in Appendix B of this book.

Like the internship agreement, the internship plan is also a formal written document and in some ways is a type of contract between the intern and his or her supervisors. However, the purpose of an internship plan is to map out the year with reference to the intern's knowledge and performance skills in various domains matched with various opportunities available at the internship site. The internship plan is formative, and individualized changes are made during the year to fit with the intern's developing needs. Let us look more closely at what ingredients go into creating an effective internship plan.

Features of an Effective Internship Plan: The Big Ideas

As indicated in Chapter 1, every school psychology internship experience is in some ways different. Variations relate to (a) the intern's prior training, including coursework, fieldwork, supervision, and interests; (b) unique opportunities available at the school or district site; (c) field supervisor areas of expertise and preferences for school psychology practice; and (d) school or district initiatives that inform school psychology practice. Although an internship plan should be designed to match with available opportunities and individualized needs, there are several common underlying features, or big ideas, that can guide interns and supervisors in the successful development of an internship plan. An effective internship plan:

- Includes the *intern as an active contributor* to plan development by incorporating the intern's *self-identified needs, strengths*, and *goals*.
- Includes *formative evaluation* so that the internship experience is adaptive to the intern's developing needs.
- Includes *summative evaluation* to determine the intern's readiness to enter the field at the end of the year.
- Covers a *breadth* of training experiences in an *integrated* and *practical* manner.
- Incorporates at least one area of professional focus or interest (i.e., *depth* of training) as determined by the intern.
- Promotes *accountability* with regard to (a) the intern's developing competencies, (b) the support provided by supervisors to promote skill development, and (c) professional standards.
- Is *useful for all parties* involved in supporting the internship year including interns, field supervisors, and university supervisors.

It is not coincidental that the big ideas behind effective internship plans tie back to the big ideas that are woven throughout the book (see Preface). In the sections that follow, the central features of internship plans are explored in depth.

Interns Should Actively Contribute to the Internship Plan

Optimally, interns are engaged as active planners, coordinators, and shapers of their own internship experiences. The development of an internship plan presents an opportunity for interns to meaningfully influence what they are doing from early on in the year. Using data to assess one's own needs and strengths and setting goals are two logical starting points for interns to contribute to the plan.

Assessing Skills

From its initial creation, an internship plan should be informed by the intern's needs and strengths as determined through various forms of assessment. A first type of assessment is self-assessment, the appraisal of one's own skills as a school psychologist in various domains of knowledge and practice. Self-assessment is a learned process and ideally occurs throughout one's professional career (Falender & Shafranske, 2017). Therefore, learning to apply self-assessment skills should be supported by supervisors during the internship year. For example, at the beginning of the internship year, interns might be required to (a) read an annotated description of the NASP domains of graduate education and practice (NASP, 2010d, pp. 11–16), (b) consider their perceived competency in each domain, and (c) use this information to prioritize three broad goals for the internship year. This process promotes self-reflection regarding deficiencies and strengths and allows interns to see the year as an integrated whole instead of multitudes of isolated activities. Self-assessment provides "evolutionary information" – data that may change interns' self-perceptions, perceptions of the world around them, and of their thoughts and actions (Levitov & Fall, 2009, p. 54). In other words, self-assessment is directly related to interns becoming increasingly critical thinkers.

However, self-assessments are limited due to their inherent subjectivity and the fact that many interns simply are not aware of what they do not know as they embark on their internship journey. Therefore, it is beneficial to simultaneously consider data from other sources. First, interns may consider data they receive from field and university supervisors. For example, Stephanie, a second-year practicum student, received summative feedback (verbally, and using a university-created tool) from her field supervisor regarding concerns with her presentation style in front of parents and teachers (e.g., a lack of eye contact, excessive use of jargon, not being collaborative). The concerns were also communicated between the practicum supervisor and university supervisor with Stephanie's knowledge. The feedback was critical to Stephanie self-prioritizing work in the NASP domain of Consultation and Collaboration at the beginning of her internship year. Her skills in this area will be supported through ongoing supervised practice.

Another type of assessment comes from peers who can provide helpful insight into one's own entry-level skills through informal and formal discussions (Levitov & Fall, 2009; Oberman, 2016). For instance, training program cohorts often create online groups, such as chat groups, through which students ask for and offer each other support; this process provides a gauge for each intern's skills as compared to his or her peers.

Yet another type of assessment comes from individuals who are impacted by the intern's services. At a school site this can include students, parents, teachers, and administrators. For example, a survey can be given to a counseling intervention group to understand how the participants felt about or experienced the group (Oberman, 2016) or a teacher may rate the intern's skills as a consultant (Klose, Plotts, & Lasser, 2010). Of course, as with self-assessment, other types of assessment are also subject to limitations such as reporter bias. Therefore, it is helpful to triangulate various forms of assessment data in consideration of entry-level skills and skill development over time.

To summarize, there are many ways for interns to assess their skills upon beginning the internship as well as throughout the year, including self-assessments, field and university supervisor assessments, peer assessments, and client assessments. Assessments provide critical information for initially creating an internship plan, and can be used throughout the year (i.e., formatively) to adapt the plan to fit with the intern's developing needs.

Setting Goals

Skill assessment should be directly linked to goals that are identified by the intern. Goals may focus on (a) skills that are absent or deficient and need to be gained for the intern to be ready to enter the field and (b) professional strengths that the intern wants to enhance. Self-identifying and setting goals and formatively evaluating whether goals have been met helps interns determine their ongoing effectiveness in the work they are completing (Oberman, 2016).

There is no hard and fast rule for how many goals should be created and different interns will likely approach the goal setting process in different ways. As an internship supervisor, I have found that interns benefit from setting at least three broad goals for their year after reflecting on and assessing their skills across the ten domains of the NASP (2010a) practice model. Obviously, having three goal areas does not mean that these are the only areas that the intern will work on during the year. Once interns have determined three priorities they can make the goals more specific to the work they are doing at their internship sites, as well as consider their needs in other domains.

Interns know themselves best (especially at the beginning of the year prior to developing a relationship with field supervisors) and should take the lead in developing their own goals. However, supervisors are likely more familiar with various components of the internship context (e.g., specifics about the site, training program expectations, available opportunities) and may have their own perspectives on goals that would be beneficial for the intern. Further, interns are not always aware of what they do not know and accordingly might not realize that they need work in a particular area. Therefore, once the intern develops goals, a collaborative discussion that includes the field supervisor(s), university supervisor, and the intern is beneficial for all parties.

Goals should be considered formative. They are expected to develop and change throughout the year. There are a variety of reasons goals may change, such as the intern determining that opportunities to meet the goal are not available, postponing a goal until later in the year, making developmental progress with regard to a particular skill or set of skills, or meeting the goal. The number of times goals should be discussed in supervision over the course of the year varies; *at least* three (beginning, middle, and end of the year) is a reasonable expectation. However, given the formative nature of goal setting, interns and supervisors likely benefit from discussing goals at other times during the year as well.

Using the Plan to Evaluate Intern Progress

The collection of assessment data and discussions about goals are not finished when the internship plan is created. The plan is a living document that should be modified during the year according to the intern's development of skills. As defined by Harvey and Struzziero (2008), "evaluations that occur at the end of a specified time period and emphasize conclusions and gatekeeping are *summative* [italics added], while those that occur on an ongoing basis and emphasize corrective feedback are *formative* [italics added]" (p. 410).

Formative Evaluation

Interns should be evaluated continuously and evaluation data should be used to tweak the internship plan as needed (Harvey & Struzziero, 2008). This process has been described as a "continuous loop in which evaluation information guides decision making, development of serviceable alternatives, implementation of treatments, and assessment of effectiveness" (Levitov & Fall, 2009, p. 45). Formative evaluation helps interns and supervisors to identify deficiencies and strengths and to note specific means for improvement through discussions in supervision.

Summative Evaluation

As defined earlier, summative evaluations are used to draw conclusions at the end of a period of time. At the end of the internship, a summative evaluation may be used to determine the intern's readiness to enter the field. Since summative evaluations may be used for high-stakes decision-making, formative evaluations should be linked to summative evaluations. Likewise, goals should be linked to outcomes and the internship plan should be explicitly clear on what support is needed for the intern to achieve goals (Levitov & Fall, 2009). For example, an intern who feels she is lacking knowledge about special education law may request from her supervisor recommendations for supplementary readings about special education law and additional time to observe IEP meetings or to discuss in detail how a special education eligibility decision was made. When it is time for summative evaluation, the intern will have already collaborated with supervisors on an internship plan and goals, documented progress towards goals, and determined actions to address any concerns that arose along the way. Therefore, the summative evaluation should not be surprising to the intern but rather a cumulative reflection of ongoing assessment and feedback, anchored in data (Falender & Shafranske, 2017).

Breadth of Training

In addition to promoting goal setting and providing a structure for meaningful evaluation, effective internship plans cover a breadth of experiences in an integrated manner without being impractical. The consensus from school psychology educators is that internship experiences should provide sufficient exposure to "the full spectrum of services" so that "graduates feel effective across all domains" (Harvey & Struzziero, 2008, p. 19). The impetus for interns to have multiple experiences is understandable considering (a) the multi-faceted nature of the school psychologist role and (b) non-doctoral trainees (the majority of school psychology interns) will have had only two years of coursework and a nine-month long internship before entering the field as full-time practitioners.

There are two major barriers to the incorporation of breadth of experiences in the internship plan. The first problem is that sometimes attainment of breadth is emphasized without sufficient consideration given to the intern's overarching goals. In such instances, the plan is devoid of context and it risks becoming nothing more than an exhaustive list of isolated activities. Such a plan is likely not meaningful for interns. The second problem is that the role of a school psychologist is ever-expanding and complex; it is not realistic that an intern will engage in every activity that a school psychologist may encounter in every domain of practice.

Despite these barriers, it is essential for interns and supervisors to incorporate a variety of activities and roles into the internship year. A narrow internship experience may create a practitioner with a narrow perspective on practice. Take for example an intern who spends the internship year engaged primarily in special education "refer-test-place" practices. It would not be far-reaching to predict that the intern's practices upon entering the field would emphasize special education assessment and placement and thereby neglect other school psychologist roles (Curtis, Hunley, & Grier, 2002). To paraphrase Abraham Maslow, if the only tool you have is a hammer, you tend to treat everything as if it were a nail. To incorporate breadth into the internship plan, interns and supervisors should treat activities as integrated and cutting across domains. Discussion and planning should move beyond *what* activities are occurring to a consideration of *why* and *how*. Similarly, breadth of activities should be informed by broad-based goals and should be accomplishable. The concept of breadth of experience will be revisited in Chapter 8.

Depth of Training

Even though having a wide range of experiences during the internship year is important, it is also essential for interns to pursue one or more areas in greater depth. Depth of training can be defined as progressing developmentally in a professional domain area, achieved by accessing increasingly advanced coursework or other professional learning opportunities and by applying one's knowledge and skills with a variety of individuals. According to this definition, achieving training depth in a given domain first requires trainees to develop content knowledge through continuing coursework or other forms of professional learning. Introductory coursework in a given area is likely not enough to facilitate depth of training. Second, trainees at each level of training (e.g., practicum and internship) need to apply clinical skills with individuals from a variety of backgrounds. Without sufficient content knowledge *and* multiple and differential opportunities for practice, a given trainee may only have developed surface-level knowledge or skills in a given domain (i.e., an awareness level of understanding [Joyce & Showers, 1980; 2002], as described in Chapter 1). Developing internship goals and an internship plan provides an ideal opportunity for interns to determine a specialized area of interest to pursue in greater depth than other areas.

Accrual of Hours: A Misleading Number

It is critical to note that "the passage of time, in and of itself, does not produce professional competence" (McCutcheon, 2009, p. S51), nor does it indicate one's depth of experience or the quality of supervision received (Callahan & Watkins, 2018). Take, for example, an intern named Marcella who engaged in consultation with teachers and parents for approximately 400 of her 1200 internship hours. On the surface, it may appear that Marcella achieved depth of training in consultation during the internship year and perhaps developed competence in the NASP (2010a) domain of Consultation and Collaboration. However, by taking a closer look at her experiences we can see that the number of hours is deceiving. First of all, Marcella only completed one quarter (10 weeks) of consultation coursework at the preservice level with a brief applied consultation experience and no individual supervision. Second, she did not complete any additional professional learning activities on the topic of consultation during the internship year. Third, Marcella did not discuss processes of consultation (e.g., systematic application of communication skills) during internship supervision. Lastly, Marcella did not learn a specific consultation model in her coursework, or apply a model in practice. Although Marcella engaged in consultation for a greater number of hours than other activities, it can be argued that she is not yet a competent consultant nor has she achieved sufficient depth of experience in this area (see Newman & Rosenfield, 2019 for further description of building competence in school consultation).

To summarize, supervisors should be aware that looking at number of hours to assess an intern's depth or competence can be misleading. As described by McCutcheon (2009),

> competence is achieved by engaged participation in structured educational activities and closely supervised experiences that, in fact, do occur over time. That is, competence is a product of both intentional educational interventions and a sufficient passage of time to allow for development. Both are necessary; each alone is insufficient.
>
> *(p. S51)*

This point is ironic given the emphasis on completing a specified number of internship hours to fulfill graduation and licensure (state and/or national) requirements. Instead of focusing solely on number of hours completed, an internship plan should be used to make explicit goals regarding depth and spell out clearly how depth will be achieved.

Doctoral-level Interns

Doctoral-level school psychology interns are distinguished from those at the non-doctoral level given their unique positioning to achieve depth of training. First of all, doctoral trainees take more coursework than non-doctoral trainees; this presents opportunities for doctoral-level trainees to achieve greater depth of content knowledge in particular clinical areas. Second, doctoral trainees likely spend more time engaged in fieldwork prior to the internship and therefore have a greater number and diversity of experiences within specific domains. Third, doctoral trainees are required to engage in research, the focus of which ideally connects to one's primary practice interests. Achieving depth in one or more areas can be particularly important for doctoral-level school psychology trainees who may wish to pursue opportunities other than school-based positions following their training. For example, an individual who wants to take on a research or academic position following the internship may seek out opportunities to be involved in activities such as action research, program evaluation, and data analysis during the internship year. An individual who is more clinically oriented may seek out experiences in alternative settings such as a community mental health clinic or a children's hospital to supplement his or her work in schools (Wasik, Song, & Knotek, 2009).

VIGNETTE 3.1 **RODNEY'S INTERNSHIP DEPTH**

School psychology student Rodney's interests in social-emotional assessment and intervention were sparked during his graduate training while taking two counseling courses (one required, one elective) and co-facilitating a counseling group on issues of bereavement with his practicum supervisor. In addition, in conjunction with his university's counseling center, Rodney conducted intake evaluations under supervision from a faculty member in the school psychology program; he also engaged in peer group supervision with students from the university's Counseling Psychology and School Counseling programs.

When beginning the internship, Rodney sought out counseling experiences to help him gain additional depth in this area. He co-facilitated a group with his internship field supervisor to support boys with Autism Spectrum Disorders at a middle school (including goal setting, progress monitoring, and evaluation

(continued)

(continued)

of effectiveness), attended a full-day workshop on using Cognitive Behavioral Therapy (CBT) in schools at the NASP convention, and applied what he learned in providing therapy to two individual high school students while receiving ongoing supervision. Additionally, Rodney worked with a faculty member in researching school climate and its impact on the social-emotional health of students and completed a presentation on this topic during his training program's end of the year research symposium.

Notably, Rodney's training focus in the area of social-emotional assessment and intervention did not preclude his involvement in a breadth of school psychology experiences at the elementary, middle, and high school levels over the course of his training, including the internship. What is more, Rodney's well-developed skills in counseling were viewed favorably by the internship sites to which he applied. His specialization will also make Rodney distinguishable from other interns when he begins the job application process later in the year (see Chapter 10).

Accountability

An internship plan should promote accountability for interns, field supervisors, and university supervisors. The plan documents what the intern has done during the year and how supervisors have formatively responded to the intern's needs. The notion of accountability integrates several components already addressed in this chapter, including regular documentation of intern activities and formative and summative evaluation of the intern's developmental progress. Clear documentation of the internship year is beneficial to the professional development of interns and demonstrates the impact of internship sites and training programs on the intern's skill development. Further, in instances where there are any internship concerns such as an intern demonstrating problems of professional competence (PPC, see Chapter 9), an ineffective internship training program, or insufficient university support, the intern or supervisors can respond pragmatically using informational evidence from the internship plan (Cruise & Swerdlik, 2010).

Useful for Interns and Supervisors

The final big idea to keep in mind when developing an internship plan is that a useful plan provides a roadmap for *all* internship navigators, not only the intern. The plan should be a catalyst for dialogue between the intern and his or her supervisors during supervision sessions, site visits, university internship seminar discussions, and other points during the year. The plan can be used by all parties to consider the intern's development and whether or not opportunities provided are meeting the intern's needs. If not, site supervisors and university supervisors should work

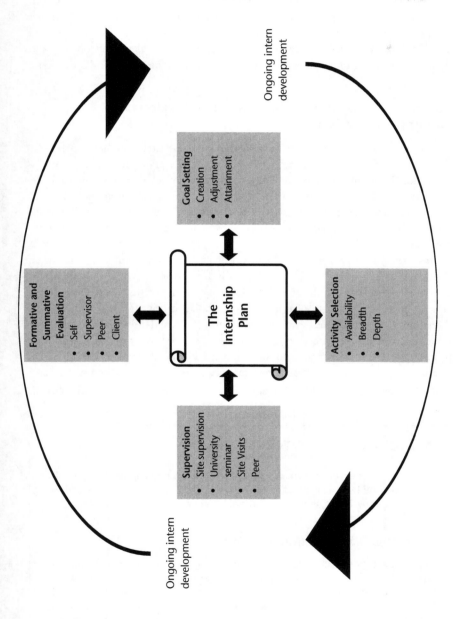

FIGURE 3.1 Developing an Internship Plan.

with the intern to adapt the internship experience. In order for a plan to be useful to all parties, it must be accessible. Accessibility requires a succinct plan rather than a laundry list of activities, and a plan that is readily available to pull out for discussion. One way to make the plan easily accessible is to use technological innovations that promote collaboration. Using such programs, the document can be easily shared and collaboratively adjusted. In short, a useful internship plan is an organic and dynamic document rather than an archived document to be autopsied at year's end.

Putting it All Together: Internship Plan Development and Implementation

The process of internship plan development is illustrated in Figure 3.1. The rounded arrows on the outside of the figure demonstrate an intern's ongoing professional learning (i.e., content knowledge, professional dispositions, applied skills) over the course of time. The intern's developmental progress influences four interrelated processes, each of which also influences the internship plan: (a) formative and summative assessment; (b) goal setting; (c) activity selection/ completion; and (d) supervision. As previously described, assessment can come from a variety of sources (e.g., self, supervisors, peers, clients) and helps determine the intern's needs and strengths. Assessment is directly tied to what goals the intern and supervisors set to be accomplished during the internship. Both assessment and goal setting influence what activities are taken on by the intern during the internship year. Lastly, assessment, goal setting, and activities are all important topics determined and discussed during ongoing supervision interactions. All four processes formatively inform and are informed by the internship plan. In sum, assessment, goal setting, activities, and supervision are naturally linked together and with the internship plan; changes made to any one process result in changes to all.

VIGNETTE 3.2 **LAURA'S INTERNSHIP PLAN**

Now that the theoretical process of internship plan development and implementation has been illustrated and explained, the chapter concludes with an overview of one intern's internship planning process.

Internship Site Selection and Entry

Laura was a specialist-level school psychology graduate trainee who was successful both academically and in her field work in her first two years in her school psychology program. She was offered and accepted an internship at Riverton School District, a medium-sized district (8,000 students) in the suburbs of a large city. Laura selected Riverton because it was conveniently located (a 10-minute drive from her home) but more importantly because she determined during the internship application and interview process that the opportunities which would be available to her overlapped greatly with her interests. In other words, before the internship even began, Laura had already reflected on her interests, skills, and professional development, which helped inform her internship decision.

Initial Assessment, Goal Setting, and Drafting the Plan

In the first university-based internship seminar, interns were asked by the university internship supervisor to review the ten NASP (2010a) practice domains and to consider their own needs, strengths, and goals. Students rated themselves as either beginner, advanced beginner, or competent in each of ten domain areas. Laura prioritized the domains of (1) Interventions and Mental Health Services to Develop Social and Life Skills; (2) Family-School (and Community) Collaboration; (3) Research and Program Evaluation; and (4) Legal, Ethical, and Professional Practice as key areas to focus on during the year. Next, using these four domains as a starting point, Laura developed broad-based goals for her year. The results of Laura's initial assessment process including self-assessment and self-identified goals are shown in Table 3.1. Although the self-assessment listed in this table reveals the overall self-rating for each domain area, note that Laura rated herself on sub-domains as well and then determined an aggregate rating for each broader domain.

The Formative Process

After completing a self-assessment and developing goals, Laura discussed prospective activities with her site supervisor and then with the site supervisor and university supervisor during a site visit. Together, Laura and her supervisors determined that all of the activities seemed feasible to accomplish during the year and matched well with her goals. The activities that were identified to achieve Laura's goal in the domain of Interventions and Mental Health Services to Develop Social and Life Skills are listed in Table 3.2. Formative changes to goals and activities are also illustrated. For the purpose of keeping this vignette succinct, the remainder of the narrative focuses only on the goals and activities within this domain area. However, note that Laura identified activities related to goals in each of her prioritized domain areas in a manner similar to what is shown in Table 3.2. Further, Laura planned to, and did in fact, engage in activities across *all* domain areas, thereby completing a breadth of activities during her internship experience.

Looking at Table 3.2, formative changes made to Laura's plan from the beginning to end of the year are evident. For instance, immediately prior to winter break, Laura realized that she had not yet completed a school-based needs assessment regarding social-emotional concerns. However, Laura had

(continued)

(continued)

TABLE 3.1 Laura's Self-Assessment and Goal Setting at the Beginning of the Internship

NASP Domain	Self-rating	Self-identified goals
Data-based Decision Making and Accountability	Advanced Beginner	
Consultation and Collaboration	Advanced Beginner	
Interventions and Instructional Support to Develop Academic Skills	Advanced Beginner	
Interventions and Mental Health Services to Develop Social and Life Skills	Advanced Beginner	• I will learn and support the best practices offered by the district for social-emotional prevention and intervention across all grade levels and with students of varying abilities.
School-wide Practices to Promote Learning	Advanced Beginner	
Preventive and Responsive Services	Advanced Beginner	
Family-school (and Community) Collaboration	Advanced Beginner	• I will increase my familiarity in working with families from different cultures and family systems. • I will learn more about the link between schools and community resources.
Diversity in Development and Learning	Advanced Beginner	
Research and Program Evaluation	Advanced Beginner to Competent	• I will engage in research and program evaluation during the internship year.
Legal, Ethical, and Professional Practice	Beginner to Advanced Beginner	• I will increase my knowledge of special education law.

started consulting with the assistant principal at the middle school to learn about perceptions of bullying in the school and worked with him and her supervisor to design and implement a school-wide bullying prevention program. She and her site supervisor decided that this experience met and exceeded the experiential intentions of the needs assessment initially described on Laura's plan. By midyear, Laura and her site supervisor determined that Laura had

TABLE 3.2 Example of Formative Internship Planning

Goal	Examples of Activities Initially Identified	Formative Adjustments/ Additional Activities Completed
I will learn and support the best practices offered by the district for social-emotional prevention and intervention across all grade levels and with students of varying abilities.	• Attend a professional development presentation on social-emotional prevention and intervention. • Review social-emotional curriculum used in the district. • Complete a site-based needs assessment regarding social-emotional supports in place for students.** • Review crisis plans at school- and district-level • Participate in training on the NASP PREPaRE model for crisis prevention and intervention. • Facilitate counseling groups at middle school and high school.** • Conduct individual counseling at middle school and high school.	• Laura determined she wanted to see how the district's social-emotional programming linked with best practices, so she researched national and state social-emotional learning standards through the Collaborative Academic, Social, and Emotional Learning website (www.casel.org). • Although Laura was initially set to co-lead a group with her internship supervisor, she instead collaborated with the school social worker to support social skill development for students with Autism Spectrum Disorders. • Laura was able to conduct two individual counseling cases at the high school level but none at her middle school site. • A student from a district middle school was killed in a car crash. Although it was not Laura's primary site, since she was part of the district's crisis planning process and was trained in the NASP PREPaRE model, she participated in the crisis response.
I will learn best practices of working with gifted and talented students.*	• Observe in multi-needs, general education, and gifted programs at the middle school and high school.	• After observing in a gifted and talented class at the middle school, Laura decided she wanted more experience working with this population. She observed some pull-out classes in an elementary school as well as advanced placement classes in the high school, interviewed teachers of gifted and talented students, learned more about the gifted and talented eligibility process, and completed a research project for an end of the year university-based symposium regarding best practices in working with gifted and talented students in schools.

Note. *Indicates a goal that was added during the year. **Indicates an initial activity that was not fully completed by the end of the year.

(continued)

(continued)

been making progress in all goal areas based on their own perceptions, a university-based intern assessment, and the progress of several students with whom Laura had been working.

As winter turned to spring, Laura had completed several activities that were not part of her initial plan, including being part of a crisis response within the district. In addition, after observing in a gifted and talented classroom, Laura realized this was a specific area of interest. Laura discussed this interest with her supervisors and she created a new goal on her internship plan. Collaboratively they determined additional ways for Laura to gain knowledge and experience on this topic including completing additional classroom observations across age levels, interviewing teachers of gifted and talented students, learning more about the gifted and talented eligibility process, and completing a research project for a university-based research symposium. By the end of the year, Laura and her supervisors felt that Laura had gained a specialized depth of knowledge and skills in working with this population of students.

Summative Use of the Plan

At the end of the school year, Laura and all of her supervisors met to discuss Laura's progress over the course of the year and her readiness to enter the field. Since Laura and her supervisors had all been in constant contact throughout the year, no one was surprised that Laura had met all of her internship goals, completed a breadth of activities during the year, and achieved competence in her prioritized domain areas. The domain which has been described in this vignette became Laura's primary area of interest. Laura gained specialized experiences in crisis prevention and intervention and working with gifted and talented students. Before terminating her internship, Laura and her supervisors looked back at the formatively developed plan and used it as a starting point to discuss appropriate goals and activities for Laura as she prepared to enter her first year of practice.

Summary

An internship plan provides a guide to navigate the internship from beginning to end. Like a driver traveling in a new city without a map or GPS, interns and supervisors who do not plan for the internship year risk driving along aimlessly and getting lost along the way. Although internship plans should be differentiated to create individualized internship experiences, there are some features that make an internship plan optimally effective.

The intern should be an active contributor to the plan from the very beginning of the year, including processes of assessment (e.g., self, supervisors, peers, and clients) and goal setting. Both formative (i.e., used to make adaptive decisions throughout the year) and summative (i.e., used at the end of the year) evaluation are tied to the internship plan. The plan should include a breadth of experiences in an integrated and pragmatic fashion (i.e., not be a laundry list) but also allow the intern to prioritize one or more areas to learn and practice in greater depth. An internship plan should promote accountability for interns and supervisors by leaving a trail of evidence of progress. Lastly, the plan should be useful for the intern and supervisors in being sufficiently accessible and in promoting productive dialogues in supervision between interns and supervisors.

Critical Thinking Questions and Activities

The following are critical thinking questions for interns, field supervisors, and university supervisors to ponder immediately prior to the beginning of the internship year.

For Interns:

- What experiences during the internship year are non-negotiable for you? Are these reflected in your plan?
- How will you ensure your goals are met over the course of the year?
- What skill area(s) would you like to focus on in greater depth than other areas?

For Field Supervisors:

- Specify the process you will use in supporting the development of an internship plan. How often and in what ways will the plan be revisited during the internship year?
- How do the intern or interns you are supervising this year vary from previous interns you have supervised? How is this reflected in the internship plan?
- If the intern's goals do not match with your skills or the opportunities available at your site, what steps will you take?
- What experiences during the internship year do you feel are non-negotiable for interns?

For University Supervisors:

- How can the internship plan be used to help structure meetings (e.g., site visits) with the intern and field supervisor(s)?
- How will you ensure interns' goals are being addressed over the course of the year?
- How might interns' internship plans inform university-based supervision and/or internship seminar content?

4

ENTERING THE INTERNSHIP SITE

Entry is the process by which interns become a part of their internship sites, generally during the first few weeks of the school year. As explained by Marks (1995), "it is hard to have an effective impact on teachers, administrators, and programs (and thereby students) without first being accepted into the school and its social system" (p. 22). Although this idea was expressed with reference to external school consultants, the same logic holds true for school psychology interns. That is, upon entering the internship, interns are challenged to become part of a system that already has an established identity and way of functioning. Therefore, an intern's potential to make an impact during the internship year is facilitated by successful entry into the internship site.

The chapter begins with a consideration of school culture and its role in internship entry. Various characteristics of school culture are considered, with an emphasis on collaboration, and examples of potential collaboration between school psychology interns and school staff are provided. Next, actions that both interns and supervisors can take to promote a successful entry process are illustrated. The chapter concludes with critical thinking questions and activities for interns and supervisors.

School Culture

The level of ease or difficulty with which the intern enters into the internship is related to school culture. School culture consists of

> unwritten rules and traditions, norms, and expectations. The unofficial pattern seems to permeate everything: the way people act, how they dress, what they talk about or consider taboo, whether they seek out colleagues

or isolate themselves, whether they work together, and how teachers feel about their work and their students.

(Deal & Peterson, 2016, p. 7)

Further, as explained by Sarason (1969/2003),

school culture refers to those aspects of the setting that are viewed by school personnel as 'givens' or essential features, which they would strenuously defend against elimination or marked change, and which to them reflect psychological concepts and value judgments

(p. 81)

Like the air we breathe, school culture is often taken for granted and overlooked (Deal & Peterson, 2016).

Sarason (1996) referred to the most important norms in school culture as regularities and suggested that regularities have *intended* outcomes which are not always the *actual* outcomes achieved. Sarason (1996) offered examples of programmatic regularities, such as the school schedule of Monday through Friday with weekends off, and behavioral regularities such as educators' tendencies to ask lots of questions of students without students themselves having sufficient opportunity to ask questions.

To further demonstrate school culture, consider the divergent experiences of two interns: one intern entered a school where the school psychologist was viewed as a collaborative problem solver who was welcome in teachers' classrooms and was constantly sought out by teachers for consultation. In contrast, a second intern entered a school where seeking support from colleagues was viewed as a weakness and teachers were wary of being evaluated or deemed incompetent if they asked others for assistance. Variations in school culture have implications for the way interns are perceived by others in the school, which actions are seen as acceptable for interns to take, and how communication interactions and relationship building are approached. For interns, understanding norms, regularities, and intended outcomes is critical for understanding school and district culture and understanding school and district culture is essential for navigating entry into the internship.

Sarason's (1996) point was not that we should always be critical of existing regularities but rather that in order to understand school culture we need to identify regularities, think about the rationales behind them, and consider the universe of alternatives. In so doing, we better understand intended outcomes and are perhaps in a better position to effect positive change. The work of Sarason (1996) is of primary interest to reformers interested in introducing change in schools; it is also relevant to individuals who may have a limited opportunity to introduce change, such as school psychology interns. That is, even though interns have limited opportunity to be change agents during (especially at the beginning of) the internship year, their navigation of the year is in part contingent on understanding the school culture in which they are embedded.

Thinking Critically about "Blinders"

A common theme in writings about school entry and school culture (e.g., Caplan, 1970; Marks, 1995; Newman & Rosenfield, 2019; Sarason, 1996) is that an individual's own culture (including values, beliefs, and prior experiences) influences his or her perspective on the school and interpretation of school culture. Prior assumptions and beliefs have been called "distortions" (Caplan, 1970, p. 59) or "blinders" (Sarason, 1996, p. 136) and inevitably influence one's perspective when entering a school setting. For example, those entering schools tend to view experiences through the lens of their own prior experiences as students, parents, or educators (Caplan, 1970; Sarason, 1996). School psychology interns should think critically about (a) the assumptions, values, and beliefs they hold about the world, (b) their prior experiences in schools and resulting perceptions about school culture, and (c) how these perspectives influence their work in the schools. Being aware of one's own cultural values is a fundamental component of being a psychologist (APA, 2017b) and school psychologist (NASP, 2010a) and is vital to successful school entry.

School Culture and Collaboration

Hargreaves and Fullan (2012) distinguished between *individualistic* and *collaborative* school cultures. Individualistic cultures are consumed by isolation. Teachers work alone, do not frequently (if at all) receive feedback from their colleagues, and may experience increased feelings of professional stagnation and uncertainty. As opined by Hargreaves and Fullan, isolation and individualism act as armor for staff members against scrutiny, intrusion, and evaluation from the outside, and are limiting to professional growth.

In contrast, in schools with collaborative cultures, teachers engage in joint work, are interdependent, and are open to giving and receiving support (Hargreaves & Fullan, 2012). In collaborative schools, ongoing professional learning and improvement are prioritized, and teachers therefore are more likely to experience enhanced professional growth. The most effective collaborative cultures create and sustain more satisfying work environments for teachers. What is more, collaboration and professional development for teachers have been shown to result in positive academic outcomes for students (Babinski, Amendum, Knotek, Sanchez, & Malone, 2018; Egodawatte, McDougall, & Stoilescu, 2011; Farbman, 2015; Darling-Hammond, Wei, Andree, Richardson, & Orphanos, 2009).

According to Hargreaves and Fullan (2012), there are varying levels of collaboration in schools – some that are more ambitious and fruitful than others. Interns will enter sites with varying levels of collaboration permeating the school culture.

While some interns may enter highly collaborative schools, others may enter balkanized schools where groups of teachers function collaboratively in cliques but there is not much building-wide collaboration. Other interns may enter schools with norms of comfortable collaboration, where teachers celebrate each other's birthdays and other milestones but collaboration does not seem to relate to professional work. And yet other interns may be in buildings or districts where collaboration is contrived from the top down and not valued by staff. Interns are advised to pay attention to the nature of collaboration in their schools and districts and to use this information as a starting point for actions taken during the entry process.

Interdisciplinary Collaboration

Although the value of collaboration is emphasized in the preceding sections, the majority of graduate courses that students take during their school psychology training tend to be isolated from other disciplines, in terms of both subject matter and composition of trainees. This is ironic considering that collaboration is placed at the core of NASP (2010d) training standards and the NASP Blueprint III (Ysseldyke et al., 2006). It seems that many school psychology programs inadvertently model cultures of individualism or isolation. However, when trainees enter a practicum, the internship, or early career practice, they are expected to successfully collaborate with others in the school despite not having prior modeling or practice. Therefore, the internship (and prior fieldwork) can provide ideal opportunities for trainees to learn about and engage in interdisciplinary collaboration.

In Table 4.1, some of the individuals school psychologists will work with in schools are identified, and examples of collaborations are described. Although Table 4.1 provides some ideas for interns and supervisors about collaborating with others in schools, it should be remembered that collaboration is not prescriptive and, if too contrived, may be less successful (Hargreaves & Fullan, 2012). On the other hand, when supervisors encourage interdisciplinary collaboration during the internship year it may enhance the internship experience, increase the intern's capacity as a collaborator, and contribute to a more positive and collaborative school and/or district culture.

Actions to Promote Entry

In addition to challenges in understanding and being responsive to the complexities of school and district culture, entry to the internship can be difficult for a variety of reasons. For one, the beginning phase of the internship naturally brings heightened anxiety for interns (Scott, Boylan & Jungers, 2015). Anxiety is expected because the role of school psychology intern is brand new and expectations may be unclear. For supervisors, especially novice supervisors, overseeing interns may also be anxiety provoking. The intern requires a significant amount of attention and time, especially at the beginning of the year. Further, the intern's

TABLE 4.1 The Internship: An Opportunity to Practice Interdisciplinary Collaboration

School Professionals	Examples of Collaboration with School Psychology Interns
Administrators (e.g., principals, vice principals, superintendents, directors of psychological services)	Dr. Roberts, the school principal, sought school psychology intern Emily's assistance when he noticed a pattern of excessive office referrals of fifth-graders from the lunchroom on Friday afternoons. Emily worked with her supervisor and the principal to re-teach lunchroom expectations to the fifth-graders, reward positive lunchroom behavior, and assign appropriate consequences to students not meeting expectations.
Teachers (e.g., general education teachers, special education teachers, related arts teachers)	As often as his schedule permitted and was appropriate, Jordan, the intern, attended grade-level team meetings for all grades, as well as special education team meetings. As the year progressed, Jordan became increasingly more comfortable at the meetings and spoke up to a greater extent; his input was valued by his teacher colleagues.
Administrative support staff (e.g., main office secretaries; guidance office secretaries; bookkeepers)	Whenever intern Isabella needed information about students, Mrs. Dougherty, the guidance office secretary, was supportive. This was helpful to Isabella when she needed to review records as part of a special education evaluation for a student.
Academic specialists (e.g., reading specialist, math specialist)	The school psychologist, Mr. Dewey, and the school psychology intern Marisa worked together with the school's reading specialist to research core reading programs that would be most effective to use in their school.
Social workers and pupil personnel workers	School psychology intern Olivia co-facilitated a group with the school social worker, Mrs. Stevens, to support LBGTQ high school students.
School counselors	The school psychologist, school psychology intern, and three of the four school counselors at Limestone High School were all a part of the school's crisis prevention and intervention team and worked together to develop a systematic crisis plan.
Nurses	School psychology intern Alex worked in combination with the school nurse and the school social worker to make sure that a student, Mike Williams, got the reading glasses he needed. Together, they supported Mike's parents, Mr. and Mrs. Williams, who did not have transportation to get Mike to the eye doctor and could not afford to purchase new frames and lenses.
Lunch aides	Bullying was a concerning issue at Worth Elementary School. Intern Ava worked with four lunch aides to be clearer on behavioral expectations and to increase their consistency in providing feedback to students

	on student behavior. The lunch aides were grateful for Ava's support and felt more effective in their role, and Ava felt she now had allies in the lunchroom to help her work with several students who needed extra assistance.
Paraeducators	Intern Chloe collaborated with a first grade paraeducator, Mrs. Guerrero, to provide drill and practice on sight words for three students who began the year behind their peers.
Custodians	Intern Lizzy worked with Mr. Hooks, a custodian who was popular with students and staff, to coordinate a behavioral intervention for a group of seventh-grade boys. By meeting predetermined behavioral expectations, the students earned the opportunity to play basketball with Mr. Hooks.
Librarian	Mrs. Newton, the school librarian, coordinated a committee to plan Dr. Seuss Day in the school. She invited school psychology intern Sophia to be a part of the planning committee and to take an active role in facilitating the day.
Technology Specialist	Mrs. Lopez, the technology specialist, taught intern Mark how to use the district's email system and helped him learn several tricks in Microsoft PowerPoint that he used when making professional presentations to the staff and at local and national conferences throughout the year.
School security/ resource officers	Running Town High School's school resource officer, Mr. Martinez, took three school psychology interns employed by the district for a ride around the community one evening after school. The interns saw several of the neighborhoods that students talked about in school and witnessed economic disparities that existed in the community.

actions are seen by those in the school as an extension of the supervisor. A wise supervisor carefully gauges the intern's entry-level skills and provides appropriate scaffolding as the year begins. Despite challenges during internship entry, there are several actions that supervisors and interns can take to support the intern's acclimation to the internship site.

Before the Internship Begins

The entry process begins as early as the internship interview. During the interview, interns should be sure to ask questions to learn more about the internship site, including demographics, opportunities that may be available, and perspectives on school psychology practice and supervision. All of this information can be considered when determining whether a particular site will be a good match for the intern's specific interests and skills. Although not every facet of the internship year can be precisely predicted, explicit dialogues between interns and supervisors may limit surprises and curb anxiety. As described in Chapter 3, the internship contract and the internship plan are two tools used to clarify and align expectations and to specify non-negotiable aspects of the internship year.

Successful internship entry can also be facilitated by supervisors planning in advance for interns to participate in various activities that take place prior to the beginning of the school year. For instance, an intern may visit and tour the school, meet some key staff members, and have a meeting with last year's intern before the internship begins. In some districts, interns are required to attend summer events such as new staff orientations, to meet with other interns, or to participate in (or even help to facilitate) professional learning sessions that occur during the summer. Such activities can help the intern network with other personnel in the district, ask lingering questions about school or district policies or procedures, and also allay the anxiety that comes with starting a new position.

VIGNETTE 4.1 **TAMARA'S FRAGMENTED ENTRY PROCESS**

School psychology intern Tamara entered a district where two school psychologists (one of whom was to be the primary internship supervisor) took maternity leave as the year began. Based on district needs and poor planning, Tamara was thrown into the two schools without the availability of direct supervisory support. Although the situation did not directly violate her contract (e.g., she still received two hours of supervision from a school psychologist outside of her buildings), Tamara had been told during her internship interview that she would be at two schools, each with its own full-time school psychologist. Instead, Tamara was forced to enter two new schools at the beginning of her internship without a school psychologist in either building, not an ideal circumstance to start off the year. Fortunately, Tamara was a talented school psychologist-in-training as well as a vocal self-advocate. She worked with the internship site and her university supervisor to improve the situation. In the end, Tamara stayed in one school where the supervisor would return in a few weeks, and was moved to work four days a week in a school with a full-time school psychologist present. However, Tamara's fragmented entry process could have been prevented with better planning and more consideration for the intern's needs.

Defining the Intern Role

One challenge that interns face when entering schools is defining what it means to be an intern. Although intern role definition will be clarified in greater depth in Chapter 5, for now it is helpful to describe the process of *how* interns can describe their role to others. Even interns with a clear intuitive understanding of their roles may have difficulty verbalizing what exactly it is that they do. The role of school psychologist is not well understood by those outside of schools (e.g., "So, you're a school counselor?"), or even those within them (e.g., "School psychologists do more than test students?"). The role of school psychology intern is perhaps more confusing given that:

- The term "intern" is generically used to describe trainees in various professional fields at varying levels of training (e.g., high school, undergraduate, and graduate) and conjures distinct schemas, some of which may be negative (e.g., "Grande coffee, pronto!");
- Interns are both students and young professionals at the same time; and
- Internships last only one full year (or two years, part-time), which has implications for relationship building and for perceptions regarding what can and cannot be accomplished.

Given these challenges, it is important for interns to be able to tell others (i.e., staff members, students, and parents) what a school psychology intern does. Having a clear understanding and definition of one's role is critical to entering schools (Marks, 1995; Newman & Rosenfield, 2019).

Once a definition is clarified, interns should be able to briefly describe their role to others when asked what it is that they do at the school. Further, an intern's self-description should be consistent with the supervisor's description of what the intern does. In retrospect, I wish I had been more thoughtful about my role definition when I was completing a field work experience at a large high school for a few hours a week. I was stopped in the hallway by a teacher who, thinking I was a high school student, asked if I had a hall pass. Unsure how to respond, I showed my university identification and disjointedly described my role until she let me move on. Although this experience did not occur during my internship, the anecdote speaks to my own lack of a defined role in a field-based experience, as well as a larger issue of a poor entry process. Most teachers, students, and administrators in the school had no idea who I was or what I did and I was unable to explain my role coherently. What is clear to me now, but I did not know it then, is that I had not successfully entered the system.

Let me provide some examples of how a new intern might describe his or her role. An intern named Sarah and her supervisor Margaret O'Donnell got a chance to discuss Sarah's internship role before staff began school for the year. At the first staff meeting, Sarah met some teachers and other staff members and introduced herself. An example dialogue shows Sarah's preparedness to briefly discuss her role:

Intern:	Hi, I'm Sarah. I'm the new psychology intern working with Maggie O'Donnell.

First Year Teacher:	Nice to meet you. I'm Jackie Burgess, a new kindergarten teacher. So, you are an intern?
Intern:	Yes. I am finishing up the school psychology graduate program at the University of Cincinnati.
First Year Teacher:	Oh, excellent. I just finished my teaching certification at UC last year! So – what will you do this year?
Intern:	Well, lots of things I hope. I will be involved in implementing academic and behavioral interventions and hopefully will get to run some counseling groups with Mrs. O'Donnell. I think I am going to be involved with the problem-solving team and the PBIS team. I think in the next couple of weeks I will help collect some benchmarking data for students. I'm also hoping to do some consultation work with teachers.
First Year Teacher:	That sounds great! I know I will need you for some consultation! It's really nice to meet you – I'm glad to know there's someone else who is new here. It feels like everyone knows each other already!
Intern:	Nice to meet you too! It sounds like we can learn the ropes together!

A second dialogue exemplifies Sarah talking with another teacher who was already familiar with the school psychology internship position. In this case, the teacher already had expectations of what Sarah would be doing during the year. Sarah was prepared to have this conversation because she previously spoke with last year's intern, Jeannie, and knew in advance that she would have some large shoes to fill.

Teacher:	Hi, I'm Betty Travis – I teach fourth grade.
Intern:	Nice to meet you! I'm Sarah, the new psychology intern working with Maggie O'Donnell.
Teacher:	Oh – so you're the new Jeannie! Jeannie did a lot of work to help my students. She did a great job! We're going to miss her this year.
Intern:	Yes, I'm the new Jeannie! I actually got to meet Jeannie and she told me about some of the things she did. Hopefully I will take on some of those pieces this year. I will be involved in working with some fourth-grade students to support interventions, and I think I will be working with Maggie to go to some of the grade level team meetings. I am hoping to get involved with the implementation of PBIS this year too. I know Jeannie loved working with the fourth-grade team!
Teacher:	Yeah – we have a great team and Maggie and Jeannie really helped us last year. Let me know if you need anything as you get oriented!

As is evident from these very brief dialogues, Sarah was prepared to introduce herself and her role, and began to develop relationships that helped solidify her successful entry process.

Supervisor Actions: Scaffolding for Empowerment

There are several actions internship supervisors can take to help support an intern's acclimation to the school once the year has begun. As has been emphasized already, the primary field supervisor is responsible for providing structured guidance and clear expectations to the intern. Some may argue that by the time trainees reach the internship year they have been in the schools for a while and no longer require extensive handholding. However, even though most interns have spent parts of at least two years in schools, even the most independent of interns need some guidance as they begin the internship experience. Supervisors are challenged to decipher what is the appropriate amount of scaffolding (i.e., support) for the intern and how best to use scaffolding to *empower* interns to be more effective problem solvers in the future. Although supervisor actions should be differentiated to meet specific intern needs, there are several general areas that are important for supervisors to consider during entry.

Administrative Support

One way for supervisors to scaffold interns is to provide guidance on the many administrative details of the internship. Although administrative pieces may be mentioned in the internship contract, some interns are left to fend for themselves once the year begins. Supervisors can support interns' entry by providing a map of the building and introducing them to key administrative personnel, such as the building's administrators, administrative support staff, and custodians. In addition, supervisors can help interns obtain keys (e.g., school building, office) and an identification badge, advocate for interns to have access to personal office space, and if applicable a computer. Additional support might be needed regarding issues such as how and where to get fingerprinted and a background check, how to obtain a district email account, how to contact human resources regarding salary and benefits, and how to access informational databases such as those related to school scheduling or Individual Education Plans (IEPs).

It is not solely the supervisor's responsibility to support the intern through every administrative detail. After all, the intern is a burgeoning professional who should be beginning to take on various responsibilities. Further, other personnel such as administrative support staff may also be in a position to guide the intern on his or her administrative way. However, administrative kinks are common and can be detrimental to the intern starting the year off successfully. Field supervisors may be in the best position to help interns navigate around such roadblocks or at the very least connect them to other individuals who can.

Including Interns from the Beginning

It is helpful for supervisors to include interns as part of beginning of the year activities that occur for all staff. This seems intuitive given that the school psychology intern will be a part of the school staff for the year to come. Unfortunately, interns are sometimes unintentionally excluded from various activities that would otherwise make them feel like a welcome part of the district. A list of suggestions for how supervisors can make interns feel like a valued part of the school and district is provided in Table 4.2.

First and foremost, interns should be introduced at school meetings that take place at the beginning of the year. This way, even if the intern has not met every single staff member in person, his or her face is recognizable to others. Further, interns should be included in activities that include all staff, such as the taking of a staff photo and the distribution of staff gifts such as a school shirt. On the first day of my internship, during staff orientation, the school principal greeted me with a firm handshake and a Cradlerock School polo shirt. From that moment, it was clear to me that I was part of the school team.

Another time supervisors can include interns is during lunch. It can be helpful for supervisors to be explicit about what they do for lunch and invite interns to join them. For example, one of my internship supervisors and I would eat lunch with the speech language pathologist on some days of the week and with the rest of the student services department at other times. At another one of my sites, I ate lunch on most days with a small group started by the school counselor. We even had potluck Fridays! These experiences contrasted greatly with one intern I supervised who was unsure about what to do for lunch. She would sit in her office by herself and eat while working; meanwhile her supervisor was in the teacher's lounge with a small group of staff members. The supervisor assumed the intern did not want to join them and the intern was not sure if she was invited.

Continuing to Include Interns Throughout the Year

In addition to taking actions at the beginning of the year to facilitate entry, field supervisors can take actions throughout the year to include their interns in school

TABLE 4.2 Ways Supervisors Can Help Interns to Enter and Feel Welcome in the School and District

Activities

- Introduce the intern at meetings (e.g., school-wide, grade-level, parent teacher association) early in the year.
- Make sure the intern is included in gifts given to the entire staff (e.g., school t-shirt).
- Have lunch with the intern the first few weeks of school.
- Invite the intern to take on responsibilities given to other staff (e.g., bus or carpool duty, lunch or recess duty, chaperone at school dance).
- Invite the intern to participate in celebrations inside and outside of school that include school staff.
- Invite the intern to contribute to cards or gifts provided to other staff.
- Encourage the intern to be part of school, district, and community teams.
- Include the intern in a staff-wide school photo.

happenings. For instance, interns can be invited to participate in celebrations that take place inside and outside of school, such as Secret Santa exchanges, a special education department happy hour, or a teacher's retirement party. Since interns do not always know about these opportunities, supervisors can make sure interns are informed and invited. Further, interns can be encouraged to take on various optional responsibilities, such as bus or recess duty, running part of a school-wide field day, or participating in school, district, or community teams. Many staff members will look favorably at the intern's contributions and the intern will feel integrated into the school and larger community.

It should also be made clear by the supervisor that it is okay for interns to turn down optional opportunities. It can be challenging to contribute to every party or gift on an intern salary and an intern's schedule may not permit being a part of teams that meet late in the evening after school. However, if the intern is not invited to participate, he or she may feel like (and may be perceived by others as) an outsider to the school community.

Supervisors Are Advocates, Not Babysitters

In identifying supervisor responsibilities surrounding interns' entry into schools, the point is not that supervisors should be babysitters, permanent hand-holders, or attached to their interns at the hip. Instead, supervisors should be advocates for their interns. An advocate supports or intervenes on behalf of the intern. Through their actions, supervisors should aim to empower interns with the skills to tackle similar problems in the future with more independence (i.e., self-advocate).

Some supervisors may think that interns desire independent functioning and may be concerned about being too smothering of the intern. This concern contrasts greatly with my anecdotal experiences as a university supervisor. I have seen concerns frequently arise from interns about not having enough supervisory support at their internship site but rarely have I heard about "helicopter" or "lawnmower" supervisors who are overbearing or do not let the intern spread his or her wings or engage in problem solving. In fact, I believe it is the small actions taken by internship supervisors, especially during the first days and weeks of the internship, that go a long way in making the entry process, and the year as a whole, a positive experience.

Intern Actions During Entry

There are several strategic actions interns can take, in tune with supervisor actions, to increase the likelihood that the intern successfully enters the internship site.

Proactive Behaviors

One overarching theme regarding intern actions for successful entry is that interns should be proactive self-advocates rather than passive recipients during the internship year. The concept of proactive behavior is expanded upon in Chapter 6. Proactive interns are self-reflective, aware of their own goals, and actively work with field and university supervisors to ensure the year is fulfilling the intern's needs and expectations. Proactive interns share responsibility for entry with supervisors and are active planners, coordinators, and shapers of the internship experience (a big idea stated in the book's Preface).

Move Beyond Comfort Zones

A second overarching theme regarding actions interns can take during entry is that it is important for interns to step outside of their comfort zones. The comfort zone is "a place where we feel at ease, with no tension, have a good grip on the topic, like to hear from others about the topic, know how to navigate occasional rough spots with ease [and] it is also a place to retreat" or escape when things are not comfortable (National School Reform Faculty, n.d., p. 122). The comfort zone is safe and when interns spend a significant portion of time in their comfort zones, they may limit opportunities for professional growth. In contrast, when interns take risks and step outside of their comfort zones, it is theorized that they will augment their professional growth. The internship is an ideal time to take such risks given that interns are still trainees and ideally have access to a great deal of supervisory support. The concept of comfort zones is revisited in greater depth in Chapter 6.

Walk Around the School and Meet People

The learning curve for interns during the first few days and weeks of school is steep; there are new names, faces, roles, procedures, and systems. If other suggestions from this chapter have been put into action, the intern may have met some staff members already and hopefully has been introduced at a staff meeting. Regardless, during staff week, before students arrive, it can be helpful for the intern to get to know others in the school. Although meeting people happens somewhat informally and organically, the process may be easier for some interns than others. Therefore, it may be helpful to have a structured approach to meeting others in the school.

To begin with, interns can ask their supervisors for a staff list and school map. When the intern meets other staff members, he or she can write down information such as their role in the school, classroom location, and personal characteristics that will help the intern remember his or her new acquaintances. As teachers are preparing their classrooms, the intern can walk around the school and peek in to quickly say "hello" and introduce him or herself. Some teachers may have more time than others to have a brief conversation but most will appreciate the effort the intern has made. What is more, the intern will have begun to develop relationships that will facilitate entry and collaboration during the year to come.

Another way interns can introduce themselves to the staff is via a letter that can be placed in faculty mailboxes or sent out via email. An example of an introductory letter sent out to staff is featured in Figure 4.1. An introductory letter is an excellent supplement to personal introductions and is also quite useful if the intern is in more than one school. The letter gives others a chance to learn more about the intern and the intern's role in the school and provides an impetus for in-person introductions and discussion ("So you are Sarah, the new intern working with Maggie this year. I saw your letter in my mailbox. Welcome to our school!").

Ask Questions

Perhaps the best way to demystify the school psychology internship is to ask lots of clarifying questions. Schools are unique systems with their own cultures and

August 28, 2019

Hello!

My name is Maya Villa and I am a School Psychology Intern pursuing my Specialist's degree at San Diego State University. I have the privilege of working with Anastasia Goodman, the School Psychologist, along with teachers and staff at Suffolk Elementary during the 2019-2020 school year.

Under the supervision of Anastasia, I look forward to working collaboratively with Suffolk's staff to provide services to children, teachers, and parents. I offer my support to the staff at Suffolk Elementary School and look forward to a wonderful school year.

Sincerely Yours,

Maya Villa
SDSU School Psychology Intern

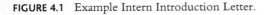

FIGURE 4.1 Example Intern Introduction Letter.

vernacular. Assumptions can be made by supervisors and other staff in the school about what interns know coming into the internship. Educational jargon and acronyms are tossed around with great frequency and in a manner that can feel daunting for trainees (Torki & Nese, 2010). Interns are encouraged to ABC – always be clarifying – in order to learn the language spoken around them. It may be outside of an intern's comfort zone to clarify something that he or she feels should already be known. However, asking clarifying questions prevents misunderstandings and helps the intern integrate into the school culture with greater ease. The process of clarifying is revisited in depth in Chapter 5.

VIGNETTE 4.2 **DOUG'S RELATIONSHIP BUILDING**

A week before students began school, school psychology intern Doug was introduced, along with other new staff members, at a full staff meeting at his school. Following the meeting, teachers were given time to get their classrooms organized. Doug had a staff list and map which were provided by his supervisor and he began to walk around the school to meet teachers and other staff as his supervisor suggested. Doing so was outside of Doug's comfort zone, in part because at his practicum site from the year before teachers did not understand why he would enter their classrooms.

After meeting and talking briefly with a teacher named Deborah Yawkey, Doug noted on his staff list: "Kids call her Mrs. Y, she is fourth grade team leader, is a huge baseball fan, and has twin daughters in Kindergarten." When Doug entered Mrs. Y's classroom to do an observation during the first week of school, he asked how her daughters were adjusting to school so far. Doug ended up working with Mrs. Y in several ways throughout the year including several consultations, completing classroom observations, and participating together in grade level team meetings. They developed a close relationship. Of course, introducing himself and taking notes were not the only reasons this relationship developed but doing so certainly got their relationship off to a strong start.

Summary

In this chapter, entry is defined as the process by which interns become a part of and are accepted into their internship sites. The ability to successfully enter into a setting, such as a school, likely influences the intern's ability to make an impact during the internship year. Interns must be cognizant of school culture, including the unwritten rules, norms, and regularities that exist at their schools. The nature of collaboration in the school is a key feature of school culture for interns to consider during entry. In addition, interns should think critically about their own assumptions, beliefs, and values. Increasing self-awareness helps to reduce the "blinders" that may otherwise hamper the entry process.

There are several specific actions that supervisors and interns can take to facilitate an entry process in which interns successfully become part of their schools and districts. Before the school year begins, interns can visit the building, meet with graduating interns, and participate in various meetings that take place over the summer. Interns and supervisors should work together to be clear on how the intern role is defined so that the intern is able to communicate that to others. Supervisors can support interns in completing administrative tasks and include them in a variety of activities – especially those that include all staff members. Supervisors are challenged to provide sufficient support to the intern without hovering over the intern at every step, and to help interns become better critical thinkers, problem solvers, and self-advocates. Interns also have many responsibilities during the entry process, including meeting staff members, asking clarifying questions, self-advocating regarding needs they may have, and challenging themselves to move beyond comfort zones.

Critical Thinking Questions and Activities

The following critical thinking questions and activities for interns, field supervisors, and university supervisors are intended to help encourage an intern's successful entry into the internship site.

For Interns:

- With a peer, practice how you would describe your role as a school psychology intern to a staff member who asks what it is that you do.
- How will you know if you have successfully entered into your internship site(s)?
- If you feel like you have not yet successfully entered into your internship site(s), what actions can you take?

For Field Supervisors:

- How do you describe the role of psychology intern to other school staff? Is your definition consistent with how your intern would define his or her role?
- What is the appropriate balance between "babysitting" and not providing enough support? How will you achieve this balance?
- How will you know if the intern has successfully entered into the internship site?
- If you feel like the intern has not yet successfully entered into the internship site, what actions can you take?

For University Supervisors:

- What is the role of university supervisors in supporting interns' site entry?
- In your training program, when and how do students learn about school culture, if at all?
- How can interdisciplinary collaboration be encouraged during students' school psychology training?

SECTION III

Clarifying Roles, Developing Relationships

5

INTERN IDENTITY AND EXPECTATIONS

The first two sections of this book are intended to orient the reader to the internship year by introducing and defining key terminology, exploring issues that commonly arise for interns and supervisors before the internship and during its earliest stages, and suggesting preventative and responsive actions for interns and supervisors to take. In the third section of the book (Chapters 5 through 9), the focus shifts to key role and relationship variables present during the internship. In this chapter, the concept of intern identity is explored, including its complexities and contradictions. The achievement of explicit expectations during the internship is discussed and exemplified. The chapter concludes with critical thinking questions and activities for interns and supervisors.

The Complexities of Intern Identity

Interns are charged with a complex undertaking. They are engaged in multiple roles simultaneously, such as being both trainees and professionals (Olk & Friedlander, 1992). Accordingly, they must navigate between training and practice, worlds which sometimes are not well linked (Hughes, Kaufman, & Hoover, 2010). Moreover, interns take on a variety of tasks, many of which are new, and they are expected to develop competence, self-efficacy, and a clearer sense of professional identity during the internship. All the while, interns have an eye on the fast approaching first year of practice and may ask themselves, "Will I be able to do this on my own next year?" Supervisors may share the same question regarding their interns' readiness to enter the field. Put succinctly, there is a whole lot for interns to learn in a limited amount of time. It follows that an intern's professional identity may be in a state of flux.

Role Conflict and Role Ambiguity

Research in the field of counseling psychology suggests that when trainees are engaged in multiple roles at the same time, difficulties arise (Ladany & Friedlander, 1995; Olk & Friedlander, 1992). A first type of difficulty, *role conflict*, surfaces when "the supervisee has specific expectations for herself or himself and/or the supervisor, but these expectations contradict those of the supervisor" (Ladany, Friedlander, & Nelson, 2016, p. 38). For instance, on one hand, school psychology interns are expected to alert supervisors to areas of self-perceived weakness in need of support. On the other hand, supervision is an evaluative process during which intern competencies are assessed, therefore interns may be hesitant to share their challenges to avoid being poorly evaluated (Mehr, Ladany, & Caskie, 2015).

A second type of difficulty, *role ambiguity*, is "a lack of clarity regarding the expectations for one's role, the methods for fulfilling those expectations, and the consequences for effective or ineffective performance" (Olk & Friedlander, 1992, p. 390). Expectations may be unclear for a number of reasons. The district may never have hosted an intern before and leadership is unclear about how to best provide support. A site supervisor may never have supervised an intern before or may not have thought strategically about what it means to do so. There also may be any number of gaps in communication, such as between the university supervisor and field supervisors, the university supervisor and the intern, or field supervisors and the intern. In sum, role conflict and role ambiguity often stem from unclear expectations. A helpful starting point for overcoming unclear expectations may be breaking down the intern role into various components and making explicit what is otherwise implicitly embedded within each role.

Interns Are Trainees

Interns are graduate students, or trainees, enrolled in a school psychology program. In fact, consistent with guidelines from the APA (2015b), CDSPP (2017), and NASP (2010d), interns are supposed to hold a title such as "school psychology intern" to designate their trainee status because they are not yet certified practitioners. Unfortunately, at some sites, interns are exploited as inexpensive sources of labor, not provided sufficient opportunities for training, or may be compelled to take on responsibilities for which they are not prepared (Sullivan et al., 2014). Being thrown into a "sink or swim" circumstance without appropriate support is unethical and is not consistent with the fact that interns are trainees. Even when an intern has advanced levels of skills in one or more areas of practice, supervisors and interns should carefully collaborate to create an experience that sufficiently supports the intern's continued professional growth.

Interns Are Extensions of Supervisors

Since interns are trainees, they are in many ways extensions of their supervisors. Consistent with NASP's (2010b) *Principles for Professional Ethics*, "when supervising graduate students' field experiences or internships, school psychologists are responsible for the work of their supervisees" (p. 7). The work of interns that supervisors bear responsibility for includes products such as written reports, services delivered by the intern, such as assessment, counseling, and consultation, and interns' professional interactions with children, parents, and colleagues. Given supervisors' legal and ethical responsibility for interns, providing a sufficient quantity and quality of supervision, including ample scaffolding for professional growth, should be prioritized.

Perception by Association

The point that supervisors are responsible for intern actions may seem obvious to readers. What is less apparent is that others may automatically see interns as similar to their supervisors in various ways, such as values, beliefs, and approaches to practice, whether or not such associations are valid. Interns who enter sites with venerated supervisors may experience a "halo effect" in which they are instantly perceived positively by others in the school. On the other hand, it may be challenging for interns to be viewed favorably if their supervisors are not well regarded by others. It should be noted that perceptions of the school psychologist, positive and negative, arise for a variety of reasons. For instance, a highly competent school psychologist who is implementing a controversial systems-level change may not be popular. Regardless of how the school psychologist is perceived, it seems likely that others may automatically meld interns with their supervisors. Such perceptions should be considered as the intern enters the school and engages in various professional activities.

The Supervisor's Spy?

Another aspect of interns being extensions of supervisors is that some staff may view interactions with the intern as non-confidential, assuming that anything discussed with the intern is automatically shared with the supervisor. To some staff, the intern may even be viewed as a spy. For example, a teacher may worry that an intern completing a classroom observation will report back to the school psychologist that the teacher did not have control of the classroom or did not implement an intervention with fidelity. The perception that interns share information with supervisors is based in reality. After all, supervisors are responsible for intern actions and need to be aware of the work that interns are doing. However, concerns regarding confidentiality can make it difficult for staff members to trust the intern and for collaborative relationships to be developed.

To facilitate the building of trusting relationships (a) the intern and supervisor can explicitly identify situations where concerns about confidentiality in working with staff may arise and (b) the intern, in advance, can be up front with staff about information that might be shared with the internship supervisor. For example, the intern may ask a teacher: "Is it okay if I observe in your class this afternoon to see how Rafael is doing academically? The observation is part of a special education evaluation and I will touch base with my supervisor Dr. Thomas after the observation to see how the observation fits with the other data we have collected."

Interns Are Reflections of their School Psychology Programs

The fact that interns are graduate students/trainees means that they are associated with a particular university and its school psychology program. More specifically, the intern's skill level when entering the internship reflects on the quality of preparation and supervision received during pre-internship training. An intern who is a critical thinker and has a strong training background may bring to the internship innovative perspectives on practice and engage in a reciprocal learning process with his or her supervisors. Conversely, trainees that exhibit significant skill deficits may reflect poorly on their school psychology programs. It is the ethical responsibility of the training program, in concert with the internship site and intern, to (a) collaboratively discuss concerns and (b) develop a plan to make sure that before entering his or her first year of practice the intern has achieved entry-level competence (Armistead, Williams, & Jacob, 2011; NASP, 2010b).

So Much to Do, So Little Time

Another implication of interns being trainees is that the intern role lasts only one year. Even those interns who are fortunate enough to be hired by their internship districts may be placed at a different school or schools the following year.

Establishing Relationships

Because interns are at their sites for only one year, the nature of relationships formed with staff, students, and parents may be affected. For example, while a full-time school psychologist may develop a relationship with a student and the student's family over the course of many years, the intern will only work with them during a single school year. However, the brevity of the internship does not necessarily preclude interns from developing meaningful relationships. As described by Denicola and Furze (2001), "each intern will approach and deal with these issues of closeness and intimacy in his or her own way. It is helpful to be cognizant of both the rich opportunities for relationships and the limits of the training year" (p. 341). The initiation, development, and termination of relationships during the internship are challenging processes that should be explicitly strategized during supervision (see Chapter 11).

Making an Impact

The limited time window of the internship may also impinge upon the perceived and actual impact that the intern can make during the year. For instance, the implementation of sustainable systems-level change may take three to five years (Hall & Hord, 2010). Consequently, although interns may contribute to processes of change, they may not see their efforts bear immediate fruit. However, as many internship supervisors would attest, interns can be significant contributors to, and perhaps even catalysts for, school and district change. Moreover, while every service delivery outcome may not be immediately visible, a training goal for interns is to provide "services that result in direct, measurable, and positive impact on children, families, schools, and/or other consumers" (NASP, 2010d, p. 8). That is, interns should conclude the year with clear evidence that they made an impact.

In addition to their immediate impact, interns should think about the long-term outcomes of their work. Critically thinking interns may ask themselves: "If I came back to this school or district or community in five years, would there be evidence that I was once here? What actions can I take that will have a positive impact on this school, district, or community?" Making a significant footprint, even if it is not instantly evident, is still possible in a limited time frame.

VIGNETTE 5.1 **JENNI'S LASTING IMPACT THROUGH A SYSTEMS-LEVEL ANTI-BULLYING CAMPAIGN**

School psychology intern Jenni joined the PBIS committee at her middle school placement and became an active team member. In the fall, the committee created and distributed a bullying survey for all middle schools in the district. In Jenni's school, the committee analyzed the data, noted locations where, according to students, bullying happened most, and worked to increase staff supervision in all identified locations. The committee devised the acronym STAND (Stand Together and Never Disrespect) to promote an anti-bullying campaign including posters, t-shirts (worn by students and staff the last Friday of every month), and a theme song as voted on by students. Eighth grade students in a mixed media class created their own anti-bullying videos (including student role-plays and subtitled statistics gathered from the survey) and submitted them to the building's administrators. One video was selected, mixed to the theme song, and played at a school-wide assembly in the spring. The STAND campaign delivered powerful information in a way that incorporated student voices.

(continued)

(continued)

Through her contributions as part of the PBIS team, Jenni made a wide-reaching impact in her school that will likely last far beyond the end of the internship year. Jenni also presented on this topic as part of her university-based internship seminar and inspired several of her peers to think about how to approach anti-bullying efforts and systems-level change during their internships and early careers.

Interns are Burgeoning Professionals

Although school psychology interns are still graduate students, they are also blossoming professionals who work in schools on a full-time basis. Children, especially younger students, likely do not distinguish between the intern and other staff members. Competent interns will quickly gain the trust of staff members and may be treated as on equal footing with their colleagues. In fact, some staff members may even defer to the intern, especially in areas where the intern is perceived to have expertise (e.g., issues related to mental health). Although the fact remains that the intern is engaged in a supervised *training* experience, the reality is that the intern is on the cusp of being a full time *professional*. Therefore, as a key meeting point between training and professional practice, the internship is an ideal time for interns to continue their professional identity development.

Professional Identity Development

Establishing a professional identity involves conceptualizing oneself as a professional, integrating skills and attitudes as a professional, and perceiving oneself in the context of a professional community (Gibson, Dollarhide, & Moss, 2010; Moss, Gibson, & Dollarhide, 2014). Professional identity development is an intrapersonal and interpersonal process and includes the integration of personal characteristics and professional training (Gibson et al., 2010; Moss et al., 2014). An intern's professional identity development is considered one of the most important goals of the school psychology internship (Sullivan et al., 2014).

It is reasonable to presume that an intern's professional identity development begins long before the internship commences and will continue throughout his or her career (Kaslow & Rice, 1985). In fact, assumptions and beliefs ingrained at the core of the intern's identity may be in place for many years prior to beginning school psychology training and perhaps even provided the impetus for choosing to pursue a career in school psychology. To paraphrase Dr. Mark R. Shinn, a former colleague of mine at National Louis University, for university educators and field supervisors, one goal of internship training may be to disrupt trainees' belief systems in order to broaden trainee perspectives and encourage trainees to become more critical thinkers regarding professional practice. In other words, field and university supervisors may consider professional identity development to be a key facet of the internship year and actively work with interns to continue the professional identity development process.

Critical Incidents: Developing Perspectives on Practice

Conceptualizing the role of school psychologist – including *what* school psychologists do and *how* they do it – is a part of professional identity development. In addition to classroom learning, field-based experiences such as observing and rehearsing models of practice demonstrated by field supervisors can influence trainees' future school psychology practices (Tarquin & Truscott, 2006). Professional identity development for interns is presumably linked to *critical incidents* (CIs), or "significant learning moments, turning points, or moments of realization" which occur during training, and make a significant contribution to trainees' professional growth (Howard, Inman, & Altman, 2006, p. 88). Reflecting on CIs, which may be a part of supervision expectations (Harvey & Struzziero, 2008), has been linked to increased self-awareness, increased reflective practice, and professional growth for school psychologists-in-training (Griffin & Scherr, 2010) and in turn may lead to an enhanced sense of professional identity.

Cultural Identity Development

Cultural awareness is an essential training component for psychologists (APA, 2015b, 2017b), is described as a critical component of school psychology internship training and supervision (Eklund, Aros-O'Malley, & Murrieta, 2014; Proctor & Rogers, 2013), and of course is related to professional identity development. Indeed, cultural competence is considered to be one of the four foundational domains of competency delineated in the NASP Blueprint III (Ysseldyke et al., 2006), and Diversity in Development and Learning is a foundational domain of the NASP (2010a) Practice Model. However, understanding the nuances of culture, cultural diversity, and working with culturally and linguistically diverse families and children is not a straightforward task and, frankly, can be overwhelming. As described by Miranda (2014),

> The journey to developing cross-cultural competence is not necessarily smooth or easy. It requires school psychologists to be self-reflective, open-minded, patient, and open to new knowledge . . . [and] . . . a professional commitment to address the challenges that [culturally and linguistically] diverse students may encounter.
>
> *(p. 14)*

Miranda (2014) provided a helpful framework for school psychologists' cross-cultural competency development, and the internship is an excellent opportunity to engage in such training. According to Miranda, working competently across cultures begins with interns analyzing and understanding their own cultures and cultural impacts on others, including acknowledging prejudices and biases; becoming aware of cultural standards, attitudes and beliefs outside of one's own; valuing diversity; reaching out to the community; and developing increased comfort in new situations that involve cultural/ethnic minority populations. Next, it is essential to build knowledge of other cultures, while simultaneously resisting stereotyping or overgeneralizing this knowledge. Further, delving into what Miranda terms "deep culture" (e.g., thoughts, beliefs, and values of a group) in addition to "surface culture" (e.g., foods, traditions, and celebrations) provides a better understanding of the diverse groups school psychologists will be working with. Finally, cultural knowledge must be applied in practice, with ongoing supervisory support, including designing and implementing culturally responsive interventions.

Canady et al. (2011) described an activity called a Cultural Roadmap that provides opportunities for interns to become skilled at a non-linear process for learning about cultural groups. The Cultural Roadmap activity contrasts with other activities that focus solely on learning specific facts about a cultural group or groups. In brief, interns learn a set of questions to be used to gain knowledge of other cultures; research a general overview about a specific cultural group; meet with community representatives, gatekeepers, and other subgroups; and produce a final product that addresses an area of concern for the culture (Canady et al., 2011). The reader is referred to the original article for a more in-depth description of how to incorporate a Culture Roadmap activity in internship training.

Although the Cultural Roadmap training approach is promising, the exercise seems to lack a consideration of one's own culture and its impact on others. One way that awareness of one's own culture can be incorporated as part of internship training is through explicit discussions in supervision. Keep in mind, however, that for supervision around cultural issues to be successful, supervisors too must address the development of their own cultural competencies (Eklund et al., 2014; Falender, Shafranske, & Falicov, 2014; Simon & Swerdlik, 2017). In sum, developing cultural competence is an essential task during internship training and is a central component of interns' professional identity development. Interns and supervisors are encouraged to work together to incorporate cultural awareness and understanding as part of the internship experience. Issues of cultural competence and supervision are revisited in greater depth in Chapter 7.

Achieving Separation-individuation

Although interns are extensions of their supervisors, they tend to establish their own distinct identities as the internship year progresses. Kaslow and Rice (1985) analogized professional identity development to child development and theorized that interns move through a process of separation-individuation from "professional adolescence" to "professional adulthood" (p. 253). Three developmental phases of the internship (Early Phase, Separation, and Individuation) are described in Table 5.1, along with challenges interns may face in each stage and actions supervisors can take to support interns' professional identity development.

TABLE 5.1 Developmental Phases of Internship: Challenges for Interns and What Supervisors Can Do

Phase of Internship (Time of Year)	Descriptive Hallmarks	Challenges for Interns	What Supervisors Can Do
Early (pre-internship / beginning of year)	• Stressful time for interns: encountering new experiences, new expectations, and beginning to develop a sense of professional identity. • Interns depend on supervisors and other staff for frequent feedback.	• Internship application and selection process. • Intern-supervisor relationship building. • Confusion regarding administrative tasks. • Apprehension about clinical skills. • Feeling the need to prove themselves • Being evaluated.	• Create a nurturing environment with appropriate limits. • Provide orientation meetings, information packets, and other adjustment activities. • Answer questions, normalize anxiety, and validate perceptions. • Encourage former and current interns to meet. • Wait for a few weeks before formally assessing the intern. • Provide constructive feedback and sensitive evaluations. • Allow time for interns to reflect on and to integrate what they are learning. • Develop a trusting supervisor-supervisee relationship.
Separation (middle of year)	• Interns less frequently check in with supervisors, are less dependent and more autonomous than at the beginning of the year. • Interns' sense of professional identity continues to develop. • Area(s) of interest, or depth, may be selected and pursued.	• Self-doubt, including questioning professional identity and clinical skills. • Experience of tension between university and practice settings.	• Emphasize continued availability to support intern supervisees. • Acknowledge intern's unique identity and individual needs including strengths, weaknesses, and goals. • Serve as a scientist-practitioner role model.
Individuation (end of year)	• Interns achieve their own individuality and sense of professional identity, and function more independently. • Interns are more autonomous in delivering services, and take on more leadership actions. • Planning for next year begins.	• Expectation to function independently without competence in all areas. • Confusion or turmoil regarding professional next steps. • Termination with students and staff.	• Encourage interns to take initiative but continue to provide support. • Provide information and support regarding professional opportunities for the upcoming year. • Explicitly discuss termination process. • Plan a farewell occasion such as a dinner or party.

Note. Adapted from "Developmental Stresses of Psychology Internship Training: What Training Staff Can Do to Help," by N. J. Kaslow and D. G. Rice, 1985, *Professional Psychology: Research and Practice, 16,* pp. 253–261.

During the Early Phase (encompassing the time prior to the internship through the beginning of the year), interns experience a great deal of stress; there are many new expectations and tasks. As interns move towards the Separation Phase they become more independent but still experience self-doubt and become more acutely aware of gaps between the world of training and the realities of practice. By the end of the year, interns reach the Individuation Phase, marked by increased autonomy and a greater sense of professional identity. Through all three phases, interns experience feelings such as confusion, anxiety, and stress, and benefit from ongoing supervisory support, including explicit modeling, guidance, and feedback. Interns' continued need for supervision indicates that irrespective of a given intern's increasing role individuation, identity development, and competence, a supervisor's ethical responsibility for the intern's actions does not change.

An example of an intern named Rose's movement through the developmental phases of the internship (demonstrated through her increasing participation in the school problem-solving team) is shown in Table 5.2. Rose began the year unsure of her role on the problem-solving team. She was hesitant to speak up during meetings despite her well-developed knowledge of problem solving, opinions about cases discussed, and thoughts on how to improve the team's functioning. Her supervisor, Sharon, encouraged Rose to participate in meetings, gave her explicit responsibilities, and provided structured guidance and feedback. Rose took on more independence as the year went on and became a highly valued team member. In fact, by the end of the year, Sharon viewed Rose as a vital advocate in promoting effective problem solving in the school.

The Complexities of Internship Supervision

In addition to being trainees and almost-professionals, interns are supervisees. Scott et al. (2015) argued that supervision expectations are often unclear to interns, creating anxiety and apprehension. When interns and supervisors engage in clear discussions about supervision expectations, that presumably can alleviate supervisee anxiety and increase effective learning. The complexities of internship supervision will be considered in significantly greater depth in Chapter 7. For now, some questions that can illuminate supervision expectations and trigger discussion about processes of supervision are listed in Table 5.3. The questions about supervision are organized into four thematic categories: logistics, evaluation, developmental considerations, and troubleshooting.

Logistics

Different supervisors approach the process of supervision in different ways. For example, some supervisors prefer regularly scheduled closed-door time with their supervisees, while others improvise supervision meetings as time becomes available during the week, or when the intern requests assistance. Interns may be engaged in various types of supervision (e.g., individual; group, with a supervisor;

TABLE 5.2 Developmental Phases of Internship Exemplified

Phase of Internship	Intern Behaviors	Supervisor Behaviors
Early	Rose was a vocal contributor to her school-based problem-solving team during her second-year practicum but hesitant to contribute at problem-solving team meetings at the start of her internship due to doubts about her clinical skills and worrying what her supervisor might think.	During a supervision meeting early in the year, Rose's site supervisor Sharon clarified the problem-solving team process at the school and expressed hope that Rose would be a contributor this year. Prior to the second meeting, Sharon and Rose discussed what cases would be on the agenda and shared perspectives. Sharon encouraged Rose to participate in the meeting, and gave Rose encouraging feedback immediately following the meeting.
Separation	By December, Rose became a strong contributor during problem-solving team meetings. She increasingly took the lead on presenting cases and helped the team work through the problem-solving process. However, Rose was frustrated because team members often did not satisfactorily identify problems and instead tended to jump directly into suggesting interventions. The problem-solving process looked different from what Rose learned during her school psychology coursework.	Sharon asked for Rose's perspective regarding the problem-solving team's functioning, and found they both shared similar concerns. Together they planned to address these issues in the next problem-solving team meeting; Sharon took the lead and Rose made supporting contributions.
Individuation	By the end of the year, Rose attended and led some problem-solving team meetings without her supervisor present. At the same time as finishing her internship, Rose actively applied for school-based positions for next year.	Rose and Sharon debriefed on the meetings during supervision time. Rose took the lead in prioritizing what she wanted to discuss. Sharon checked in regarding Rose's job prospects, provided feedback on her CV and cover letters, and offered suggestions of potential job interview questions.

TABLE 5.3 Examples of Questions to Clarify Internship Supervision Practices

Category of Concern	Examples of Questions that Can be Clarified
Logistics	• How often and for how much time will the intern and supervisor meet for supervision? • What model of supervision and supervision techniques will be used by the supervisor? • How should the intern prepare for supervision meetings? • What happens during a site visit?
Evaluation	• How will formative and summative evaluation be incorporated as part of supervision? • What are the intern's goals and how will the intern and supervisor know if those goals have been met? • How is evaluative feedback communicated? • How do field requirements relate to university requirements?
Developmental Considerations	• Does the supervisor know the intern's current level of skills in various areas of practice? • How are appropriate levels of independence and scaffolding determined and provided? • How does the supervisor support the intern's development in an area where the supervisor may not be competent? • How are supervision interactions different during the beginning, middle, and end of the year, if at all?
Troubleshooting	• What should an intern do if he or she disagrees with a supervisor's perspective on a case? • What should an intern do if he or she receives different messages from different supervisors? • What should the intern do if he or she is receiving too much or not enough supervision? • How can the supervisor and intern improve their relationship?

non-hierarchical peer group) and there may be multiple supervisors, each with unique styles. Without explicit discussions about how supervision will be provided, interns simply will not know what to expect or how to be well-prepared supervisees. Discussions about logistics get at the nuts and bolts of supervision, such as who is the primary supervisor, when and where supervision will take place, and how many hours per week supervision will occur. Other considerations include how the supervisor approaches supervision, including models and techniques, and the coordination of supervision across various supervisors. The potential consequences of various supervision structures are explored in significantly more depth in Chapter 7.

Evaluation

It is the responsibility of field and university supervisors to evaluate interns (a) formatively and summatively, (b) formally and informally, and (c) along numerous dimensions, such as competence, professional dispositions, and ethical practice (Scott et al., 2015; Sullivan et al., 2014). Although it is normal for interns to feel anxious about being evaluated, providing a structured approach to evaluation, including setting clear criteria for assessment, providing ongoing feedback that is explicit and constructive, and using a variety of techniques, mitigates apprehension (Scott et al, 2015).

Developmental Considerations

As described in Chapter 1 and in this chapter, frameworks of development provide a lens to view interns' personal and professional growth during the internship year. Developmental models of supervision describe how interns' levels of skills in various areas can be matched with developmentally appropriate supervision strategies (Simon & Swerdlik, 2017). Supervisors can make explicit how developmental progress will be determined (e.g., how progress is tied to evaluation data and the intern's goals) and discuss how supervision may look different based on intern skills in a particular clinical area, or time of year.

Troubleshooting

Supervision issues that are difficult to navigate, for both supervisors and interns, sometimes arise during the school psychology internship. Such circumstances include ethical dilemmas such as the intern not receiving enough supervision time, or precarious interpersonal situations such as a poor supervisor-supervisee relationship. Interns and supervisors may be well served by being upfront about what to do if challenging situations should arise. For example, during a site visit I recently conducted, the field supervisor told the intern: "If you are not sure why I took an action, please ask. Talking through my decisions helps me continue to grow as a school psychologist." Such discussions also present excellent opportunities for teaching interns to be problem solvers, critical thinkers, and ethical practitioners.

Clarifying Internship Expectations

Given the complexities of intern identity and processes of supervision described thus far, the need for explicit and clear expectations during the internship seems apparent. In fact, the importance of clearly communicated expectations during the internship is asserted by several authors (e.g., Scott et al., 2015; Harvey & Struzziero, 2008; Sullivan et al., 2014; Simon & Swerdlik, 2017) and the need for (a) clear training goals and objectives and (b) timely and specific supervisory feedback are highlighted within the APA's (2017a) Ethical Code. Although the importance of clear internship structures appears evident, *how* to achieve clarity is less apparent. Therefore, the second part of this chapter focuses more precisely on how interns and supervisors can communicate effectively to elucidate expectations and demystify the school psychology internship.

The Influence of Language

Words shape our experiences, actions, and the actions of others. The misuse of oral or written language, whether by mistake or deliberate (i.e., for purposes of persuasion), can contribute to poor decision making in clinical practice (Gambrill, 2012). There are numerous examples of fallacies, or mistakes in thinking, that are related to the use of language. Examples of some of the language fallacies described by Gambrill (2012) are presented in Table 5.4. The table includes a brief definition of each term and examples of how the errors may arise when interns and supervisors negotiate internship expectations.

The information in Table 5.4 serves several purposes. First, it is helpful for interns and supervisors to be aware of potential errors of language, including giving them specific names, in order for them to avoid committing such fallacies while communicating (Gambrill, 2012). Second, many of the errors listed can be addressed by *clarifying*, using questions or statements that help break down the inferential or abstract into observable and measurable terms (Newman & Rosenfield, 2019). Third, it is important to stress that language fallacies are often committed by mistake. For instance, communicators make assumptions about meaning even though what is meant by the speaker and what is understood by the listener may not be one and the same. Some communicators may even pretend to understand in order to avoid embarrassment. To prevent pitfalls of communication, it is important for interns and supervisors to be conscientious in their verbal and written interactions.

Clarifying Down the Ladder of Inference

To illustrate fallacies of misunderstanding, Argyris (1990) and later Senge, Kleiner, Roberts, Ross, and Smith (1994) described a heuristic called the ladder of inference, illustrated in Figure 5.1. At the bottom of the ladder is sturdy ground, including observable and measurable data as might be captured by a video recorder. Moving up the ladder, an observer filters the data through his or her own lens, adds meaning (e.g., personal, cultural, professional) to the data, makes assumptions about what is observed based on the added meaning, draws conclusions, changes his or her beliefs, and takes actions based on his or her beliefs. New beliefs affect the observer's future perceptions, a process called the "reflexive loop" (Senge et al., 1994, p. 243). When perceptions and actions are far removed from the bottom of the ladder, the observer may find himself or herself on shaky ground. In other words, the observer takes actions based on inferences rather than facts. Applied to the school psychology internship, when expectations are not clearly discussed, interns and supervisors may inadvertently find themselves atop the ladder of inference, engaged in misinformed actions.

TABLE 5.4 Fallacies Related to Language that can Obscure School Psychology Internship Expectations

Fallacy	Definition	Example
Predigested Thinking	Oversimplifying complex topics, issues, or perspectives.	An intern reports in her university seminar that her district "does not do RTI" so she cannot be involved in "RTI activities" during the internship.
Jargon	Using complicated, technical, or obscure language.	On the internship plan, it is written that the intern will engage in "Data-based decision making and accountability" but what this means is not clarified.
Use of Emotional Words, Buzzwords, or Imagery	Using words, metaphors, or imagery that are emotionally laden or convey strong feelings.	A site supervisor tells the intern, "Students frequently come to our office when they are in crisis. We do our best to prevent and put out fires and make sure no one gets hurt."
Labeling	The misapplication or inaccurate use of a classification term.	An intern tells her supervisor, "I want to do a group with Aspergery-type kids this year."
The Assumption of One Word, One Meaning	Failure to recognize that the same word may mean different things to different people, or in different contexts.	The intern and supervisor agree on a goal for the intern to work with "diverse children and families." The intern is interested in working with bilingual students but the supervisor thinks the intern wants to work with economically diverse populations.
Misuse of Verbal Speculation	Relying on conjecture and assumptions rather than observable and measurable facts.	An intern tells his supervisor that he feels he has made significant growth in his counseling skills this year but no assessment has been conducted.

(continued)

TABLE 5.4 *(continued)*

Fallacy	Definition	Example
Use of Vague Terms	Use of terms that are broad, unclear, or may have multiple meanings.	The university supervisor tells students in the internship seminar that he expects they will engage in "evidence-based practice" during the internship experience and does not clarify further.
Conviction through Repetition	Hearing, seeing, or thinking about a statement multiple times, which increases a belief that the statement is true.	The site supervisor frequently tells the intern, "Forget what you learned in school . . . now you are in the real world."
Bold Assertions	Firmly and confidently declaring a position or stating a conclusion regardless of evidence.	The intern states that he feels ready to conduct a threat assessment independently even though he has not done so before.
Primacy Effects	The first thing we hear or see influences what we attend to and the attributions we make.	An intern gets nervous presenting aloud at meetings (e.g., stumbling, turning red, relying heavily on notes), especially at the beginning of the year. The site supervisor rates the intern poorly in this area on an end of year evaluation rubric even though the intern has made significant growth during the year.

Note. The text in columns 1 and 2 is adapted from *Critical Thinking in Clinical Practice: Improving the Quality of Judgments and Decisions* (3rd ed., pp. 133–148), by E. Gambrill, 2012, Hoboken, NJ: John Wiley and Sons.

An illustration of the ladder of inference concept applied to the school psychology internship is featured in Figure 5.2. Early in the internship year, an intern named Tricia got nervous at IEP meetings – she stammered in her speech, turned red, and looked extensively at her notes rather than making eye contact with parents. Both Tricia and her supervisor, Anne, recognized Tricia's nervousness but the beliefs and actions that each of them developed in response to the performance diverged as they moved up the ladder of inference. Tricia was self-critical, labeling herself as incompetent and assuming others (including her supervisor) viewed her in that light. Although Tricia recognized her continued need to practice presenting evaluation data, she worried about potential implications of requesting Anne's guidance and support. On the other hand, Anne empathized with Tricia's experience. However, given Anne's own prior experiences, she chalked up Tricia's nervousness to Anne being too overbearing as a supervisor. Actions resulting from inferences suggest that Anne will take a more hands-off supervisory approach and Tricia may not receive the modeling and scaffolding support that might otherwise contribute to her growth of skills.

As argued by Newman and Rosenfield (2019) with regard to school consultation, the ladder of inference is a helpful heuristic to aid school psychologists in unpacking language and clarifying the nature of problems. The authors also described requesting clarification as an essential skill for facilitating effective

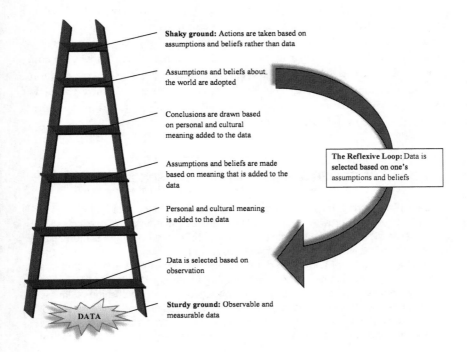

FIGURE 5.1 The ladder of inference.

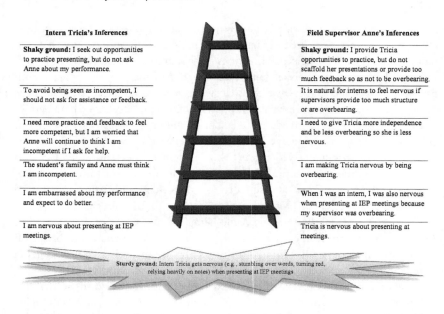

Intern Tricia's Inferences		Field Supervisor Anne's Inferences
Shaky ground: I seek out opportunities to practice presenting, but do not ask Anne about my performance.		**Shaky ground:** I provide Tricia opportunities to practice, but do not scaffold her presentations or provide too much feedback so as not to be overbearing.
To avoid being seen as incompetent, I should not ask for assistance or feedback.		It is natural for interns to feel nervous if supervisors provide too much structure or are overbearing.
I need more practice and feedback to feel more competent, but I am worried that Anne will continue to think I am incompetent if I ask for help.		I need to give Tricia more independence and be less overbearing so she is less nervous.
The student's family and Anne must think I am incompetent.		I am making Tricia nervous by being overbearing.
I am embarrassed about my performance and expect to do better.		When I was an intern, I was also nervous when presenting at IEP meetings because my supervisor was overbearing.
I am nervous about presenting at IEP meetings.		Tricia is nervous about presenting at meetings.

Sturdy ground: Intern Tricia gets nervous (e.g., stumbling over words, turning red, relying heavily on notes) when presenting at IEP meetings

FIGURE 5.2 The ladder of inference applied to school psychology internship expectations.

communication. Clarifying can be done through a statement (e.g., "Tell me more about what you mean by data-based decision making and accountability"), or a question (e.g., "What do you mean when you say 'diverse families and children'?"). Clarifying brings forward valuable information and moves the communicators down the ladder of inference towards explicit goals, expectations, and actions. Looking again at Figure 5.2, Tricia or Anne could have clarified at the bottom of the ladder by explicitly discussing Tricia's performance at the IEP meeting, as well as their shared concerns.

VIGNETTE 5.2 **ROGER'S MISUSE OF VERBAL SPECULATION**

Late in the spring, Roger reported to his supervisor, Mary, that he felt he had made significant growth in his knowledge and application of counseling skills. Roger in fact *had* made significant strides in counseling during his internship. He had co-facilitated a bereavement group with the school counselor at the middle school level and worked individually with three high school students with counseling minutes written into their IEPs (although the counseling goals were somewhat unclear to Roger). He engaged in brief discussions with his site supervisor about the cases, but mostly discussed his work with the school counselor and his university supervisor. Roger also completed several relevant outside readings and learned new counseling strategies that he successfully applied in action. Mary assumed Roger had done an excellent job in his counseling work and affirmed Roger's assertion. However, Mary had not observed or viewed recordings of Roger counseling; they had only briefly discussed counseling techniques in supervision; she had not completed an evaluation of Roger's counseling skills; and he had not self-assessed his counseling skills.

In retrospect, it may have been beneficial for Mary to clarify Roger's speculation (e.g., "Tell me more about your perceived skill growth . . .", or "How do you know you've made growth in your skills?"). In so doing, the dyad would have identified concrete examples of Roger's growth as well as experiences that Roger could continue to work on with supervisory support. Without clarification, it is not readily apparent what skills Roger needed to continue to work on for the remainder of the year and as an early career school psychologist. Moreover, if Roger was not becoming a more skilled counselor, the combination of verbal speculation and a faulty assumption might have been harmful to his professional development and could have resulted in negative outcomes for children.

The Internship Agreement and Plan: Clear Writing Leads to Clear Expectations

Internship expectations should be written in explicit and unambiguous terms on the internship agreement and the internship plan. As described in Chapter 3, the internship agreement holds the university, internship site, and intern together under a contract that clearly spells out administrative and logistical details of the internship. An internship agreement should be completed before the internship program begins so that all parties are immediately on the same page. Unlike the internship agreement, the internship plan is formative and changes during the year in tune with the intern's developing goals and needs. Ideally, the internship plan includes several features that augment clarity such as (a) a statement of the intern's goals, (b) a statement of how the intern will be evaluated, and (c) a consideration of how the intern will achieve a breadth and depth of experiences. As in oral communication, the use of vague terminology, jargon, or implicit assumptions should be avoided when composing written documents.

Further, after the internship agreement and internship plan are written, it is important for there to be an oral discussion between intern and supervisor regarding what is agreed upon. A discussion gives all parties the opportunity to ask questions about anything that remains unclear (e.g., University Supervisor: "The plan says Amy will engage in peer group supervision at the internship site. What will that consist of?"), add anything that is missing (e.g., Intern: "The agreement says that I will be at Western Middle School but on the phone we said I would also be at Western High School"), or to overtly address any concerns that may otherwise be implicit (e.g., Field Supervisor: "How will site visits work? Do you observe Amy doing work, or do we just talk about how things are going?").

Multiple Supervisors, Multiple Expectations

Coordination across an intern's supervisors (both within the internship district and between the district and university) can also help facilitate clearer internship expectations. Coordination is challenging because interns may have several supervisors, each of whom may approach practice and supervision differently. Further, the intern may have different relationships with each supervisor, some of which may be positive while others may be strained. When supervisors do not communicate with each other it may put the intern in a precarious position, or even worse, be detrimental to training. For example, an intern named Renya had positive relationships with her two site supervisors but the two supervisors had divergent perspectives on practice. Each supervisor vented to Renya about the other's practice and the supervisors frequently argued about what training areas should be prioritized. Renya ended up having a fragmented internship experience and a confused sense of professional identity entering her first year as a school psychologist.

Depending on how the internship is coordinated, having supervisors with different perspectives can be a *positive* experience for interns. Exposure to multiple ways of practicing expands the intern's professional repertoire and allows the intern to think critically about what practices result in positive outcomes for children, and what practices fit best with his or her developing professional identity. Internship coordinators (or others who are responsible for assigning site supervisors) may wish to purposefully select supervisors who expose interns to different school contexts and approaches to practice, get along with each other, and will be in frequent communication during the year. Ongoing communication between supervisors can promote clear expectations, diminish feelings of confusion and contradiction, and create an integrated web of support for interns during this capstone experience.

Expectations from the University

Internship expectations should also be clear from university supervisors. At the very least, university educators can establish clear internship guidelines in their school psychology program handbooks. Many training programs even provide trainees with an internship manual to explain procedures and guidelines for the internship year (McMahon, Jenkins, & Styles, 2018). Handbooks or manuals can include information about how to secure an internship, templates and examples of an internship agreement and internship plan, guidelines for site visits, procedures for university supervision, a clear description of how successful completion of the internship will be evaluated, and steps for obtaining state and national certification.

In many school psychology training programs, interns are required to participate in a university-based internship seminar. The course syllabus can be explicit about what is expected of interns in the seminar, and should be consistent with expectations listed in the university handbook or internship manual. Through the seminar, the instructor (often the university internship supervisor) can provide information and answer questions about what may be considered confusing processes, such as taking state or national examinations and procedures for attaining licensure. It may also be helpful for the instructor to invite a former intern or interns to present at an early internship seminar regarding what new interns need to know and to answer new interns' questions.

When internship seminars are offered, university supervisors should think carefully about how seminar expectations are aligned with the field components of the internship. Items for consideration are numerous, and may include:

- How often and what time does the seminar meet? Does the schedule interfere with the interns' professional responsibilities?
- What assignments should be included in the seminar? Do assignments support the interns' field experiences?
- What time, if any, is provided for peer group supervision and how is it structured?
- How are field supervisors included as part of the university seminar or the overall university-based internship supervision process?

By contemplating such questions, university supervisors can contribute to a transparent and integrated internship experience.

Summary

Interns are student trainees, emerging professionals, and supervisees all at the same time. Having multiple facets of identity presents numerous challenges for interns, including conflicting or ambiguous expectations. As trainees, interns are extensions of their supervisors and reflections of their school psychology programs. As soon-to-be professionals, each intern's professional identity, including cultural identity, is formatively developing towards an individuated sense of self as a professional school psychologist. As supervisees, interns are engaged in supervision processes both in the field and with their university. It is useful for interns and supervisors to explicitly discuss logistical details of supervision, procedures for evaluation, developmental considerations, and how sensitive concerns will be navigated should they arise.

In order to establish clear internship expectations, matters of communication are critically important. Errors of language, both oral and written, should be avoided. Using clarifying questions and clarifying statements can help interns and supervisors break down vague or inferential language and make expectations observable and measurable. Unambiguous written language should be used on the internship agreement and internship plan. Further, all supervisors should engage in ongoing communication in order to promote consistent expectations across settings. University supervisors should also be careful to provide transparent and comprehensible expectations regarding the internship.

Critical Thinking Questions and Activities

The following are critical thinking questions for interns, field supervisors, and university supervisors to ponder regarding intern identity and internship expectations.

For Interns:

- On a continuum from trainee to professional, where would you mark your identity? How do you suppose this will change over the course of the internship year, if at all?
- Identify five *critical incidents* from your training experience that have shaped your development as a school psychologist.
- If you recognize a fallacy of language in interactions with a supervisor or written in internship paperwork, how will you respond?

For Field Supervisors:

- What is your approach to supervision? Have you made your supervisory approach clear to your intern(s)?
- What are school psychology internship expectations from the district level?
- How do internship expectations differ for different interns, if at all?

For University Supervisors:

- How are internship expectations provided to students in your program (e.g., written, oral, other)? Is the process of explaining expectations sufficient?
- If you recognize a fallacy of language in interactions with a field supervisor or written in internship paperwork, how will you respond?
- What are some ways you can enhance your communication interactions with field supervisors?

6

THE PROACTIVE INTERN

One of this book's big ideas is that interns should be active planners, coordinators, and shapers of the internship experience. That is, interns should self-advocate for their personal and professional needs, contribute to decision making processes regarding the internship, take initiative, and constantly seek out opportunities for learning. This big idea does *not* mean that interns should fly solo, completing their internships independently without supervisor support. The point is that interns should actively influence the internship as opposed to being passive recipients of their supervisors' plans. Stated another way, the internship should happen *with* interns, not *to* interns. The focus of Chapter 6 is on (a) what it means to be a proactive intern and (b) how the intern can be a proactive contributor to the internship. Actions supervisors can take to facilitate interns' proactive behavior are also explored. The chapter concludes with critical thinking questions and activities for interns and supervisors about intern proactivity.

What Does it Mean to Be a Proactive Intern?

Proactive behavior is a complex construct that has been extensively explored in the Organizational Psychology research literature (see Parker & Bindl, 2017 for a summary) and has been applied to numerous professional fields (e.g., Accounting, Business, Engineering, and Nursing, to name a few). Proactive behavior is defined as taking "self-directed and future-focused action in an organization, in which the individual aims to bring about change, including change to the situation . . . and/or change within him- or herself" (Bindl & Parker, 2011, p. 568). Being proactive therefore involves being future-focused, change-oriented, and self-starting in one's behaviors (Parker & Bindl, 2017). Proactivity is shaped by an individual's personality as well as numerous situational forces such as job demands and expectations and is conceptually and empirically linked to superior job performance (Crant, Hu, & Jiang, 2017; Parker & Bindl, 2017).

Applied to school psychology interns, being proactive may be thought of as thinking critically about the internship experience and using that information to advocate for changes to enhance learning. Changes may include *changes to self* (e.g., seeking out additional professional development opportunities or resources; purposefully asking more clarifying questions; developing a process for self-assessment; or engaging in networking opportunities) and *changes to the environment* (e.g., taking on additional opportunities or activities; making schedule changes in order to alleviate stress; or requesting additional time for supervision).

Proactive Personality

The construct of *proactive personality* is the dispositional tendency for individuals to take actions in order to influence their environments (Bateman & Crant, 1993). According to Bateman and Crant (1993), prototypically proactive individuals "scan for opportunities, show initiative, take action, and persevere until they reach closure by bringing about change," while those who "are relatively passive react to, adapt to, and are shaped by their environments" (p. 105). Research demonstrates proactive personality is predictive of factors related to career success, such as overarching job performance, satisfaction, and organizational commitment (Thomas, Whitman, & Viswesvaran, 2010). Interns with proactive personalities may have a professional advantage in how they are perceived and evaluated by supervisors. For example, in a qualitative study of the learning experiences of medical interns by Deketelaere, Kelchtermans, Struyf, and De Leyn (2006), supervisors tended to view interns' proactive attitudes as evidence of commitment and motivation and perceived it as easier to provide proactive interns with learning opportunities.

It seems likely that school psychology interns, like other individuals in an array of professional fields and levels of training, differ in their dispositional tendencies to be proactive. Variations in proactive personality may have implications for the actions interns take or do not take, the way they are perceived by their supervisors, and the overall success of the internship year. However, personality alone does not account for the presence or absence of proactive behaviors; proactive behavior is also a function of situational variables (Bindl & Parker, 2011; Erdogan & Bauer, 2005). Therefore, it is reasonable to presume that professional practice skills such as how to be proactive can be "harvested, grown, and sustained" (Bateman & Crant, 1999, p. 66) during the internship year.

Contextual Considerations

The school psychology internship takes place in a context with its own situational variables to be accounted for. For instance, as described in detail in Chapter 5, interns are still trainees, a status that may inhibit the ability to be proactive. They may worry about overstepping the boundaries of the intern role (especially if such boundaries are not clearly delineated), may not have a sufficient understanding of their school or district culture to take certain actions, or may be concerned about processes of evaluation. Although there are some universal features of the school psychology internship for all interns, the internship is also in some ways unique for each individual. Therefore, each intern's distinct internship context provides varying opportunities for proactive behavior.

VIGNETTE 6.1 **DIFFERING CONTEXTS, DIFFERENT BEHAVIORS**

Interns Susan and Noah were in the same cohort of a training program and were interning at different school districts. Both were highly rated by their supervisors with regard to professionalism and could be described as motivated interns. Neither had worked at the early childhood level during their school psychology training so far but both wanted such an experience. During a supervision session in the early fall, Susan inquired with her field supervisor to see if an early childhood experience was possible. Together, they adjusted Susan's schedule to include a half-day a week at a preschool in the district where there was a school psychologist in the building. Susan was proactive in making a change in her environment, had the support of a flexible supervisor to do so, and there was an opportunity available nearby.

In contrast, Noah felt constrained by his already busy internship schedule (he was split between three schools over five days) and numerous responsibilities. Although he had a positive relationship with his supervisor, Noah assumed changing his schedule was not possible. He also knew there was not an early childhood location in the district where he could work. As a result, Noah did not pursue his interest and did not get to engage in an early childhood experience. Noah's passivity was based on realistic assumptions regarding his internship context. However, it may have been helpful for Noah and his supervisors (field and university) to strategize ways to creatively provide Noah's desired experiences (e.g., visiting a different district, collaborating with a community agency, or working at an early childhood center on the university campus).

Examples of Interns' Proactive Behaviors

Although defining personality and contextual variables helps to conceptualize what it means to be proactive, it is also important to describe specific proactive actions interns can take to enhance their internship experience. For interns, being proactive includes seeking out information, seeking out opportunities, having a proactive attitude, and attending to self-care needs.

Seeking Information

One behavior that interns can engage in to be proactive is seeking information. Information-seeking behaviors contribute to organizational newcomers' process of socialization, or "learning the behaviors and attitudes necessary for assuming a role in an organization" (Morrison, 1993a, p. 173). Socialization for school psychology interns can be defined as learning the behaviors and attitudes needed to be an effective school psychology intern and eventually a professional school psychologist. For interns, socialization includes entering into internship sites, establishing relationships with colleagues, developing content and applied knowledge of school psychology, and taking on professional responsibilities with increasing independence over time. Like other professional newcomers, it seems important for school psychology interns to seek information from others, such as university supervisors, field supervisors, school staff, and peers, to support their socialization.

What Types of Information Should Interns Seek?

According to Morrison (1995), there appear to be seven types of information that newcomers to organizations, such as interns or early career professionals seek: technical; referent; social; appraisal; normative; organizational; and political. *Technical information* refers to how one executes his or her job. *Referent information* includes requirements and expectations specific to a particular position. *Social information* is knowledge about colleagues and one's relationships with them. *Appraisal information* refers to how one's performance is evaluated, including self-assessment and evaluation by others such as supervisors. *Normative information* encompasses an organization's cultural norms and *organizational information* gets at the structures, procedures, and services provided by the organization. Lastly, *political information* is the distribution of power in the organization. Examples of information school psychology interns may seek in each of the seven categories are provided in Table 6.1.

Passive and Active Approaches to Obtaining Information

Clearly, there is an overwhelming amount of information for school psychology interns to seek out. There are also numerous ways interns can successfully obtain information. For one, interns may receive information in a passive manner through means such as unobtrusively observing, including listening, watching, and monitoring. Being a passive recipient of information can be a helpful behavior for interns. For example, intern shadowing and observation combined with supervisor modeling are suggested to be important components of the early stages of the school psychology internship (Simon & Swerdlik, 2017). In addition, interns with supervisors who provide clear expectations and explicit, timely feedback may not always have to be proactive to gather information.

However, relying primarily on passive information seeking can be problematic, especially when not combined with any proactive behaviors. Sometimes interns are passive because they are concerned about the implications of directly asking for information. They are wary of being a burden to their supervisors

TABLE 6.1 Types of Information Sought Out by Proactive School Psychology Interns

Type of Information	Information Potentially Sought by Interns
Technical	• How do I perform particular parts of my job? • How do I balance job demands? • How do I obtain administrative and informational resources? • How do I work most efficiently and effectively? • What are the acronyms and technical language I need to know?
Referent	• What are the performance standards I am accountable for? • What specific responsibilities do I have? • What are my goals and objectives? • What are my supervisors' goals and objectives? • What levels of dependence or independence are expected of me? • Are there rewards (e.g., scholarships) for excellent performance? • What are my supervisors' expectations?
Social	• How do I go about developing and maintaining relationships with colleagues? • Who do I trust and not trust? • What behaviors/personalities can I expect from colleagues? • How do I best fit-in with colleagues?
Appraisal	• Do I possess adequate skills and abilities as an intern, or as a school psychologist? • Are there any problems in my job performance? • Am I performing well? • What evaluation processes do my supervisors use? • How is successful internship completion determined?
Normative	• What is the history of my internship site? • What is the internship site's philosophy and goals? • What customs or rituals should I be aware of? • Am I performing well? • What evaluation process do my supervisors use? • How is successful internship completion determined? • What behaviors and attitudes are expected at the internship site? • Is there potential for me to be hired next year?
Organizational	• What are the internship site's policies and procedures? • What is the organizational structure of the internship site? • What services are provided by the internship site? • Where are people and/or services located? • What will be my salary and benefits?
Political	• Who makes important decisions at the internship site? • Who controls resources at the internship site? • Who's who at the internship site?

Note. Adapted from "Information Usefulness and Acquisition During Organizational Encounter," by E. W. Morrison, 1995, *Journal of Applied Psychology*, 78, pp. 151–152.

or do not want to be perceived as naïve or incompetent. In fact, research on newcomers to organizations (e.g., interns) suggests that individuals would rather misinterpret or misunderstand information than endure negative perceptions that may be associated with asking questions (Morrison, 1995).

Regardless of the reason for passivity, even in contexts with formalized processes for providing information to newcomers (i.e., environments where it may be easier to be passive), proactive information seeking is demonstrated to have a positive effect on newcomers' socialization, task mastery, and role clarity (Morrison, 1993b; Morrison, 1995). Therefore, interns are encouraged to combine passive behaviors with proactive behaviors in order to maximize the learning process. For example, as opposed to sitting back and watching supervisors in action, interns can take notes while they are observing and in turn use their notes to stimulate discussions regarding content, process, or decision making. Additional examples of proactive information seeking behaviors for interns include:

- using clarifying statements and questions to understand supervisor expectations (see Chapter 5);
- contacting/meeting with former interns from the internship site;
- accessing and reading documents (e.g., policy manuals) from the school, district, or other site;
- asking questions to better understand how the supervisor arrived at a decision (e.g., "Would you explain how you determined that the student qualified for special education under the category of Specific Learning Disability?")
- gathering assessment data to monitor one's own performance, including feedback from supervisors, other staff, peers, and self (see Chapter 3);
- keeping abreast of developments in the field by reading professional newsletters, journals, and books, and by attending professional workshops and conferences.

These are only a few of numerous examples of how interns may proactively seek out information. In sum, there is a wealth of information that may be helpful to interns' socialization as interns and burgeoning school psychologists. Even though some information may be acquired through passive means, interns benefit from engaging in proactive information seeking behaviors.

Seeking out Opportunities

In addition to seeking out information, being a proactive intern means seeking out opportunities. The countless opportunities available to interns during the internship include delivering a broad array of school psychology services (including those outside of one's comfort zone), participating in professional learning opportunities, networking with colleagues, and taking on leadership roles.

School Psychology Services

With a move towards broad-based service delivery roles for school psychologists (e.g., Fagan & Wise, 2007; Minke & Rossen, 2018; Sheridan & Gutkin, 2000; Ysseldyke & Reschly, 2014), the array of activities interns can take may be quite wide. Although interns will not complete every possible school psychologist activity during the internship, they certainly can be involved in a breadth of activities. Interns can also seek out additional practice in a particular area or areas in order to achieve a depth of experience. When interns seek out practice opportunities, it should be in a purposeful manner that is consistent with their formative and summative internship goals. For example, an intern named Serena set a goal to take on a systems-level consultation case during her internship. Not having completed this activity by midyear, Serena revisited the goal with her supervisor during a midyear supervision session. Together they strategized how Serena could consult with the fourth-grade team leader who requested support in addressing increased bullying behaviors in the fourth grade.

Seeking Opportunities Outside of One's Comfort Zone

In addition to seeking out breadth and depth, proactive interns seek out experiences that are outside of their comfort zones. An activity protocol used to support the professional growth of educators called *Zones of Comfort, Risk and Danger: Constructing Your Zone Map* (National School Reform Faculty, n.d.) distinguishes between comfort zones, risk zones, and danger zones:

- *The comfort zone* [italics added] is usually a place where we feel at ease, with no tension, have a good grip on the topic, like to hear from others about the topic, know how to navigate occasional rough spots with ease [and] it is also a place to retreat from the danger zone.
- *The risk zone* [italics added] is the most fertile place for learning. It is where most people are willing to take some risks, not know everything, or sometimes not know anything at all, but clearly know [that] they want to learn and will take the risks necessary to do so. It is where people open up to other people with curiosity and interest, and where they will consider options or ideas they haven't thought of before.
- *The danger zone* [italics added] is an area . . . full of defenses, fears, red-lights, [and] desire for escape . . . it requires too much energy and time to accomplish anything . . . The best way to work when you find yourself there is to own that it is a Danger Zone and work on some strategies to move into the Risk Zone (either on your own or with colleagues).

(p. 122)

A contrast of practices between two interns, Jasmine and Carla, provides a concrete example of the comfort zone concept (see Figure 6.1). Carla seeks

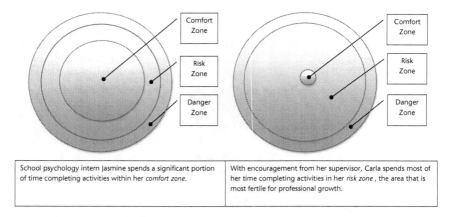

| School psychology intern Jasmine spends a significant portion of time completing activities within her *comfort zone*. | With encouragement from her supervisor, Carla spends most of her time completing activities in her *risk zone*, the area that is most fertile for professional growth. |

FIGURE 6.1 Moving outside of comfort zones: A contrast of two interns.

opportunities outside of her comfort zone with more frequency than Jasmine, who tends to practice primarily from a place of comfort. In theory, by taking more risks with the support of supervision, Carla may be in a better position to achieve professional growth. The zones of comfort heuristic can be helpful for interns to map out what areas of practice fall in each zone, and then proactively seek out activities that are beyond their comfort zone. Supervisors can encourage interns to function more frequently in risk zones than comfort zones or danger zones and emphasize that they will provide interns with a safety net of supervision.

Professional Learning Opportunities

Interns should continuously seek out opportunities for professional learning. In fact, access to professional learning may be required as part of the internship agreement. Professional learning may take a variety of forms and cover a multitude of topic areas. For example, many training programs include school psychology internship seminars that provide interns with relevant course content as well as ongoing supervisory support. For those completing out of state internships, it may be possible to hook into a local university's school psychology internship seminar (university supervisors can help make this connection) or to video conference into their home training program's seminar should other supports not be available. Interns should stay attuned to university happenings, including speakers or workshops hosted by the training program or university, and take advantage of such opportunities for learning.

Professional learning activities may also be available through schools, districts, community agencies, and APPIC internship sites. Some school districts provide ongoing training on particular topics for all school psychologists in their district and school psychology interns should be encouraged to participate.

For professional learning opportunities that are not free, some districts may provide a stipend for interns to attend. In addition to universities and school districts, school psychology organizations, local, national, and international, offer workshops and conferences that interns may be able to attend. Registration fees are often reduced for graduate students, or even waived in exchange for volunteering at the event. Professional conferences provide excellent opportunities for learning as well as for networking.

APPIC internship sites are often thoughtful about how professional learning is structured for interns. For example, Hickey, Basch, and Huber (in press) describe how they developed a professional learning curriculum, focused on professionalization and self-care, which was well received by supervisors and intern supervisees. It is appropriate for prospective APPIC interns to inquire during the interview process about professional learning structures at the internship site (see Chapter 2), as the provision of unique professional learning opportunities is often a strength of APPIC sites.

Networking

Throughout their professional training, graduate students are frequently reminded that networking is a critical task. Networking is a process of proactively establishing and maintaining relationships with others who can potentially provide professional supports that are of benefit in the present or throughout a career (Forret, 2018). Summaries of networking research (e.g., Forret, 2018; Sonnetag, 2016) point to connections between engagement in networking behaviors and positive outcomes such as increased salary level and growth, positive perceptions of growth potential by managers, professional advancement, job offers received and accepted, and overall career satisfaction.

Despite the clear value of professional networking, like many other internship actions, *how* to engage in networking is not particularly clear. As such, networking may be a daunting task for students, especially for those students that are introverted. The networking process can be demystified by illustrating how to network using the acronym *APPLE*: *A*cknowledge opportunities; *P*repare; be *P*ersonable; *L*eap/take risks; and *E*ngage in follow up.

First, interns must *a*cknowledge opportunities for networking. This means seeking out chances to meet other people in both professional and social contexts. Networking does not consist of meeting only "celebrities" in the field (although this may be a part of networking) but also other graduate trainees, practitioners, and faculty members; such connections may grow into friendships and collaborations, and be helpful in career development. Next, interns should be *p*repared to network. Being prepared to network means the intern can briefly and confidently speak about him- or herself to others, including the intern's current role and interests. To talk about oneself may feel awkward, perhaps even conceited. Thinking about what to say and practicing doing so in a way that feels genuine can be helpful. Preparation also means having materials such as business cards readily available so that exchange of information is easily accomplished.

The second P of *APPLE* stands for being *p*ersonable. Although some networking situations may be formal (e.g., a job fair), treating networking as a series of reciprocal discussions can make the process easier, perhaps even enjoyable. As in any conversation, it is important to remember to smile, listen, and ask questions; some social skills may inadvertently get neglected if one becomes too rigid while networking. *L*eaping is another important part of networking; leaping means moving outside of one's comfort zone into a risk zone. For example, while it is easy to talk with fellow students from one's own program at a conference, it is much more difficult to introduce oneself to strangers. However, networking involves taking risks, including meeting new people. Finally, *e*ngaging in follow-up is a critical component of networking. Interns may wish to stay in contact with others they have met, even with a simple email saying "It was nice to meet you," "I enjoyed our conversation," and "I look forward to seeing you again soon." Follow-up efforts may also include connection using any of a variety of social media resources such as Facebook or LinkedIn.

Forret (2018) offered a few additional, helpful points of guidance for the process of networking. First, a networking intern should be clear on emerging professional goals and types of positions of potential interest for the coming year. Doing so will help the intern reflect on his or her professional network and consider how to expand contacts in a systematic manner. Although such a focus is in many ways strategic, Forret (2018) also recommended networkers develop a diverse social network to expand beyond their own characteristics and career goals, which enables increased emotional support. Other networking strategies based on the literature include staying organized and up-to-date, such as on social media sites; accessing networking opportunities with relative frequency (e.g., weekly); and seeking knowledge and opportunities to remain marketable so others feel strongly about providing the intern with a positive reference.

Leadership

Interns can be both learners and leaders during the internship year. At their internship sites, interns can seek out leadership opportunities such as sitting on school or district teams, consulting at the systems-level with administrators, or leading professional learning sessions for staff. State school psychology organizations, as well as the APA and NASP, also offer opportunities for students to be involved in leadership activities. Examples of such activities include joining the Student Affiliates of School Psychology (SASP; the student-led organization of Division 16 of the APA) or seeking a leadership position on the SASP board; being a NASP student leader; volunteering to review convention proposals for the upcoming NASP convention; or writing an article for an organization's professional newsletter, such as the *NASP Communiqué*. Taking on leadership roles may enhance an intern's professional identity development, increase opportunities for networking, and enrich the internship experience overall.

Achieving Balance

Hammer and Hammer (2009) suggested that in order for psychology graduate students to maximize their training experience, they should make "yes" a default response when presented with opportunities. Certainly, proactive interns are open to a variety of new experiences, even (or perhaps especially) those outside of their comfort zones. On the other hand, there is no shortage of potential experiences and activities for interns to take on during the internship year. Interns need to be strategic in seeking out opportunities, including (a) prioritizing opportunities based on assessed needs and (b) self-advocating when feeling that an experience will be particularly important. Since it can often be challenging for interns to discriminate between opportunities (i.e., is this something important for me to do, or a poor use of my time?), guidance from supervisors is vital.

VIGNETTE 6.2 **HELENA'S BALANCE OF PROFESSIONAL LEARNING OPPORTUNITIES**

At Newton School District there were countless opportunities for professional learning for school psychologists, including school psychology interns. In addition, the four school psychology interns in the district engaged in their own group supervision session once a month and intern Helena's training program required a monthly internship seminar at the university. If Helena had participated in every training opportunity, she would rarely have been in her two school buildings. Knowing this was the case, in early fall, Helena and her supervisor discussed which opportunities Helena should attend during the year.

Having already determined Helena's goals, identified some of Helena's strengths and areas for improvement, and developed an internship plan, they worked together to (a) match professional learning opportunities with Helena's interests and needs and (b) create a schedule that was not too fragmented. For instance, since Helena wanted to gain a depth of experience in working with students with autism, she prioritized attending a professional learning session on this topic. On the other hand, she and her supervisor agreed that Helena would not attend an optional training on the topic of executive functioning because this was being covered during an internship seminar session and would mean being out of her buildings three days in one week.

Proactive Behaviors in Supervision

Proactive behaviors for interns extend to actions they can take during the supervision process. According to Corey, Haynes, Moulton, and Muratori (2010) some proactive behaviors supervisees can take to maximally benefit from supervision include:

- knowing the purpose of supervision and recognizing that different supervisors will take different approaches to achieve that purpose;
- clarifying what the supervisor expects of supervisees and how the supervisee will be evaluated;
- being honest and forthright regarding supervisee needs, and;
- preparing for supervision sessions in advance by thinking about questions and prioritizing issues to be discussed.

When interns are proactive supervisees, the supervision process may become more individualized, applicable, and accessible. The role of the intern as supervisee is revisited in greater depth in Chapter 7.

Self-care

Advocating for self-care needs is also an essential behavior of proactive interns. Most helping professionals will find themselves working while under significant stress at some point during their training or career (Baird, 2016) and school psychologists are no exception (Boccio, Weisz, & Lefkowitz, 2016; Schilling, Randolph, & Boan-Lenzo, 2018; Silva, Newman, Guiney, Valley-Gray, & Barrett, 2016). Huebner, Gilligan, and Cobb (2002) suggested that school psychologists may be at a greater risk for burnout than other psychological service providers and that younger, less experienced school psychologists (including trainees) may be particularly vulnerable to burnout. Preventing or mitigating stress and burnout for school psychology interns requires putting protective mechanisms in place to increase the intern's resilience. In contrast, an intern's failure to attend to self-care needs may be detrimental to the effective completion of professional responsibilities, including providing services to others (Barnett & Cooper, 2009; Smith & Moss, 2009).

Although "surviving" the internship requires a collaborative effort by interns, field supervisors, and university supervisors, for now the focus is on how interns may take the lead in incorporating self-care behaviors during the internship. Self-care begins with awareness of one's own needs, including recognition of the importance of one's own emotional and physical health. In addition to self-awareness, interns can engage in numerous behaviors to promote self-care, such as:

- becoming more effective at time management;
- recognizing and coping with cognitions such as having realistic expectations for oneself;
- maintaining physical wellness through exercise and healthy eating;
- staying attuned with one's emotional needs at a given moment;

- seeking out support from loved ones, peers, and supervisors;
- finding time to have fun with colleagues outside of work; and
- seeking out personal therapy as needed.

(Baird, 2016)

This section offers an introduction to the importance of self-care and a quick glance at some self-care strategies for interns. These strategies, as well as several others (including how supervisors can support interns' self-care), are described more extensively in Chapter 9.

Additional Considerations Regarding Interns' Proactive Behaviors

Thus far, the chapter has focused primarily on what interns can do to be proactive. However, there are also numerous actions *supervisors* can take in order to encourage intern proactivity. In addition, there are several cautions that should be reflected upon by interns and supervisors when discussing proactive behaviors.

Supervisors Can Generate Proactive Behaviors

Since proactive behaviors are a product of both intern dispositions and internship context, it makes sense to turn attention to what supervisors can do to promote proactive behavior. Bateman and Crant (1999) identified (a) selecting, (b) training, (c) liberating, and (d) inspiring as important components of how managers generate proactive behaviors in organizations; these four areas can be applied to the school psychology internship and potential supervisor actions.

Selecting

Consideration can be given to interns' proactive behavior as early as the internship interview. For example, during the interview, supervisors might ask prospective interns to describe a time they took initiative during their practicum, or to talk about a time they encountered resistance and how they responded (Bateman & Crant, 1999). Prospective interns should think about their own proclivity to be proactive and how during an internship interview they might provide examples of times they have acted proactively. Discussions about proactive behaviors should (a) introduce proactivity as an important quality of interns and (b) help both supervisors and interns think about how to promote intern proactivity during the internship.

Training

As the internship gets underway, supervisors can encourage interns to continue to think about their proactive behaviors, self-assess the extent to which they occur, and identify additional ways they might be proactive. Attempts to be proactive can be supported by supervisors, both in words and through actions. For example, if a usually reticent intern makes a valid suggestion at a meeting the supervisor may wish to publicly recognize the intern's comment, discuss ways to follow up on the idea, and provide any support needed for follow up.

Liberating

According to Bateman and Crant (1999), proactive behaviors are often invalidated by others rather than being allowed to flourish. Internship supervisors should encourage interns' attempts at being proactive. First, supervisors can challenge themselves to "loosen the reins," allowing interns to set priorities and sometimes take the lead, especially as the year goes on. Second, supervisors can attempt to reduce overly burdensome workloads and too many short-term requirements in favor of providing interns opportunities to take initiative. An intern that is overwhelmed with too much work or is constantly putting out fires may never have an opportunity to be proactive.

Inspiring

In order to inspire proactive behaviors by their interns, supervisors can make it clear that such actions are valued at the internship site. Ladany, Mori, and Mehr (2013) found evidence that *"empowering* the supervisee via encouraging autonomy and facilitating openness to the supervisee's ideas is valued by supervisees" (p. 41). Supervisor responses to interns' *ideas* and *mistakes* have implications for generating proactive behavior (Bateman & Crant, 1999). With regard to ideas, supervisors can "squash the ideas (and the people) on the spot, or they can ask questions and explore possibilities" (Bateman & Crant, 1999, p. 67). The same reactions hold true for intern mistakes. A supervisor attitude of "Let's learn from this mistake" encourages further proactive behavior, while a culture of blame can make interns feel defensive or worse, fearful to act.

Passive Behavior Can Be Misleading

As mentioned earlier in this chapter, interns' proactive behaviors tend to be viewed positively by supervisors, while passive behaviors may be viewed by supervisors as signifying an intern's lack of motivation, lack of commitment, or even laziness (Deketelaere et al., 2006). However, interns may engage in passive behaviors for a variety of reasons. Some interns take a more passive stance because they are concerned with whether or not they are completing tasks correctly and are waiting for explicit supervisor feedback. Other interns may be unsure about what is expected of them or perhaps they are unclear about where their role begins and the supervisor's role ends; as a result, they are hesitant to act in order to avoid stepping on their supervisor's toes. And yet other interns may believe that, as the old adage goes, it is better to be thought the fool than to prove it by speaking up.

In short, passive behaviors from interns may arise for a variety of reasons not related to negative intern attitudes. Changes in context initiated by supervisors or by interns, such as enhancing the clarity of expectations or encouraging proactive behaviors, can assist the dyad in turning passivity into proactivity. Further, passive behaviors may sometimes be very appropriate, such as when the intern is observing the supervisor complete a task that is outside of the intern's boundaries of competence. However, passive behavior (e.g., observation) can be combined with proactive behavior (e.g., taking notes during the observation) to maximally benefit the intern.

Summary

Proactive behavior for school psychology interns involves thinking critically about oneself and one's internship and advocating for changes to enhance the internship experience. Although proactivity may be considered a dispositional personality characteristic that falls on a continuum, contextual factors also influence proactive behaviors. As such, it is reasonable to presume that how to act proactively can be taught and learned during the internship year.

One way interns can be proactive is by actively seeking out information. There are numerous types of information that interns may seek out to learn about internship expectations, the intern role, and the role of school psychologist. Seeking information helps interns socialize into the internship and into the profession of school psychology. A second way interns can be proactive is by seeking out opportunities. This includes engaging in a breadth and depth of school psychology activities based on interests and needs, engaging in activities outside of one's comfort zone, taking advantage of professional learning opportunities, networking, and taking on leadership roles. Since so many opportunities abound, prioritizing activities is critical for interns to achieve balance. So too is engaging in proactive self-care, which acts to support one's own physical and mental health.

Proactive behaviors can be discussed as early as the internship interview and highlighted as an important and expected behavior of interns. Supervisors can encourage interns to think formatively about and assess the extent to which they are proactive, and reflect on how they can become more proactive during the year. Proactive behaviors can be validated and supported when supervisors provide interns with opportunities for independence, respond positively to interns' ideas, and consider mistakes as opportunities for learning. It is normal for interns to engage in some passive behavior during the internship for a variety of reasons; supervisors are cautioned to be understanding of these behaviors, create open lines of communication with interns, and encourage interns to combine passive behaviors with proactive behaviors that enhance the overall internship experience.

Critical Thinking Questions and Activities

The following are critical thinking questions for interns, field supervisors, and university supervisors to ponder regarding proactive behaviors during the school psychology internship.

For Interns:

- What proactive behaviors do you currently engage in? What additional proactive behaviors would it be beneficial to engage in?
- What do you need to promote your own emotional and physical wellness during the internship?
- Map out internship activities that fall in your comfort zone, risk zone, and danger zone in a diagram similar to Figure 5.1. Where do you spend most of your time? What are the implications?

For Field Supervisors:

- What actions would you take to support an intern that does not proactively seek out opportunities?
- Looking at Table 6.1, what types of information do you feel are most important for interns to seek out?
- How are interns best supported to practice in areas outside of their comfort zones?

For University Supervisors:

- How are proactive behaviors taught during the school psychology training program, if at all? If they are not, how might they be incorporated as part of training?
- How does interns' contact with the university during the internship support their emotional and physical health, and self-care practices?
- What opportunities do university internship seminars potentially provide interns?

7

THE SUPERVISION PROCESS

A brief overview of supervision is provided in Chapter 1 of this book, including defining supervision, identifying types of internship supervisors, and introducing developmental models of supervision. In addition, consistent with the dynamic and integrated nature of the school psychology internship, various considerations regarding supervision are interwoven throughout the text. However, processes of supervision are explored in significantly greater depth in this chapter than in other chapters of this book.

The chapter begins by highlighting the importance of supervision as a training tool during the internship, and identifying key goals of supervision. Components and outcomes of effective supervision are described, as are processes for evaluation and remediation. Models, formats, and techniques of supervision are presented with the intent of helping supervisors think about how to most effectively structure supervision during the internship. Means for supervisors to seek out continued professional learning on supervision are offered. The chapter concludes with critical thinking questions for interns, field supervisors, and university supervisors around pertinent supervision issues. Given the fundamental nature of supervision during the internship, Chapter 7 may be considered a keystone chapter in this book.

Supervision in School Psychology

While fields such as clinical and counseling psychology boast a robust base of supervision research, a research gap has existed for decades regarding supervision in school psychology (Knoff, 1986; McIntosh & Phelps, 2000; Newman, Simon, & Swerdlik, 2019). McIntosh and Phelps (2000) suggested that the paucity of supervision research in school psychology may reflect the endeavor being perceived as daunting: There are numerous variables involved, several complications in research design, and complexity in implementation and analysis. Difficulties in conducting supervision research have also been noted by authors in related psychology disciplines such as clinical and counseling psychology (e.g., Bernard & Goodyear, 2019; Holloway & Neufeldt, 1995; Wheeler & Richards, 2007; White, in Goodyear et al., 2016).

Regardless of challenges in researching supervision and its limited research base in school psychology, it is generally recognized that supervision is vital to supporting the training and practice of school psychologists (Harvey, Struzziero, & Desai, 2014; NASP, 2018; Simon & Swerdlik, 2017). For example, NASP's (2018) *Supervision in School Psychology* position statement asserts that "school psychologists should have access to clinical supervision throughout their careers, particularly when engaging in new areas and modalities of practice" (p. 1). Further, the statement specifies that clinical supervision should be provided to school psychologists by school psychologists at all levels of training and practice. In other words, as suggested by Knoff (1986) in a seminal article on supervision in school psychology, "supervision should be an ongoing activity from one's preservice entrance into the field to one's retirement after years of productive service" (p. 533).

Supervision During the School Psychology Internship May Be Seen as Unique

Supervision in school psychology may be viewed as different from supervision in related mental health fields, given the complexities of working in an educational context. Funding limitations, legislative and educational mandates, the increased need for mental health services, increasingly diverse student populations, and school psychologist roles that vary according to personal values and systemic philosophy are some of the unique contextual considerations for school psychologists (Crespi & Dube, 2005; Harvey & Struzziero, 2008; Newman et al., 2019). In a study of challenges to providing supervision in school psychology, Harvey and Pearrow (2010) concluded that successful school psychology supervisors must be systemic change leaders and incorporate consideration of systems-level variables in supervision; in so doing, they create a supervision role that is perhaps broader than supervision in non-school settings. Furthermore, school psychologists engage in three main areas of practice: assessment, counseling, and consultation, each of which may require some unique supervision considerations as was illustrated in a special section of *The Clinical Supervisor* (Crespi & Kaufman, 2004).

Supervision during the school psychology internship is also in some ways distinct from supervision at other levels of school psychology training and practice. Although supervision during practicum experiences is provided primarily by the university and supplemented in the field, internship supervision is predominately provided in the field and supplemented by the university. Of course, internship supervision is not solely the responsibility of field supervisors (Sullivan et al., 2014). The importance of a close relationship and ongoing communication between internship site supervisors and university supervisors cannot be overstated (Guiney, 2018; Hebert & Patterson, 2010). For example, while field supervisors engage in daily contact with interns and hold immediate responsibility for intern actions, it is the university that certifies successful internship completion. Furthermore, the intricacies of the intern role, such as having a hybrid identity of trainee and burgeoning professional (see Chapter 5), make the process of internship supervision particularly complex.

Finally, the receipt of intensive and individualized supervision distinguishes internship supervision from the supervision generally provided to school psychology practitioners (Strein, 1996; Sullivan et al., 2014). In other words, when graduating interns enter the field, supervision will likely look quantitatively (there will probably be less) and qualitatively (it will be more administrative than clinical in focus) different than it did during internship training. Of note, such realities are not consistent with the NASP's (2018) *Supervision in School Psychology* position statement and may not meet post-doctoral supervision requirements for licensure for independent practice, or even renewal of the National Certified School Psychologist (NCSP) credential (see Chapter 11).

Goals of Supervision

Five goals of supervision in psychology are identified in this chapter, two of which are recognized as central: (a) fostering supervisees' growth and development through teaching and (b) protecting the welfare of clients (Bernard & Goodyear, 2019; Corey et al., 2010). The first goal suggests that through supervision, supervisee learning and development of competence is achieved via advising and instruction from supervisors (Holloway, 1995). Bernard and Goodyear (2019) point out that although supervision and teaching share similarities, they are not the same thing: "teaching is driven by a set of curriculum or protocols, [and] supervision is driven by the needs of the particular supervisee and his or her clients" (p. 10). The authors also suggest that for less experienced supervisees (e.g., practicum students and interns), teaching will be a larger component of supervision than for supervisees further along the developmental continuum (e.g., practitioner-level supervisees).

The second main goal of supervision is to protect the welfare of the individuals served by the supervisee. In other words, the supervisor's actions must ensure that clients (e.g., children, families, teachers) receive services that are delivered with both professionalism and competence. If the supervisor has reason to believe the supervisee's actions are not in the best interest of clients, it is the supervisor's legal and ethical responsibility to intervene (Corey et al., 2010). For example, a female intern named Maureen, working at the high school level, frequently wore revealing clothing, was ogled by several male students, and teased behind her back by some of the school staff. Worried about how this might affect Maureen's relationships with staff and students as well as her ability to effectively deliver services, her supervisor intervened. She sensitively broached her concerns with Maureen early in the year, gave examples of what may be deemed appropriate and inappropriate dress in the school setting and noted Maureen's ongoing professional dress following their conversation. Acting to ensure client welfare via prudent supervisee monitoring is consistent with the ethical responsibility supervisors maintain for supervisee actions according to the APA (2017a) and NASP (2010b).

A third goal of supervision, related to promoting client welfare, is *gatekeeping* for the profession, or monitoring supervisee performance to make sure only those who are ready to be credentialed/licensed and enter the field are permitted to do so. The gatekeeping goal is particularly relevant in the consideration of school psychology internship supervision because the internship is likely the last stop for intensive, individualized supervision before trainees enter the field and practice independently (Sullivan et al., 2014).

A fourth goal of supervision is empowering supervisees with the capacity to self-supervise in the future (Bernard & Goodyear, 2019; Corey et al., 2010). Being able to self-supervise includes valuing and employing self-evaluation; trusting one's own clinical judgment; acknowledging one's assumptions and beliefs and how they influence practice, and proactively working to reduce bias; and recognizing limits of competence, including seeking out consultation or supervision as needed. To expand on this goal, supervisees should also learn about effective processes of supervision by way of supervisor actions and modeling so that one day they too can be effective supervisors. The reality is that many school psychology supervisors have limited to no formal training in supervision (Cochrane, Salyers, & Ding, 2010; McMahon et al., 2018; Silva et al., 2016), and supervisors' supervision practices are often informed by prior life experiences such as how they were supervised (Falender & Shafranske, 2017). Therefore, it is likely that the internship supervision process modeled by site and university supervisors will be applied to the intern's future practice as a supervisor for others in a few short years.

Finally, a fifth supervision goal is to provide emotional support to supervisees to prevent or mitigate burnout. The restorative goal is consistent with the importance of self-care behaviors described in Chapters 6 and 8 of this text. According to Norcross and Vandenbos (2018): "Supervision should address not only case problems but also you as a person" (p. 85). Further, supervisors can model self-care behaviors in order to promote such actions in supervisees. An internship supervisor who does not take time for him or herself, who is often stressed or overwhelmed, or who frequently complains about being burned out is likely not providing a good model of self-care (Norcross & Vandenbos, 2018). On the other hand, interns can benefit from discussing with their supervisors the sometimes hectic realities of being a school psychologist and how the supervisor best balances, both personally and professionally, the fulfillment of all responsibilities (Hickey et al., in press).

Why Is It Important to Recognize the Overarching Goals of Supervision?

To some readers, the broad goals of supervision may seem intuitive or obvious. However, as the internship gets underway, goals of supervision can quickly become neglected or ignored. For instance, although it is sometimes appropriate to have "on the fly" supervision (e.g., an intern asks a supervisor to clarify a decision-making process immediately following a meeting), this type of supervision should probably not be the only type of supervision interns receive during the internship. In order to make sure the overarching goals of supervision receive adequate consideration, making time for scheduled, closed-door, and structured supervision is important.

VIGNETTE 7.1 **JOANNE'S INTERNSHIP CHALLENGES**

A doctoral intern named JoAnne had a successful entry into her internship. Her clinical skills improved greatly throughout the beginning of the year, as documented by formative assessments, and she was well thought of by her supervisor and the school staff. Since JoAnne began the year with so much success, by mid-October she and her supervisor Jack had stopped planning supervision time in advance, instead meeting only when specific questions came up. However, as the year progressed, several challenges mounted for JoAnne. In January, JoAnne was unsuccessful in proposing her doctoral dissertation due to complications with obtaining Institutional Review Board approval. As spring approached, JoAnne began to look for job openings but, due to budget shortfalls in her state, school psychologist positions were few and far between. All the while JoAnne was planning her wedding to take place in June, one week following the end of her internship. JoAnne was frequently sick during the second half of her internship and missed several days of work. The quality of her work suffered, including not being prepared for counseling groups she was running, completing several assessment reports last minute with numerous grammatical errors, and finding herself fatigued during the school day.

JoAnne broke down crying one afternoon in March. She and her supervisor talked about JoAnne's stressors, and developed a plan to help JoAnne achieve a personal and professional balance. Jack shared some of his self-care strategies and normalized JoAnne's stress by sharing similar experiences he faced when he was an intern and that he currently tackles in his full-time practitioner role. Jack and JoAnne agreed to meet weekly for extra supervision time on Friday mornings before school. During one supervision meeting, Jack even helped JoAnne re-conceptualize her dissertation. JoAnne was able to close out the year successfully

(continued)

(continued)

with Jack's ongoing supervisory support. Although this case ended positively, explicit consideration given to the five goals of supervision earlier in the year might have preventively supported JoAnne's emotional wellbeing and the quality of her service delivery.

Components of an Effective Supervision Process

The overall research evidence demonstrating supervision outcomes in psychology, especially client outcomes, is modest but developing (Bernard & Goodyear, 2019; Watkins, 2011). Extant research suggests some agreement of elements that are contributors to effective supervision. Some pivotal elements of effective supervision include a positive supervisor-supervisee relationship, multicultural competence, and reflection from the supervisor and supervisee.

Supervisor–Supervisee Relationship

A positive supervisory relationship is at the heart of successful supervision while negative or conflictual relationships may be detrimental to supervision outcomes, both for supervisees and clients (Bernard & Goodyear, 2019; Callahan & Watkins, 2018; Corey et al., 2010; Harvey & Struzziero, 2008; Ladany, Mori, & Mehr, 2013; Swalwell & Harvey, 2017). In a series of commentaries on ethical and effective supervision practices in professional psychology, Barnett, Cornish, Goodyear, and Lichtenberg (2007) suggested that a good supervisor-supervisee relationship includes a supervisor's commitment to the professional growth and emotional support of the supervisee, a collaborative working dynamic, and the establishment of mutual trust. A supervisor's explicit and clear expectations are also critical to building a strong supervisory working alliance (Simon & Swerdlik, 2017). Ladany et al. (2013) summarized findings from their study on supervisee perceptions of effective and ineffective supervision, and the supervisory relationship came to the forefront:

> Hence, if one were to ask what an effective or highly competent supervisor were to look like, the findings [from this study] point to the following. First, the supervisor would work toward developing a strong supervisory alliance by working toward mutually agreeing with the supervisee on the goals and tasks of supervision. The supervisor would use basic counseling skills such as listening, reflection of feelings, and empathy to facilitate the development of an emotional bond. An effective supervisor would attend to and offer a balance of attractive or collegial interactions, interpersonal attentiveness, and task-oriented structure. Moreover, self-disclosure would be used judiciously and in the service of the supervisee. It would be anticipated that supervisees would offer less nondisclosures, thereby facilitating a more meaningful supervision experience. Finally, supervisors would

attend specifically to the evaluation aspect of supervision by facilitating the setting of supervisory goals and providing both formative and summative feedback.

(pp. 42–43)

Supervisors' provision of constructive feedback in a non-judgmental, supportive manner creates a safe environment and mitigates anxiety provoking circumstances that might otherwise silence a supervisee from discussing critical concerns (Barnett et al., 2007; Webb, 2000). Research suggests that strong working alliances are related to supervisees' decreased anxiety, and increased willingness to disclose to their supervisors (Mehr et al., 2015), which in turn can promote the eventual success of supervision (Ladany, Hill, Corbett, & Nutt, 1996). Self-disclosure, or the willingness of supervisors and supervisees to engage in open and constructive dialogue, is an important condition of a productive relationship in supervision (Corey et al., 2010).

The supervisor-supervisee working alliance is impacted by numerous variables including the context for supervision, supervisor characteristics, supervisee characteristics, relationship dynamics, and characteristics of the organization (Harvey & Struzziero, 2008; Holloway, 1995; Simon & Swerdlik, 2017). Characteristics of the supervisor and supervisee that are relevant include each individual's personal characteristics as well as their level of experience, development, theoretical orientation, and motivation. Variables that relate to supervisor-supervisee relationships can receive consideration as early as internship interviews (e.g., Will this candidate be a good match for our district and the supervisor[s] we can match him with?). Supervisor-supervisee relationship dynamics maintain importance throughout the internship year and should be given appropriate consideration by internship coordinators and field and university supervisors.

Multicultural Competence

Attending to issues of diversity in supervision is an important component of the supervisor-supervisee relationship and may translate into culturally competent, also called culturally responsive, practice by the supervisee (Barnett et al., 2007; Eklund et al., 2014). Attaining multicultural competence is best viewed as an ongoing journey and supervisors continue to develop multicultural competence in conjunction with supervisees (Harvey and Struzziero, 2008). Bernard and Goodyear (2019) suggested that supervisors should define all interactions as multicultural in nature and check their assumptions accordingly. For example, Arlene Silva, Chair of the School Psychology Department at William James College, argued that supervisors should acknowledge that dynamics of power and privilege frequently exist within the supervisory relationship but often do not receive adequate consideration, and address this dilemma through culturally responsive interactions with supervisees (Guiney, 2019, Chapter 7).

Multicultural Supervision

Lopez and Rogers (2010) explored a multicultural approach to supervision in school psychology, and framed its importance within the context of APA's (2017b) and NASP's (2010b) ethical codes which advocate for fairness, justice, and respect for people's rights and dignity. Lopez and Rogers (2010) defined multicultural supervision as "an approach . . . that (a) provides a forum for examining how human diversity influences quality of life and (b) uses that knowledge to improve effectiveness of services, with the goal of ensuring a just and fair environment for clients" (p. 120). Corey et al. (2010) outlined several multicultural supervision competencies that supervisors can incorporate in supervision practice. Although the competencies outlined by Corey et al. were intended for supervisors, their list is adapted with examples for supervisors *and* supervisees in Table 7.1. By highlighting specific actions, it is hoped that interns and supervisors can begin to incorporate multicultural considerations into supervision and other activities during the internship. Further, consistent with strengths-based approaches to supervision (Newman, Guiney, & Silva, 2018; Wade & Jones, 2015), addressing multicultural issues in supervision, including those focused on the delivery of cross-cultural services in schools, should be viewed as an asset to the supervision process rather than a landmine to be avoided.

Lopez and Rogers (2010) concluded that multicultural supervision may lead to (a) positive outcomes for clients through effective service delivery; (b) supervisor modeling of a multicultural approach to practice for supervisees; (c) increased feelings of efficacy for supervisees in working with diverse clients; (d) increased supervisee satisfaction and perceived quality of supervision; (e) creation of opportunities to discuss and explore bias, prejudice, and oppression; and (f) increased justice within the organizational system (e.g., school or district). Lopez and Rogers also pointed to obstacles in applying multicultural supervision such as variance in supervisors' abilities and readiness to engage in multicultural supervision, a lack of bilingual psychologists, and some environments (e.g., school cultures) that may contrast with the goals of a multicultural approach. Obstacles notwithstanding, incorporating a multicultural approach in supervision is an ethical obligation of school psychologists that has the potential to benefit supervisors, supervisees, children, and families.

Self-reflection

Self-reflection, both from supervisors and supervisees, is another integral component of effective supervision. Supervisors should reflect on their own supervision competencies and the goals that are established and monitored with supervisees, and solicit and utilize evaluative feedback from others (e.g., supervisees, peers, metasupervisors) to improve their supervision work (APA, 2015a; Falender et al., 2004). Supervision of supervisors, or metasupervision,

TABLE 7.1 Integrating Multicultural Supervision into the School Psychology Internship

Multicultural Supervision Competencies	Supervisor and Intern Actions to Promote Competencies
Explore cultural dynamics in supervisory relationships	• Supervisors can discuss cultural similarities and differences with the supervisee in a way that avoids misunderstandings. • Supervisors can model appropriate and safe communication, for example seeking permission of supervisees before asking personal questions. • Interns can share cultural experiences that may impact their perspectives on practice.
Include multicultural competencies in the internship plan	• Supervisors can think about what opportunities to develop multicultural competencies will be available during the internship and encourage interns to engage in these opportunities. • Interns can inquire about what opportunities to develop multicultural competencies will be available during the internship and engage in these opportunities. • Interns can seek opportunities outside of their cultural comfort zones.
Encourage and empower supervisees to develop cultural self-awareness	• Supervisors and interns can complete self-assessments of cultural awareness or sensitivity (e.g., see Harvey & Struzziero, 2008, pp. 93–96; Corey et al., 2010, pp. 128–129). • Supervisors and interns can reflect on how culture impacted their work and discuss in supervision.
Accept multicultural limitations	• Supervisors can seek support if needing to address challenging issues in the supervisory relationship beyond their own competence. • Interns should be careful not to practice outside of domains of multicultural competence without the support of supervision. • Supervisors and interns should be willing to own their mistakes and learn from them.

(continued)

TABLE 7.1 *(continued)*

Multicultural Supervision Competencies	*Supervisor and Intern Actions to Promote Competencies*
Model cultural sensitivity	<ul><li>Supervisors should be aware of cultural saliency instead of overemphasizing culture.</li><li>Interns should be clear with supervisors about what they need from supervision.</li><li>Supervisors and interns can practice cultural awareness and sensitivity in interactions, including supervision as well as interactions with children, families, and staff.</li></ul>
Accept responsibility to provide knowledge regarding cultural diversity	<ul><li>Supervisors can use supervision interactions as opportunities to teach and learn about cultural diversity.</li><li>Supervisors and interns can seek out ongoing professional learning opportunities to learn about culturally competent practice.</li></ul>
Treat culture as integrated in all domains of school psychology practice including assessment, consultation, and counseling	<ul><li>Supervisors and interns should view clients and cases as individual experiences, each deserving differentiated consideration.</li><li>Supervisors and interns should develop a working knowledge of cultural considerations within each domain of school psychology practice (e.g., see Jones, 2009).</li></ul>
Provide and model social advocacy	<ul><li>Supervisors can model social advocacy to interns and train interns to act as advocates for other groups.</li><li>Supervisors and interns can speak out on behalf of groups that have been oppressed or discriminated against.</li><li>Supervisors and interns can work towards reducing and ideally eliminating biases, prejudices, and discriminatory practices.</li></ul>

Note. Adapted from *Clinical Supervision in the Helping Professions* (2nd ed., pp. 125–132), by G. Corey, R. Haynes, P. Moulton, and M. Muratori, 2010, Alexandria, VA: American Counseling Association.

encourages self-reflection and includes interventions for gaps in one's supervision knowledge, skills, confidence, objectivity, and interactions (Falender & Shafranske, 2017).

Reflection is also critical for supervisees. Neufeldt, Karno, and Nelson (1996) described the reflective process in supervision for counseling psychology supervisees as "a search for understanding" of phenomena with attention to supervisee actions, emotions, thoughts, and interactions between the supervisee and clients (p. 8). A recent consideration of the implications of APA (2015a) supervision competency guidelines for supervisees pointed to reflection as critical to absorb and respond to supervision feedback, develop multicultural supervision competency, be authentic in the supervision relationship, and engage in ethical practice (Kangos et al., 2018). Reflective supervisees actively seek understanding of events, engage in active inquiry, take risks, and are open to learning as opposed to defensive. Accordingly, "reflectivity in supervision leads to changes in perception, changes in practice, and an increased capacity to make meaning of experiences" (Neufeldt et al., 1996, p. 8). In short, reflection from both supervisors and supervisees can be considered critical components of the learning cycle in supervision (Falender & Shafranske, 2017).

A Model of the Reflective Process in Supervision

Newman (2012) illustrated the reflective process in supervision for school psychology trainees learning about school consultation based on a reflective model of practice, illustrated by Bernard and Goodyear (2019). Figure 7.1 demonstrates a novice supervisee's reflective process as she worked through a consultation case with the support of university supervision. According to this model, reflection begins with a trigger event resulting in supervisee surprise, discomfort, or confusion. Supervisee reactions are connected to self-perceptions regarding clinical skills, personal issues, and/or a case conceptualization. In turn, supervisors can help supervisees critically reevaluate the situation in favor of a new perspective on how to approach similar situations in the future. Some techniques for promoting reflection in supervision are illustrated in Figure 7.1 (e.g., use of journaling, recording, modeling and rehearsal); these and other supervision techniques are discussed in greater depth later in this chapter.

Bernard and Goodyear (2019) summarized three important concluding points about reflective processes in supervision. First, it is likely that every supervisor stimulates at least some level of reflection with his or her supervisees. Second, in so doing, supervisors encourage supervisees to be reflective, which is consistent with the overarching goal of supervision to promote skills for the supervision of self and others. Third, reflection should not take place in a vacuum but rather be linked to evidence-based practices. If not, supervisees risk engaging in a *misguided discovery* process that may be detrimental to the supervisee's provision of services to clients.

A trigger event elicits	CIT reactions focus on	Critical reevaluation draws on	Achievement of new perspective
• Surprise • Discomfort • Confusion	• Skills/strategies • Personhood issues • Conceptualization	• Available skills • Content knowledge • Process knowledge • Knowledge of self	• Affects future application by CIT
Bonnie, a novice CIT, is consulting with a new first grade teacher, Mr. S, regarding a student, Harry. The initial problem identified is that Harry is out of his seat throughout the day. During a classroom observation, Bonnie notices that classroom expectations are unclear and that Harry is no more out of his seat than other students. She is surprised with what she observed and unsure about how she might address these issues with her consultee.	Bonnie watches a video-recording of her previous consultation session and writes a reflective log about the session and her classroom observation. Bonnie notes her limited use of clarifying questions when she and Mr. S talked about Harry's out of seat behavior. She also reflects on the discrepancy between Mr. S's frame of the problem and her developing case conceptualization.	During supervision, Bonnie and her supervisor use her video-recording and reflective log as points of reference. They discuss specific instances when Bonnie might have clarified to more accurately define the problem with the consultee. They discuss how Bonnie might talk about her observations with Mr. S. The supervisor models how he might address the concern and Bonnie rehearses how to do so using her own words.	Bonnie realizes the importance of clarifying, especially during the problem identification stage. She recognizes the need to observe the instructional environment, not just the child. Bonnie has learned that many problems that present as intensive individual problems can be addressed at the group or systems level. In the subsequent case session, Bonnie and Mr. S. talked about the classroom observation and developed a plan to make expectations clearer for all students.

FIGURE 7.1 Reflective process in supervision of school-based consultation. Adapted from "Supervision of Consultation Training: Addressing the Content and Process Concerns of Novice Consultants," by D. S. Newman, 2012, in *Becoming a School Consultant: Lessons Learned* (p. 51), by S. A. Rosenfield (Ed.), 2012, New York, NY: Routledge. Copyright 2012 by Taylor & Francis. Reprinted with permission.

Prescheduled Supervision and Reflection

Internship supervisors and interns often share an office space, and are therefore able to engage in discussions about cases throughout the school day. In such circumstances, supervisors and interns might think: "We are always doing supervision!" While sharing an office space allows supervisors to meet the immediate learning demands of interns, it does not always allow room for processes of reflection and learning. Therefore, it is recommended that supervisors and interns plan for supervision to include a combination of "on the fly" and prescheduled time.

Prescheduled supervision time can be scheduled at a time and in a location unlikely to be interrupted. Simon and Swerdlik (2017) described a process of advanced preparation for supervision which includes responsibilities for both supervisees and supervisors. The supervisee documents (either on paper or electronically): ongoing cases and case progress since the last supervision meeting (including case data, as appropriate); concerns and questions that would be helpful to review in supervision; and a self-assessment of progress towards internship goals (prior to some supervision meetings). This information is provided to supervisors prior to the meeting. A supervisor is responsible for reviewing this information prior to the supervision meeting, documenting the progress of the supervisee and clients the supervisee is working with, and planning developmentally appropriate supervision meetings and strategies.

Supervisors often lament, and rightly so, the difficulty in finding the time to implement structured supervision. However, prescheduled supervision time can be used creatively to implement some of the more intensive supervision techniques covered later in this chapter. For example, one supervisory dyad I recently worked with as a university internship supervisor used prescheduled time as a chance for co-consulting with a teacher. The intern took on the role of lead consultant with the supervisor acting as a backup support only to chime in if absolutely necessary. These roles were strategically defined in advance based on assessment of the intern's knowledge, skills, and comfort levels. The structured supervision time allowed the supervisor to collect live observation data regarding the intern's applied consultation skills, and to provide support, should the intern have needed it, on a difficult case.

Outcomes of Effective Supervision

Harvey and Struzziero (2008) and Simon and Swerdlik (2017) synthesized research from the fields of psychology and education to highlight broad outcomes of effective supervision that can be applied to school psychologists. The authors collectively concluded that effective supervision contributes to (a) supervisees' skill maintenance, development, and expansion; (b) reduced experience of stress; (c) increased self-reflection; and (d) increased accountability for service delivery. Applied specifically to school psychology interns, Sullivan et al. (2014) concluded that effective supervision results in supervisees

(a) developing autonomous skills in services such as assessment, counseling, and consultation; (b) learning to translate knowledge into informed, competent practice; (c) learning to apply the most recent ethics guidelines and legal standards to professional practice; (d) enhancing interpersonal skills with clients and families; (e) developing a professional identity and sense of self-confidence; (f) learning to self-reflect on areas of professional strength and weakness; and (g) receiving opportunities to share personal and professional experiences with others on a regular basis.

(p. 528)

Although there are many potential positive effects of supervision, the field of school psychology generally lacks a strong empirical base regarding supervision outcomes (Newman et al., 2019) and studies of supervision outcomes in related fields are often are of poor methodological quality (Wheeler & Richards, 2007). Nevertheless, (a) research evidence supporting supervision outcomes is burgeoning (Callahan & Watkins, 2018), (b) the potential impact of effective supervision is far reaching, and (c) supervision is generally accepted as a critical pedagogical tool in school psychology and allied fields (Bernard & Goodyear, 2019).

Evaluating Supervision Outcomes

Evaluation may be considered "the nucleus of clinical supervision" (Bernard & Goodyear, 2019, p. 222) and is considered central to achieving supervision goals (Corey et al., 2010). That is, in order to make sure school psychology interns are meeting the goals of supervision, it is necessary to measure their formative growth of skills and ability to deliver clinically and ethically competent services to children, families, and staff. Lamb and Swerdlik (2004) suggested that when evaluation is effectively incorporated in supervision, it (a) mitigates evaluation apprehension, thereby allowing for professional growth (a formative function) and (b) facilitates the assessment of trainees' competencies, skill development, readiness to function independently, and any potentially problematic behaviors (a summative function).

Evaluation Domains

Interns should be evaluated in concordance with their internship goals and plan, which will be aligned to school psychology practice domains (e.g., NASP, 2010a), as described elsewhere in this text. In addition to measuring interns' levels of competence in various practice domains, Sullivan et al. (2014) identified a number of pertinent areas for evaluation and skill-building in supervision including professional behaviors and several others (see Table 7.2). Of course, some of these areas are difficult to measure objectively (e.g., professional identity), but each remains worthy of, at a minimum, ongoing discussion in supervision given their potential impact on the intern's current and future functioning.

The pertinence of various evaluation domains likely differs per the needs of the intern, the internship site, and the training program. Therefore, interns and supervisors may wish to think about each of these domains and which are most relevant to use in their particular context. The examples of each domain in Table 7.2 purposefully exhibit different levels of intern functioning. Readers are encouraged to reflect on (a) how to interpret varying levels of intern performance and (b) what prospective supervisor responses may be most helpful to support interns' continued skill growth in that area. Further, readers can consider how each domain links to the five overarching goals of supervision.

Evaluation Tools

Several authors have provided specific tools university and/or field supervisors can use to support processes of evaluation during practica and internships (e.g., see Cruise & Swerdlik, 2010; Harvey & Struzziero, 2008; Kaslow et al., 2009; and Simon & Swerdlik, 2017). Field supervisors are responsible for evaluating interns' developing clinical competencies in the applied practice of school psychology, often with tools provided by training programs. Clinical competencies assessed by training programs likely align closely with the NASP (2010a) Practice Model (see Chapter 1).

Interns' professional behaviors or dispositions, or "professionalism," are also an important area for assessment. Many training programs request that field supervisors provide formative and summative assessment of interns' professional behaviors, either as a distinct assessment or embedded within other evaluation tools. Professionalism in psychology includes professional attitudes and values; respect for diversity; ethical and legal behavior; and reflective practice, self-assessment, and self-care (Hatcher et al., 2013). Professionalism is difficult to define with precision and is accordingly challenging to assess (Grus & Kaslow, 2014). However, the assessment of professionalism, both formatively and summatively, allows supervisors to provide feedback and support for interns and document, remediate, and evaluate the progress of interns demonstrating problems of professional competence in an accountable manner (Grus & Kaslow, 2014).

It is also beneficial for internship supervisors/sites, as well as university supervisors/training programs, to reflect on their performance so that they can continue to provide excellent training to interns in the future. Therefore, evaluation tools can be provided for interns to provide feedback about their experiences. For example, trainers and supervisors can inquire about the range and depth of training opportunities provided to interns and perceptions of ongoing support during the internship, as well as the quality of supervision. Evaluations can be completed at least twice a year, and discussed in numerous ways, including between field supervisor and trainee, university supervisor and trainee, and all three parties (e.g., during site visits).

TABLE 7.2 Evaluating Intern Skills: Domains for Supervisor Investigation

Domain	Definition	Examples Demonstrating *Varying Levels of Competence*
Competence	Performing professional functions capably, across domains, effectively based on knowledge, skills, attitudes, values, and ethics	During a classroom observation in a middle school, intern Lola intervenes immediately upon seeing two students about to get into a physical altercation. She separates the students, alerts the teacher to the situation, supports the teacher to sort out the situation, and then processes her actions with her supervisor.
Professionalism	Applying professional dispositions or behaviors in one's work	When unsure how to approach a problem, intern Eddie seeks out various resources including people (e.g., his field supervisor, school-based specialists, his university supervisor, other colleagues), and literature (e.g., research articles, books, materials available online) before intervening.
Emotional awareness	Using emotions and reactions to understand and empathize with others	Intern Roberta observes that a teacher consultee is feeling overwhelmed with a busy schedule. She acknowledges this in conversation and they reschedule to meet later that week.
Professional identity	Assimilating into the profession, including internalizing ethics and values for practice	Intern Lucy joins the International School Psychologists Association organization because her school has a large immigrant population from several Eastern African nations and she is interested in learning about the role of school psychology outside of the United States.
Respect for individual differences	Understanding and appreciating cultural, ethnic, linguistic, and sexual orientation differences, including intersectionality	Intern Allison is asked by her supervisor to meet with a student who recently immigrated from Nigeria. Prior to their meeting, Allison does background research on Nigerian culture to better understand and connect with the student.
Purpose and direction	Formulating a plan, identifying goals, and monitoring progress	Intern Tanya is part of a problem-solving team that identifies a student's reading difficulties. She agrees to take the lead in support of a struggling reader, but is not sure how to best monitor the student's reading progress during an intervention.

Autonomy	Making choices and decisions independently (when appropriate)	While Li, the intern, is administering a standardized test as part of an assessment battery, the student being tested breaks down crying uncontrollably. Li decides to stop the testing, help the student calm down, and return the student to class. She will discuss next steps with her supervisor.
Accepting supervision	Recognizing the need for supervisory support, seeking it out when necessary, and avoiding defensive reactions	On the second day of school, a teacher tells school psychology intern Preeti that she overheard a student talking to his friends about having swallowed a bottle of pills before class. Unsure what to do, Preeti immediately contacts an administrator and her supervisor.
Ethics	Integrating ethical values and standards in practice	School psychology intern Nina takes home from school a folder including various case data such as test protocols, rating scales, and interview notes. She brings the folder to a coffee shop to complete the write up of a psychological evaluation and accidentally leaves it behind. She returns to the shop two hours later and the manager, who recovered the folder, returns it to Nina. She does not speak of this incident again.
Motivation	Being enthusiastic and finding work rewarding and meaningful	Doctoral-level intern Sam is not enjoying his internship experience. He is introspective about whether he should have become a counseling psychologist instead of a school psychologist. He has been in school for 5 years and feels stuck. Although he works hard, Sam is not satisfied with his internship experience.

Note. The information in columns 1 and 2 is adapted from "Best Practices in the Supervision of Interns," by J. R. Sullivan, N. Svenkerud, and J. C. Conoley, 2014, in Best Practices in School Psychology: Foundations (pp. 527–540), by P. L. Harrison, and J. Grimes (Eds), 2014, Bethesda, MD: National Association of School Psychologists.

Addressing Supervisee Problems of Professional Competence

The majority of school psychology interns will complete the internship year ready to successfully enter the first year of professional practice. However, a small percentage of students may exhibit significant deficiencies with regard to clinical or professional competence. Although the frequency of problems of professional competence (PPC) is small, the amount of time and emotional effort it takes to address them is significant (Forrest & Elman, 2014).

Addressing problematic behaviors begins with prevention. Field and university sites should have in place clear evaluation policies and procedures, including processes for formative and summative evaluation as have already been described. It is important that evaluations address both clinical competencies and also professional behaviors. Supervisors can use evaluations to determine the level of severity of competence problems in order to determine the appropriate level of supervisory response (Cruise & Swerdlik, 2010). Problematic behaviors that are noted should be communicated both orally *and* in writing to trainees, with behaviors specified in observable and measurable terms (Cruise & Swerdlik, 2010). If a remediation plan is developed, it should include these components:

- an observable and measurable statement of the concerning behavior(s);
- an acknowledgement of ethical codes that relate to the behavior(s) of concern;
- a specification of goals to be achieved by the remediation plan;
- a constructive and educative focus that specifies replacement behaviors;
- a description of interventions to be implemented with details regarding what, who, when, where, and how;
- a statement regarding how it will be determined that goals are met; and
- a statement of what will happen if goals are not met.

The reader is referred to Cruise and Swerdlik (2010), Guiney (2018, 2019), and Lamb and Swerdlik (2004) for further information regarding prevention of and response to supervisees' PPC.

Two sample remediation plans are provided in Appendices C and D. Appendix C presents a remediation plan for a doctoral student including due process rights and personal therapy, originally developed by Cruise and Swerdlik (2010). Appendix D is a plan for a non-doctoral intern negotiated between the intern, his field supervisors, and a university faculty member in order to plan for and document progress towards successful internship completion. Notably, the plan in Appendix D begins with the intern's strengths rather than being solely focused on challenges or deficits and is ecological in that it includes actions to be taken by the intern, field supervisors, and his university supervisor.

The Structure of Supervision: Models, Formats, and Techniques

It can be argued that "the structure of clinical supervision profoundly influences its potential to be effective" (Harvey & Struzziero, 2008, p. 182). Whether or not explicitly recognized, supervisors have assumptions and beliefs about the world and school psychology practice that guide their use of specific models, formats, and techniques in supervision. Further, since school psychology interns may have multiple supervisors, they are likely to be exposed to many different types of supervision during the internship. Figure 7.2 illustrates the structure of supervision as is constructed by models, formats, and techniques. In addition to the supervisor's worldview, the structure of supervision is also influenced by supervisee developmental levels in various skill areas. In other words, models, formats, and techniques may be differentially relevant or helpful depending on supervisee developmental level.

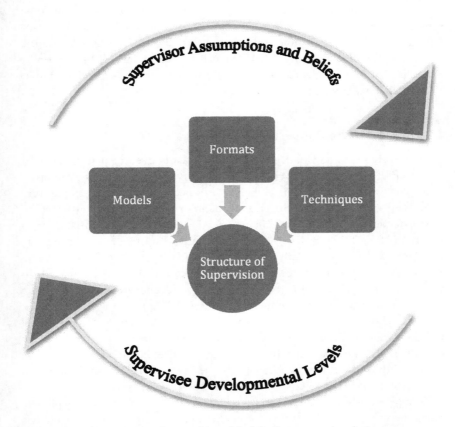

FIGURE 7.2 The structure of supervision: Models, formats, and techniques.

Supervision Models

Much is written about models of supervision in mental health fields but it is still unclear if any models of supervision are better than others (Aten, Strain, & Gillespie, 2008; Bernard & Goodyear, 2019; Kaufman & Schwartz, 2004) and there is not sufficient evidence to conclude that one model should be endorsed as the most effective for school psychology supervision (Kaufman, 2010a; McIntosh & Phelps, 2000). Examples of supervisor theoretical orientations and models discussed in the school psychology supervision literature include psychodynamic, behavioral and cognitive behavioral, ecological, person-centered, constructivist, discrimination, developmental, integrative, and transtheoretical approaches (Harvey & Struzziero, 2008; Kaufman & Schwartz, 2004; Kaufman, 2010a; Simon & Swerdlik, 2017). Given the numerous models of supervision that might apply, Sullivan and Conoley (2008) suggested that "the best supervisors may be those who . . . manage a flexible blending . . . of perspectives . . . to meet the unique needs of individual interns" (p. 1960).

In the sections that follow, competency-based supervision, strengths-based supervision, and developmental approaches to supervision are outlined, each with applicability to supervision of school psychologists. The Developmental, Ecological, Problem Solving (DEP) model (Simon et al., 2014; Simon & Swerdlik, 2017), is highlighted as a school psychology specific supervision model that incorporates components from each of these frameworks.

Competency-based Supervision

One supervision framework that has gained popularity over the past several years is a competency-based approach to clinical supervision (Falender & Shafranske, 2004, 2017). Through this lens, supervision is defined as a distinct professional competency, which "entails the creation of an explicit framework and method to initiate, develop, implement, and evaluate the process and outcomes of supervision." (APA, 2015a, p. 34). Consistent with a competency-based approach, the APA (2015a) has recently developed *Guidelines for Clinical Supervision in Health Service Psychology*, which provide guidance on the practice of supervision in psychology education and training. The guidelines are organized around seven domains: Supervisor Competence; Diversity; Supervisory Relationship; Professionalism; Assessment/Evaluation/Feedback; Problems of Professional Competence; and Ethical, Legal, and Regulatory Considerations. Each of these domains is consistent with descriptions of best practices in internship supervision illustrated throughout the text; readers are referred to APA (2015a) for more on how these domains intersect with professional psychology, at large.

Competency-based supervision is metatheoretical, meaning it is applicable across the various models a supervisor might implement in practice. The knowledge, skills, attitudes, and values of professional competencies are identified and defined, and teaching/learning strategies are implemented to meet competency standards (Falender & Shafranske, 2017). Benefits of competency-based supervision include: strengthening of the supervisory alliance; orienting supervisors and supervisees to specific knowledge, skill, attitude and value areas that underlie competence; providing a means for assessment; linking learning with assessment, feedback, and evaluation in support of supervisee growth; situating competency development as a lifelong process; and protecting the welfare of clients through increased competency of both supervisors and supervisees (Falender & Shafranske, 2017). The "culture of competency" (Roberts, Borden, Christiansen, & Lopez, 2005) that has permeated psychology for well over a decade provides the context for implementing a competency-based supervision framework, and is expanded upon in Chapter 8.

Strengths-based Supervision

Another supervision framework which has garnered recent attention is a strengths-based approach (Edwards, 2017; Newman, Guiney, & Silva, 2017; Wade & Jones, 2015). Applied to school psychology, strengths-based supervision (SBS) is defined as "a process in which supervisors and supervisees collaboratively assess and build upon supervisee strengths, including cultural assets, and in which supervisee contributions to supervision are valued." (Newman et al., 2017, pp. 21–22). As an overarching framework, SBS can work in tandem with other supervision approaches, such as DEP, to inform the school psychology supervision process. Like DEP, SBS is a new approach in psychology (Edwards, 2017; Wade & Jones, 2015) and therefore does not as yet have strong empirical support. However, SBS is built upon foundations of positive psychology (Seligman & Csikszentmihalyi, 2000), which provide several conceptual building blocks from which to understand the needs of supervisees such as interns. Newman et al. (2017) illustrated how SBS is applicable to support trainees exhibiting PPC (see Table 7.3). Although SBS focuses on supervisees' strengths rather than gaps, it is important to recognize that SBS does not ignore supervisees' training needs or challenges. Instead, SBS provides a framework for constructive feedback to be articulated within the context of a supervision relationship built on trust (Nichter & Dowda, 2017).

Developmental Approaches to Supervision

A common underlying theme across supervision models is the (sometimes implicit) recognition that supervisee development of clinical skills and professional identity is a critical component of supervision (Bernard & Goodyear, 2019; Kaufman, 2010a). Stage-based models such as the prominent Integrated Developmental Model (IDM; McNeill & Stoltenberg, 2016; Stoltenberg, 2005; Stoltenberg & Delworth, 1987) and life-span developmental models

TABLE 7.3 Strengths-Based Supervision Strategies to Support Supervisees with Problems of Professional Competence (PPC)

Strategy	Examples of Supervisor Actions
Reframe PPC from a deficit perspective to an ecological perspective	Move beyond "problematic supervisee" and consider contributions of factors such as: • Field and university training contexts (e.g., cases too difficult for stage of training, required skills not sufficiently addressed in coursework/practica). • Cultural differences (e.g., supervisee, supervisor, and clients; school culture). • Supervisor variables (e.g., insufficient formative feedback; lack of supervision training).
Emphasize prevention and early intervention	• Engage in ongoing communication and collaboration between field and university. • Establish due process *before* supervision experience, including what happens if things go well and if they do not go well. • Set norms for discussing cultural variables and inviting supervisee feedback on the supervision process at the outset of the supervision experience. • Model professional behaviors and self-care. • Engage in formative assessment, documenting strengths and areas for growth, tied to ongoing, timely, clear feedback.
Intervene within the context of a strong supervision relationship	• Establish trust within the relationship with clear expectations (e.g., a contract, an explicit supervision framework), bi-directional feedback, and shared power. • Engage in developmentally appropriate teaching: "I do it" (e.g., modeling, assigned readings), "we do it" (e.g., practicing skills together), and "you do it" (e.g., supervisee application of skills with supervisor observation and feedback). • Teach professional behaviors as you would teach professional content knowledge and skills. • Acknowledge and build upon supervisee strengths, including cultural assets, and use strengths to address PPC. • Search for solutions rather than problems. • Use practical questions to facilitate supervisee growth (e.g., "What went well that you can build upon for next time?"). • Model strengths-based approach in interactions with supervisee, parents, staff, and students.
Engage in ongoing self-reflection	Ask questions such as: • "What are my blind spots? How might they influence my supervision?" • "How might my supervisee perceive supervision differently than I intend?"

- "What is a mistake I might be making with my supervisee? Drawing upon my strengths, how might I attain a better outcome?"
- "What can I learn from my supervisee?"
- Model for your supervisee your own periodic self-assessment of skills in growing areas, such as developing cultural responsiveness or working with specific populations.

Note. SBS to Support Supervisees with Problems of Professional Competence. From Newman, D. S., Guiney, M., and Silva, A. E. (2017). Strengths-based supervision in school psychology: Accentuate the positive; eliminate the negative. *NASP Communiqué, 46(1), 1; 21–23.*SBS strategies to support supervisees with problems of professional competence. Copyright 2017 by the National Association of School Psychologists, Bethesda, MD. Reprinted with permission of the publisher. www.nasponline.org.

(e.g., Rønnestad & Skovholt, 2003, 2013) focus on distinctions between stages of development (e.g., beginning student versus experienced professional) rather than differences within stages. On the other hand, process developmental models focus on processes occurring within a limited period of time, such as the one-year window of the school psychology internship.

Process Developmental Models

Process developmental approaches to supervision include reflective models of practice (illustrated in Figure 7.1), an events-based approach to supervision (Ladany et al., 2016), and an intricate model of counselor development described by Loganbill, Hardy, and Delworth (1982). The Loganbill et al. model describes supervisees working through eight developmental issues (competence, emotional awareness, autonomy, theoretical identity, respect for individual differences, purpose and direction, personal motivation, and professional ethics) during three recursive stages (stagnation, confusion, and integration), which are typified by attitudes towards self, supervisor, and the world. The developmental issues identified by Loganbill et al. for supervisees overlap considerably with intern skills identified by Sullivan et al. (2014), defined in Table 7.2.

In the Loganbill et al. (1982) model, process-related stages are revisited more than once as part of supervision, each time with "increasing thoroughness" – like tightening the bolts on a tire until the wheel is firmly fastened to the car (p. 17). The Loganbill et al. model is illustrated in Figure 7.3 using an example of intern Tanya's development of purpose and direction. Tanya's progress through the stages of stagnation, confusion, and integration are illustrated so the reader can see how her skills progress with each recurring stage. Theoretically, "stages of the process can be gone through again and again" (Loganbill et al., 1982, p. 17). Ideally Tanya will experience skill growth in this and other domain areas over the course of the internship year.

Stagnation Stage: Supervisee is unaware of deficiencies (novice) or feeling stuck (more experienced); engages in cognitively simple thinking; and may be either highly dependent on, or neglectful of supervision.

Intern Tanya is part of a problem-solving team that identifies a student's reading difficulties. She agrees to take the lead in support of a struggling reader but is not sure how to best monitor the student's reading progress during an intervention. She seeks out supervision.

Confusion Stage: Supervisee is disorganized, confused, or conflicted about what to do; may fluctuate between feelings of incompetence and inflated confidence; and may realize that the supervisor does not have all the answers.

Tanya feels unsatisfied with supervision and the case's lack of progress. She is not sure how to move forward. She begins collecting CBM data but is unsure if she is doing so correctly. She is frustrated with her supervisor, and feeling like she is performing poorly.

Skill Domain:
Purpose and Direction

Integration Stage: Supervisee achieves a new and more accurate understanding of self, world, and supervision; increased flexibility in problem solving; and responsibility for actions. Integration is a continuous stage of growth.

Tanya and the supervisor look at the data together and determine the student is making some progress but less than expected. They reevaluate the intervention, discuss options with the problem solving team, and make changes that result in student progress.

FIGURE 7.3 Stagnation, confusion, and integration: A developmental process model applied to the school psychology internship.

Since the supervisor is expected to maintain awareness of eight issues over three stages in the Loganbill et al. (1982) model, over 24 positions are considered. Needless to say, the model is quite complex. However, the model (a) offers supervisors insight into the multitude of concerns supervisees face, (b) offers a starting point for deciding how to evaluate intern skills, (c) provides an impetus for supervisors to differentiate the process of supervision given divergent supervisee needs, and (d) demonstrates that ongoing practice and supervisory support are needed over an extended period of time for supervisees to develop competence.

Developmental, Ecological, Problem-solving Model for School Psychology

Recently, Simon et al. (2014) and Simon and Swerdlik (2017) described the school psychology specific DEP supervision model. Although yet to be empirically researched, since the DEP model is uniquely designed for the field of school psychology, it might be the most fitting for application during the school psychology internship. The developmental pillar of the model attends to the stages of intern growth, with a goal of moving interns from dependence on supervisors to independent practice over time. In short, the developmental component of the model summarizes how supervisors can adjust their role, supervision structures, and feedback mechanisms to match with interns' varying training goals and needs across different points in time.

The second pillar of DEP, the ecological domain, emphasizes that supervision must include attention to the ecology, systems, multicultural composition and diversity of schools. As asserted by Simon and Swerdlik (2017), "It is impossible to understand individual students, classrooms, or school communities without understanding their interaction with larger environments" (p. 245). Therefore, the supervisor and supervisee attend to the larger context and interactions within which supervision is nested to best consider approaches to prevention and intervention. An ecological emphasis is consistent with APA's (2017b) recently updated *Multicultural Guidelines: An Ecological Approach to Context, Identity, and Intersectionality*, as well as the Diversity competency domain described in APA (2015a) supervision competency guidelines.

Problem solving is the third pillar of DEP, emphasized in this supervision model because problem solving is *the* core activity of school psychology (Simon & Swerdlik, 2017). Interns can observe and engage in problem solving at various levels (e.g., grade, building, district) during the internship. Meanwhile, supervisors can provide ongoing, explicit instruction and modeling of data-based decision making and its role in a systematic problem-solving process, with a goal of augmenting interns' problem-solving skills. Interested readers can access more detailed markers of each of the three DEP domains from Simon and Swerdlik (2017), which could be used by supervisors for self-reflection or to obtain feedback from supervisees.

Internship Stages

To wrap up the consideration of developmental approaches to supervision, a sequential, goal-directed teaching model of supervision described by Alessi et al. (1981) and expanded on by Harvey and Struzziero (2008) is illustrated in Figure 7.4. Harvey and Struzziero (2008) described five stages of supervisor-supervisee supervision interactions: (1) Shadowing and Modeling; (2) Observation of Assessment and Professional Skills; (3) Guided Independent Practice; (4) Increasing Independent Practice; and (5) Professional Independence.

Supervisors may consider this model an "I do, we do, you do" approach to internship supervision which begins with intern entry and observation of supervisor behaviors ("I do"), moves to the intern and supervisor working together in parallel ("we do"), and concludes with an intern's achievement of increased independence ("you do"). Harvey and Struzziero (2008) noted that "supervisors should not expect that interns will function completely independently by the end of the internship" (p. 206). Therefore, at the end of the year, it may be beneficial for the intern and supervisor to discuss the intern's transition into the first year of independent practice, including how the intern may access various supports such as mentorship, supervision, and other professional learning opportunities. Such a dialogue may act to enhance the intern's feelings of readiness to enter the field.

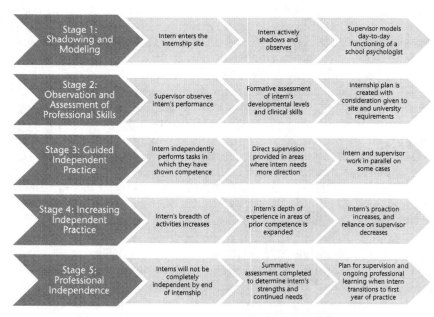

FIGURE 7.4 Five stages of the school psychology internship.

Supervision Formats

In addition to supervision models, there are several supervision formats that school psychology interns may encounter during the internship, including individual, group, and peer group supervision.

Individual Supervision

The most common format for supervision is *individual supervision* or a single supervisor working with a single supervisee to engage in case planning and to support the supervisee's formative development of clinical skills. Individual supervision can be time consuming but allows the supervisor and supervisee to focus on the supervisee's distinctive needs and permits close monitoring of the supervisee's developmental progress and of the services provided by the supervisee. Individual supervision can also take place in a small group, where the supervisor works with each supervisee individually in a rotation; this may be more time efficient than one-on-one supervision (Harvey & Struzziero, 2008). Consistent with NASP (2010d) and APA (2015b) guidelines, the majority of supervision hours during the internship will likely occur in individual supervision.

Group Supervision

Another supervision format is *group supervision*, which is defined by Bernard and Goodyear (2019) as

> the regular meeting of a group of supervisees (a) with a designated supervisor or supervisors; (b) to monitor the quality of their work; and (c) to further their understanding of themselves . . . of the clients with whom they work, and of service delivery in general . . . Supervisees achieve these goals with the help of their supervisor(s) and the feedback from and interactions with one other.
>
> *(pp. 190–191)*

There are numerous benefits and a few limitations of group supervision identified by Bernard and Goodyear, which are summarized in Table 7.4. The advantages of group supervision outweigh potential limitations, making this format useful for university and field supervisors.

Although there is great potential variability in the structure of group supervision (Mastoras & Andrews, 2011), there are some principles that may help guide its implementation. Harvey and Struzziero (2008) suggested supervisors limit group size to between four and eight supervisees and aim for relative homogeneity of developmental levels and topical interests when composing a group. Processes of group development are also important to consider (see Haboush, 2003, for

TABLE 7.4 Benefits and Limitations of Group Supervision Identified by Bernard and Goodyear (2019, pp. 191–192) Pertinent to the School Psychology Internship

Benefits	Limitations
• Supervisors make economic use of resources such as time, money, and expertise. • Supervisees' experiences are normalized through vicarious exposure to peers' experiences. • The supervisor can see the supervisee in a different way than is possible in individual supervision. • Supervisees learn from each other's experiences and application of skills. • Supervisees can learn supervision skills. • Supervisees receive greater quantity, quality, and diversity of feedback.	• Supervisees may not get individual needs addressed (e.g., if time is not managed well). • Group phenomena such as competitiveness or scapegoating among group members can potentially hinder learning. • Everything that is discussed may not be relevant to every supervisee at every interval. • There is increased risk of confidentiality violations.

further description of group theory). Finally, Harvey and Struzziero (2008) acknowledged the importance of having a formal group structure which may include supervisee case presentations and requests for assistance, peer clarification questions and feedback, supervisee response, and post-supervision feedback from the supervisor to supervisees that presented cases.

Peer Group Supervision

Peer group supervision is a type of group supervision but differs from other supervision formats because it is non-hierarchical and does not include a formal evaluation process (Bernard & Goodyear, 2019). Counselman and Weber (2004) offered insights regarding peer group structure, including the importance of developing a group contract, sharing tasks of leadership, and having a plan for case presentations. Even though the research on peer supervision groups is modest, the approach seems like a promising one for interns. First, the internship provides an opportunity for interns to learn a peer supervision process they can apply in their future practice. Since school psychology practitioners do not always receive clinical supervision in professional practice (Chafouleas, Clonan, & Vanauken, 2002; Silva et al., 2016), knowing how to effectively access peer consultation is essential. Second, the non-evaluative nature of peer group supervision can facilitate interns' openness to share with one another, thereby acting as a supplement to other forms of internship supervision. Third, opportunities for peer group supervision may naturally arise during the internship, especially if there are several interns at one internship site or if the intern attends a university-based internship seminar with other interns.

A Structure for Group or Peer Group Supervision

University-based internship seminars are one setting in which a formalized group supervision process can be implemented. Supervisors may find a structured peer group supervision model relevant to use for field- or university-based supervision. Students work in groups of three or four and the instructor rotates to participate in each group, making this approach a hybrid of group and peer group supervision. Consistent with characteristics of well-functioning peer supervision groups (e.g., Counselman & Weber, 2004) supervisees are expected to: (a) develop a working group contract; (b) stay on task during group discussions; (c) work collaboratively through problems; and (d) follow a format for group supervision. Any violations of the group contract are expected to be addressed by the group.

The following steps in the supervision process, adapted from the structured group supervision research (e.g., Borders, 1991; Wilbur, Roberts-Wilbur, Morris, Betz, & Hart, 1991; Wilbur, Roberts-Wilbur, Hart, Morris, & Betz, 1994), provide the format for the supervision:

Step 1: *Request for Help.* The intern states what assistance is being requested from the supervision group. Summary information may be presented using audio/video recordings, data from the case, written summaries, and/or verbal statements. Following the presentation of information, the supervisee makes an explicit statement of the request for assistance (e.g., "I need the group's help to. . .").

Step 2: *Asking Questions.* The group members *paraphrase* (i.e., restate in their own words to verify understanding) and *clarify* information presented in Step 1 to make sure they accurately understand the presenting concern(s). Peers should avoid asking relevant questions (e.g., those not stemming directly from information provided by the presenter) and irrelevant questions (e.g., those not related to the topic). Questions should be asked one at a time in an orderly manner until there are no more questions (i.e., the request for assistance is clear).

Step 3: *Feedback.* Group members respond to the information provided in Steps 1 and 2 by stating how they might handle their peer's concern (e.g., "If I was working with that teacher, I might. . ."). The presenter remains silent but takes notes regarding the comments or suggestions. Feedback should be provided one at a time in an orderly manner until there is no additional feedback.

Pause/Break. A break of a few minutes between Steps 3 and 4 allows for the presenter's reflection on the group members' feedback.

Step 4: *Response Statement.* The group members remain silent and allow the presenter to respond to each person's feedback, one at a time. The presenter may choose to state whether the feedback was helpful or not and why it was helpful or not. The response statement concludes with the presenter summarizing the next steps for his or her work.

Step 5: *Discussion (Optional).* Time depending, issues discussed in small groups may be discussed with the full class.

Supervision groups are more organic and flexible than may be apparent when looking at the steps in this process. For instance; the group must determine the order in which they will present; sometimes clarifying questions arise at steps other than Step 2; and the format can be used with or without a supervisor present. Further, sometimes an issue arises for which the group members do not have sufficient expertise, in which case the course instructor should be consulted. Anecdotally, I have noticed that having some structure tends to support positive group dynamics, enhance problem solving efforts, and provide opportunities for vicarious learning by exposure to a variety of case concerns.

Techniques

Supervision is considered an intervention in and of itself, but is also comprised of several interventions (also called methods, strategies, or techniques) that are delivered by supervisors. Supervision techniques are used to (a) assess supervisee needs, (b) change, shape, or support supervisee behavior, and (c) evaluate supervisee performance, and may be differentially suited to achieve these different goals (Bernard & Goodyear, 2019). Purposeful supervisors select techniques based on supervisee and supervisor goals, supervisee experience and learning preferences, and the supervisor's theoretical orientation and model of supervision. Therefore, an effective "supervisor needs to have both a repertoire of skills and the ability to be flexible in using them" (Bernard & Goodyear, 2019, p. 162).

A number of supervision techniques are featured in Table 7.5, with a consideration of their advantages as well as challenges in their application. Although there are multiple supervision techniques that may be helpful training tools, supervisors do not always apply a wide array of strategies, or choose the ones they perceive to be the most effective. For example, Romans, Boswell, Carlozzi, and Ferguson (1995) found that directors of counseling, clinical and school psychology training programs rated co-facilitation (e.g., co-therapy) to be the most effective supervision strategy but implemented that technique less than all others. On the contrary, self-report techniques (e.g., case consultation) were rated as the least effective but were the most commonly applied. Similarly, in a survey of internship supervision practices in school psychology, Ward (2001) found that both university- and field-based supervisors spent the largest chunk of their supervision time on supervisee case presentations.

TABLE 7.5 Supervision Techniques

Technique	Definition	Advantages	Challenges
Case consultation	Discussion of supervisee's cases including supervisee's description of major case issues and broad case conceptualization	• Effective in individual and group formats. • Can be applied in consideration of numerous issues. • Easily combined with other techniques.	• Supervisee self-report may not be accurate due to supervisee's limited awareness or understanding, or desire for positive evaluation.
Co-facilitation	Supervisee and supervisor(s) work together on a particular case including planning, implementation, and follow up	• Supervisor gets firsthand perspective of supervisee skills. • Supervisor can model skills.	• Potential for role confusion. • Supervisor may dominate, not letting supervisee get experience. • Clients may favor supervisor over supervisee.
Live observation	Supervisor(s) observe the supervisee's work, either behind a one-way mirror, on a video, or in person. May include in vivo supervisor feedback such as interruptions or built-in breaks	• Supervisor gets firsthand perspective of supervisee skills. • Allows supervisors to provide feedback before, during, or after. • Use of one-way mirror is amenable to group supervision processes.	• Interruptions may be distracting or anxiety provoking to supervisee. • Permission from clients may be necessary.
Audio and video recording	The supervisee is recorded while applying skills in action. Supervisee process notes are often required in conjunction with recordings.	• Recordings can be watched, paused, and replayed as needed allowing for discussion, modeling, and rehearsal. • Observable and measurable recordings provide accurate supplements to supervisee and supervisor perceptions. • Easily available on devices such as cell phones, tablets, and computers.	• Potential for technological difficulties. • Video recording is more robust than audio recording because it provides information on body language and other environmental factors. • Permission from clients is necessary.

(continued)

TABLE 7.5 *(continued)*

Technique	Definition	Advantages	Challenges
Computer and online	Use of technology for supervision in any of a variety forms such as supervisor instant messaging during live observation, email supervision, videoconferencing, and use of simulation activities	• Allows supervision and learning over far distances. • Novel, engaging, and relevant to technologically savvy supervisors and supervisees.	• Potential for technological difficulties. • Ethical challenges such as maintaining confidentiality. • May be difficult to form the supervisor–supervisee relationship. • Limited research base regarding effectiveness.
Role play	Acting out challenging case scenarios with the supervisee. May include role reversal (e.g., supervisee plays the role of client to explore case issues, or the role of supervisor to explore supervision process issues)	• Effective in individual and group formats. • Promotes perspective taking. • Provides supervisee opportunities to practice skills in a safe space.	• May feel awkward or artificial. • Skills may not transfer to real situations.
Modeling and rehearsal	Supervisor teaches the supervisee through his or her behavior, and/or demonstrates how to do something. Modeling is often combined with supervisees' rehearsal, or practice of skills.	• Supervisees see and hear how to do something rather than only talking about how to do something. • Promotes conscious reflection from the supervisor regarding modeling behaviors. • Provides supervisee opportunities to practice skills in a safe space.	• May inhibit supervisees from finding their own voice. • Supervisees may not apply what was modeled or rehearsed in actual cases.
Written information (e.g., process notes, progress notes, transcription)	Written notes may cover case issues and case progress, perceptions regarding growth in skills, challenges, successes, and supervision needs. Partial or full transcriptions can be produced using audio or video recordings of sessions.	• Promotes supervisee reflection on a number of issues. • Encourages supervisee and supervisor preparation for supervision. • Provides documentation of case progress as well as supervisee skill growth.	• May be time consuming for supervisee and supervisor. • Supervisee notes may not be accurate due to supervisee's limited awareness or understanding, or desire for positive evaluation.

Ward (2001) also noted differences between the activities of field and university internship supervisors. Field supervisors reported more involvement in clinical supervision activities (e.g., reviewing reports, modeling, live observation) while university supervisors spent more time in less-individualized activities, including general group supervision and sharing of resources. Ward (2001) concluded that "together, the field-based and university supervisors provide interns with a more extensive supervision experience than either supervisor could provide on his/her own" (p. 281). Surely, the combination of field and university supervision has the potential to be a powerful tool to support interns. However, if supervisors are not thoughtful about which techniques they implement, including when and with what purpose, supervision may be an improvised process of trial and error rather than a structured intervention.

Training and Skill Development for Supervisors

There appear to be supervision gaps at all levels of school psychology training and practice. The most recent survey of NASP members by Walcott and Hyson (2018) found that only approximately half of respondents to their national survey indicated receiving systematic professional support, mentoring, and/or peer supervision of their work. What is more, less than one third of participants had a credentialed school psychologist responsible for their performance evaluations. These data are consistent with findings from Silva et al. (2016), which indicated limited access to and availability of mentoring and supervision for early career school psychologists despite interest in receiving these supports. In short, most practicing school psychologists do not receive clinical supervision, and those who do receive it from someone who is not trained to be a school psychologist. Given these data, it seems likely that school psychologists do not receive metasupervision when providing field-based supervision to practicum students or interns.

The findings from Walcott and Hyson (2018) and Silva et al. (2016) are consistent with data by Ward (2001) who surveyed school psychology internship supervisors (239 field-based and forty-one university-based) and found that most (both field *and* university) had received little or no training in supervision and did not engage in formal metasupervision. Further, Ward reported that the vast majority of field and university supervisors had no graduate coursework in supervision and that the most common type of supervision training for both types of supervisors was informal discussions with colleagues. Silva et al. (2016) similarly found that 63% of early career school psychologists they surveyed had no training in supervision and those that did had limited exposure (e.g., part of one graduate course).

Most recently, McMahon et al. (2018) surveyed school psychology trainers and internship coordinators ($N = 93$) finding that only one quarter of the sample offered continuing education support related to supervision for supervisors and the vast majority of supervisors reportedly did not take advantage of such opportunities when offered. Yet most trainers in the sample (76%) perceived that supervisors would benefit from enhanced support and training specifically focused on internship supervision. Such gaps in supervision practice and training are inconsistent with the increasingly common expectation that supervision coursework and metasupervision be included as components of graduate training in psychology (Falender et al., 2004), and recognition of supervision as an overarching competency area for all psychologists (APA, 2015a).

For supervisors who have not or will not take a course in supervision, other opportunities for professional learning may be available, some of which may provide continuing professional development credits. Opportunities may include attending presentations or workshops, engaging in self-studies (e.g., completing relevant readings), or participating in a peer-supervision network (Harvey and Struzziero, 2008; Simon & Swerdlik, 2017). Some universities or state associations run trainings for supervisors. For example, Harvey and colleagues (2010) described a supervision institute for practicum and internship supervisors in Massachusetts which documented several positive outcomes for attendees and the state of Illinois has hosted an annual Intern Supervision Day for internship supervisors and new interns for many years (Kelly, Cruise, Newman, Swerdlik, & Simon, 2012). The Illinois School Psychology Association has also recently approved and begun implementing a Supervisor Credential program, which allows supervisors to obtain a credential for engaging in twelve hours of coursework on best practices in supervision, and metasupervision sessions, and includes a training of trainers to proliferate the availability of supervision training throughout the state (Simon, Swerdlik, Cruise, & Stein, in press).

Metasupervision is an underutilized way that supervisors can continue their ongoing professional development. Peer networks can provide opportunities to engage in peer group supervision, including consultation on complex supervision issues and matters outside of one's boundaries of competence (Annan & Ryba, 2013). No matter how knowledge and skill support is obtained, since supervision is considered a competency, professional learning on the topic of supervision should be prioritized. Attending presentations or workshops, engaging in self-studies, and conversing with colleagues offer starting points for supervision training. Supervisors are encouraged to seek out multiple opportunities and to continue to engage in learning over time.

Summary

There is a dearth of research on supervision in school psychology supervision but it is generally accepted that supervision is a pivotal training tool. School psychology internship supervision may be considered unique compared to supervision in other mental health fields as well as to supervision at other levels of school psychology training and practice.

Goals of supervision include supervisee skill growth, supporting client welfare, gatekeeping for the profession, teaching supervisees skills to self-supervise, and providing restorative support. Three pivotal, interrelated components of effective supervision include a positive supervisor-supervisee relationship, attending to multicultural considerations in supervision, and engaging in ongoing self-reflection. When effective supervision is in place, positive outcomes for supervisees include expansion of knowledge and applied skills, reduction of anxiety, increased self-efficacy, enhanced accountability and ethical practice, and the continued development of professional identity. Formative and summative evaluations help supervisors and supervisees gain awareness of supervision outcomes and the intern's progress from the beginning to end of the internship. For interns who demonstrate problems with regard to their development of competence, a plan for remediation may be necessary.

Supervision is structured by particular supervision models, formats, and techniques. Research does not support one model of supervision over others but contemporary approaches include focuses on supervisees' competency development, strengths, and practice contexts. The recently developed DEP Model focuses on supervision in the professional context of school psychology practice and therefore may be considered particularly relevant to school psychology internship supervision. Supervisors may wish to use an "I do, we do, you do" approach to supervision in order to allow interns to develop autonomy with appropriate amounts of scaffolding along the way. There are a number of techniques that supervisors can use to structure supervision and being eclectic (purposefully selecting approaches to match with supervisee needs and the supervision context) is a helpful approach. Supervision may also take place in a variety of formats such as one-on-one, in a group, or non-hierarchically with peers. It is recommended that supervisors, especially novice supervisors, continue to seek out professional learning opportunities to hone the supervision practices that they provide.

Critical Thinking Questions and Activities

The following are critical thinking questions for interns, field supervisors, and university supervisors regarding the role of supervision during the school psychology internship.

For Interns:

- What trigger events (see Figure 7.1) have stimulated reflection for you during your internship thus far? How were trigger events addressed in supervision, if at all?
- Reflect on your skill development in the domain areas identified in Table 7.2. Which areas do you feel are your strengths? How might you improve in areas that are challenging for you?
- What have you learned about supervision from observing supervisors in the past or during the internship? How do you predict this will influence who you are as a supervisor in the future?

For Field Supervisors:

- How do you incorporate multicultural supervision practices as part of the supervision you provide?
- Looking at Table 7.5, what new techniques might you apply as part of supervision? How might you combine several different techniques? Are different techniques more or less relevant for particular domains of school psychology practice? Do you use the same approaches with all supervisees?
- What opportunities are available for you to continue your own professional learning as a supervisor?

For University Supervisors:

- Reflect on the structure of supervision in your training program. What models, formats, and techniques are used to support school psychology interns? Other trainees?
- How might you decrease the anxiety many interns experience regarding evaluation?
- How can the university support field supervisors' continued professional learning about supervision?

8

BREADTH, DEPTH, AND COMPETENCE

As has been defined in previous chapters, *breadth* of experience refers to an intern's involvement in a number and assortment of opportunities and d*epth* of experience is the progression of training in a particular domain, from early coursework to skill application, working with differing populations at different levels or tiers of service. With sufficient breadth and depth of experiences that are (a) aligned with the ten domains outlined in NASP's (2010a) practice model and (b) completed in conjunction with ongoing supervision, it is expected that the intern will develop the competencies needed to begin practice as an entry-level school psychologist.

Explicitly considering breadth, depth, and competence fits within the "culture of competence" that currently impacts the broad field of professional psychology (e.g., Belar, 2009; Fouad et al., 2009; Grus, Falender, Fouad, & Lavelle, 2016; Hatcher et al., 2013; Kaslow et al., 2009; Roberts et al., 2005), including the specialty of school psychology (e.g., Daly, Doll, Schulte, & Fenning, 2011; Fenning et al., 2015; Phelps & Swerdlik, 2011). The competency movement recognizes the need to (a) clarify foundational competencies (i.e., the knowledge, skills, attitudes, and values underlying psychology practice) and functional competencies (i.e., the major functions of psychologists); (b) specify benchmarks for attaining competency at varying developmental levels; and (c) provide formative and summative evaluation of performance for psychology trainees and practitioners (Fouad et al., 2009; Kaslow, 2004).

As discussed by Kaslow (2004), when psychologists apply a competency-based approach they must be careful not to reduce "the profession to a collection of specific skills that might or might not require extensive educational/experiential training, and as a result, train technicians rather than professionals" (p. 779). Similarly, Belar (2009) expressed that too narrow a focus on articulating and evaluating competencies may result in a "stove-piping" phenomenon whereby psychologists mechanically list competencies but do not sufficiently recognize their interrelated and interactive nature. Such concerns are consistent with this book's big idea that the development of a school psychology intern's professional skills should be treated as an integrated process rather than a series of isolated activities. Therefore, although the chapter contains a number of examples of potential activities that school psychology interns may take on, it is purposely designed to be integrated, non-prescriptive, and practical.

The chapter begins by clearly defining the terms competence and competencies. Competency documents influencing professional psychology and the subfield of school psychology are briefly reviewed with consideration for how they may help shape the school psychology internship. Examples of activities completed by one intern, Raven, are provided to demonstrate how competence can be integrated into internship training. The importance of breadth and depth during the internship are explored in detail. With regard to depth, interns are encouraged to develop a *Hedgehog Concept*: the overlap between what they excel at more than anything else, what they are passionate about, and what will make them marketable upon internship completion. The chapter closes with critical thinking questions and activities for interns and supervisors regarding breadth, depth, and competence.

What is Competence?

According to Kaslow (2004), *competence* is "an individual's capability and demonstrated ability to understand and do certain tasks in an appropriate and effective manner consistent with the expectations for a person qualified by education and training in a particular profession or specialty thereof" (p. 775). Further, competence implies being able to (a) engage in critical thinking and analysis; (b) apply professional judgment in decision making; and (c) adapt decisions based on specific situations. Competence is developmental, meaning that expectations regarding competence should differ for individuals at different stages of training and practice (Assessment of Competency Benchmarks Workgroup, ACBW, 2012a, 2012b; Fouad et al., 2009). For example, what it means to be a competent practicum student likely differs in some ways from what it means to be a competent intern as well as what it means to be competent to enter professional practice. Finally, competence is context dependent; that is, different settings or environments may differentially impact the development and/or the evaluation of competencies (Kaslow, 2004). *Competencies* are "elements of competence that are observable, measurable, containable, practical, derived by experts, and flexible" (Kaslow, 2004, p. 775). Competencies correlate with one's performance and therefore can be formatively and summatively evaluated as well as augmented through training.

In a recent review of the science of psychology training, Callahan and Watkins (2018) recognized that "the bulk of the extant literature on the attainment of competency is theoretical and/or consensus based, rather than empirical" (p. 249). However, given that the internship is proximally situated at the intersection of training and professional practice, understanding the development of trainee competency is critically aligned with goals of supervision, particularly protecting the welfare of clients and gatekeeping for the profession.

Competency Guidelines Influencing School Psychology

In a consideration of evolving issues during the school psychology internship, Phelps and Swerdlik (2011) identified four documents that are particularly relevant to a discussion of competency attainment: The *Competency Benchmarks* (Fouad et al., 2009), which have since been updated (ACBW, 2012a, 2012b), and the *Competency Assessment Toolkit* (Kaslow et al., 2009), both derived from APA workgroups, and NASP's *Blueprint III* (Ysseldyke et al., 2006) and *Standards for Graduate Preparation of School Psychologists* (NASP, 2010d). Although the documents are briefly summarized in the sections that follow, a detailed exploration is beyond the scope of the chapter. Readers are referred to the original resources for a more in-depth description of standards, domains, and competencies.

APA Competency Documents

The most recent version of the *Competency Benchmarks* (ACBW, 2012a, 2012b) describes sixteen competencies (seven foundational and nine functional), across six broad clusters (professionalism, relational, science, application, education, and systems) and these are intended to be relevant to all psychology disciplines, including school psychology. Each competency is further divided into essential components and behavioral anchors are provided across three developmental levels (readiness for practicum, internship, and entry-level practice). The related *Competency Assessment Toolkit* (Kaslow et al., 2009) identifies fifteen assessment measures (both formative and summative) that can be used by multiple informants to evaluate competency, including readiness for practicum, internship, and entry into professional practice. The measures identified in the *Toolkit* are listed and briefly described in Table 8.1, and can be seen as consistent with assessment processes discussed at various other junctures in this book. The assessment approaches are described and scrutinized in greater detail in the original *Toolkit*, including psychometrics as well as steps for implementation, strengths, and limitations. Although the *Toolkit* has been criticized for potentially presenting an oversimplified view of assessment (Daly et al., 2011), supervisors and interns may find one or more of these approaches useful for evaluation, which is why they are highlighted in this book.

NASP Documents

Both the *Blueprint III* (Ysseldyke et al., 2006) and the *Standards for Graduate Preparation of School Psychologists* (NASP, 2010d) have been referenced and

TABLE 8.1 Assessment Tools that May Help Evaluate Interns' Competency Development

Tool	Brief Summary
360-Degree Evaluations	Multiple raters evaluate the intern across foundational and functional competency domains. Raters may include supervisors, peers, colleagues, supervisees, and the intern. Ratings are summed, feedback is provided to the intern, and an action plan for improvement is developed.
Annual/Rotation Performance Reviews	Faculty, field supervisors, and possibly peers provide an integrated, summative evaluation to the intern regarding foundational and functional competency domains. Multiple sources of data are used for review, integrated, and assessed with regard to developmental level (e.g., readiness to enter professional practice).
Case Presentation Reviews	The intern discusses a case s/he is working in a pre-determined format. Presentations may include client and/or system characteristics, assessment methods, intervention design and implementation, progress monitoring, and outcomes. Presentations are followed by interactive discussion by the intern and evaluators.
Client Process and Outcome Data	Client outcomes are evaluated using any of a number of measures (e.g., working alliance, symptom checklists, rating scales, diagnostic interviews). Intern and evaluator(s) determine measures, explain purpose to clients, and gather data. Data are analyzed, and used to enhance quality of services delivered to clients.
Competency Evaluation Rating Forms	The intern is rated by supervisors on behavioral indicators for selected foundational and functional competency domains in order to indicate attainment. The intern and supervisors discuss evaluation results, and pinpoint areas of need.
Consumer Surveys	Surveys are completed by clients regarding satisfaction with services received and the intern's competency results are summed and shared with the intern by supervisors.
Live or Recorded Performance Ratings	Evaluator(s) observe the intern in person or via a recording and rate the intern's performance in relevant competency areas. The observation format is determined in advance, and both the intern and client(s) consent to the observation.
*Objective Structured Clinical Examinations *and* Standardized Client Interviews	Specially trained actors play the role of clients with particular psychological symptoms. The intern interacts with the actors and completes notes or prepares other written material regarding the interaction with the "client." Performance may be evaluated by the "client," the assessor, and the intern.
Portfolios	A collection of products are gathered by the intern, providing evidence of competency attainment. The portfolio format (e.g., electronic or hard copy) is determined in advance, as are elements to be included, and the intern is evaluated based on his or her work.

Record Reviews	Client records (e.g., assessment reports, case files, counseling notes) developed by the intern are reviewed by the assessor to determine the adequacy/sufficiency of notes, as well as their quality and accuracy. A standardized rating system/protocol can be developed for record review.
Self-Assessment	The intern evaluates his or her on strengths and areas of need (e.g., limits of expertise) across foundational and functional domains of competence. The intern should be aware of the rationale for self-assessment, methods for self-assessment, and competencies to be evaluated, and should reflect on the self-assessment with field and/or university supervisor(s).
Simulation/Role Plays	A situation resembling actual practice (including competencies) is constructed – either in vivo or computer based – and the intern's practice in the simulation observed and evaluated. Immediate feedback may be provided to the intern.
Structured Oral Examinations	The intern is asked a series of questions orally in a systematic manner and is expected to respond orally. Responses are evaluated using predetermined criteria to assess foundational and functional competencies.
Written Examinations	The intern completes a paper- or computer-based examination which may include questions of varying types (e.g., multiple choice, essay, problem-solving vignettes or scenarios). Results may provide data regarding the intern's knowledge in a number of foundational and functional competency areas.

Note. Adapted from "Competency Assessment Toolkit for Professional Psychology," by N. J. Kaslow, C. L., Grus, L. Campbell, N. A. Fouad, R. L., Hatcher, and E. R. Rodolfa, 2009, *Training and Education in Professional Psychology, 3*, pp. S27–S45.

*Indicates categories were combined given their similarity; readers are referred to Kaslow et al. (2009) for further distinction.

described throughout the book thus far. The NASP documents are similar to the *Competency Benchmarks* in several ways, including the delineation of foundational and functional competencies and consideration of developmental levels. Although the *Blueprint III* is developmentally oriented, specific benchmarks for the developmental levels of novice, competent, and expert are not provided. However, the *Blueprint III* does make explicit that novice levels of competence should be expected for trainees following the completion of coursework (pre-internship), that competence to enter professional practice is expected by the end of the internship year, and that expertise may be present after practicing in the field for several years, and is perhaps to be achieved in only in a few domains (Ysseldyke et al., 2006).

With regard to development of competence, NASP's (2010d) *Standards for Graduate Preparation of School Psychologists* states that training programs should ensure "candidates demonstrate basic professional competencies, including both *knowledge* and *skills*, in the ten domains of school psychology as a result of their graduate preparation" (p. 4). Further, it is explicitly stated that interns should provide "services that result in direct, measurable, and positive impact on children, families, school, and/or other consumers" (p. 8). Taking the *Blueprint III* and the *Standards for Graduate Preparation* documents together, by the end of the internship year, school psychologists should (a) have some exposure to each NASP domain area, including the development of basic competencies (i.e., breadth), (b) pursue *at least* one area that is more well-developed than others (i.e., depth), and (c) directly contribute to service delivery resulting in positive outcomes for clients.

Non-doctoral Versus Doctoral Level Competencies

School psychology, unlike other subspecialties in psychology, produces graduates at both the non-doctoral and doctoral levels. Although NASP differentiates between non-doctoral and doctoral-level internship hour requirements (i.e., 1200 hours for non-doctoral interns and 1500 hours for doctoral-level), differences between competencies at these two levels are not explicitly stated. Since the APA competency documents are primarily intended for doctoral-level trainees (as opposed to non-doctoral), a potential challenge in alignment with NASP competencies arises (Daly et al., 2011). Perhaps one way doctoral-level competencies can be distinguished from non-doctoral competencies is skill depth or specialization (Phelps & Swerdlik, 2011), a topic that is revisited in more detail later in this chapter.

Application of Competencies During the School Psychology Internship

The four documents may be used by university educators, field supervisors, and interns for several purposes, including (a) assessing readiness to begin the internship; (b) goal-setting; (c) identifying, preventing, and responding to problematic professional behaviors; (d) designing internship training experiences; and (e) assessing a graduating intern's readiness to enter the field (Phelps & Swerdlik, 2011). The example of school psychology intern Raven helps highlight the use of competency documents to inform what happens during the school psychology internship. Given the book's focus on *school psychology* interns, competencies are primarily considered within the framework of the two NASP documents.

VIGNETTE 8.1 **RAVEN'S INTEGRATED INTERNSHIP ACTIVITIES**

A non-doctoral intern named Raven completed her internship at a small suburban school district, including spending time at the elementary and middle school levels. Four of the more involved activities Raven participated in during the year are described in detail in Table 8.2, along with their alignment with domain areas from the NASP (2010a) practice model. Even from this small sample from all activities Raven completed during

TABLE 8.2 Integration and Breadth During Raven's Internship

Detailed Description of Activity	NASP Domains
Raven and her field supervisor consulted together with the assistant principal at her middle school around a school-wide cyberbullying concern. Together they engaged in an ongoing problem-solving process that included: • clearly defining what was meant by cyberbullying; • conducting a needs assessment regarding students', teachers', and parents' perceptions of the problem and its prevalence; • analyzing the data; making relevant changes to school policies including clarifying the protocol for reporting cyberbullying and intervening; educating school staff, parents, and students about cyberbullying and its consequences; and • evaluating changes in perceptions and prevalence over the year.	• Data-Based Decision Making and Accountability • Consultation and Collaboration • Interventions and Mental Health Services to Develop Social and Life Skills • School-Wide Practices to Promote Learning • Preventive and Responsive Services • Family–School Collaboration • Research and Program Evaluation
Raven's supervisor asked her to take the lead (with ongoing supervision) on a case regarding a kindergarten student, Maria, who had not spoken for the first two days of school. Raven consulted with Maria's teacher, Mrs. Livingston, who reported that although Maria did not talk verbally, she communicated non-verbally by pointing and nodding or shaking her head. Raven and the teacher contacted Maria's parents and learned that Maria spoke at home, primarily in Spanish. Raven conducted a literature review to learn more about selective mutism, and the potential intersection with English Language Learning (ELL). She learned that ELL students may go through a "silent period" where they focus on listening strategies to facilitate comprehension (Elizalde-Utnick, 2007). In addition to learning English, Mrs. Livingston and Raven noticed that Maria often appeared terrified during opportunities for verbal communication. Raven, her supervisor, and Mrs. Livingston consulted with the ESL teacher and also planned a behavioral intervention that included contingency-based positive reinforcement to (a) decrease Maria's anxiety about speaking and (b) increase Maria's nonverbal and verbal communication (in Spanish and English). Maria made significant progress on behavioral goals, monitored together by Raven and Mrs. Livingston.	• Data-Based Decision Making and Accountability • Consultation and Collaboration • Interventions and Mental Health Services to Develop Social and Life Skills • Family–School Collaboration Services • Diversity in Development and Learning • Research and Program Evaluation

(continued)

TABLE 8.2 *(continued)*

Detailed Description of Activity	NASP Domains
At her middle school, Raven worked with a veteran school counselor, Amy, to design and facilitate a grief and loss counseling group for seventh graders who had recently experienced the loss of a loved one (e.g., a parent, sibling, or grandparent). First, they screened seven participants they thought would be a good fit for the group and selected six (one student was referred for individual counseling services outside of the school setting). Next, Raven and Amy collaboratively developed an informed consent letter that was sent home to parents, including information about the purpose of the group, the facilitators, and the meeting schedule. They developed pre- and post-assessment measures to be completed by Raven and Amy, the group participants, and caregivers. The assessments measured students' development of coping skills at school and home, as well as progress towards individual goals set by each group member. Since they did not have an evidence-based curriculum readily available, Raven and Amy consulted with a local community counseling resource center regarding potential activities to implement and Raven also conducted additional background research.	• Data-based Decision Making and Accountability • Consultation and Collaboration • Interventions and Mental Health Services to Develop Social and Life Skills • Preventive and Responsive Services • Family–School Collaboration • Research and Program Evaluation • Legal, Ethical, and Professional Practice
Raven and her supervisor participated in grade level problem-solving team meetings at the elementary school. A third-grade teacher, Mr. Douglas, expressed concerns about four students in his class that were struggling readers. Two of the students were ELLs. Raven volunteered to follow up with Mr. Douglas through a formal consultation process. After contracting to work together, they decided that Raven would observe the class during reading. Raven noticed that Mr. Douglas rapidly introduced the text, made few connections to students' prior knowledge, and did not introduce any vocabulary words. He had the students briefly read independently and rapidly asked comprehension questions using the Socratic method. Several of the students, including the four students of concern, were visibly terrified to be called on. Mr. Douglas asked for Raven's honest feedback and she shared her observations in a constructive and non-evaluative manner. They collaboratively developed alternative strategies for reading instruction, including accessing students' prior knowledge, identifying and pre-teaching challenging vocabulary, and having students demonstrate comprehension in a variety of ways. By collecting data on reading comprehension, Raven and Mr. Douglas noticed significant reading progress for three of the four students (including both ELLs) in a short period of time, as well as several other students in the class. The student who did not make progress received a tier-three intervention and eventually was determined eligible for special education services; Raven contributed to the special education evaluation process.	• Data-based Decision Making and Accountability • Consultation and Collaboration • Interventions and Instructional Support to Develop Academic Skills • School-Wide Practices to Promote Learning • Diversity in Development and Learning

the year, it is apparent that she worked towards attainment of internship breadth. Whether or not Raven achieved depth is not readily apparent from Table 8.2. Each highlighted activity supports Raven's growth in a manner that integrates several different NASP (2010a) domains or areas of competence. None of the four activities integrates all ten domains but each activity spans several. It is also possible to parse out specific competencies that fall under each NASP domain area. Interested readers are referred to the NASP (2010a) *Model for Comprehensive and Integrated School Psychological Services* which offers examples of professional practice activities representative of some professional competencies for school psychologists.

Why Breadth Is Important

As introduced in Chapter 3, there is an expectation in school psychology training that interns should be exposed to a variety of services so that they can effectively practice across domain areas once they enter the field (Harvey & Struzziero, 2008). Participating in a breadth of experiences is important given school psychologists' increasingly versatile role and the quick turnaround from trainee to practitioner (e.g., at the non-doctoral level, it is typically two years of coursework plus a nine to ten-month, 1200-hour internship). Gaining exposure to a variety of roles may increase an individual's ability and desire to practice in a broader way when entering the field. Breadth should be sought in the context of internship goals and it should be recognized by interns and supervisors that it is not possible for an intern to engage in *every* activity a school psychologist may encounter in his or her work.

Linking Breadth and Competence

Consistent with the idea that interns should gain exposure to activities across the ten NASP (2010a) practice domains, interns should be involved in a great number and variety of activities during the year. Interns and supervisors are encouraged to move beyond listing activities to be completed (e.g., "You need to do a Functional Behavior Assessment [FBA] before the year is over") to consider the meaning behind them (e.g., "Would an FBA be appropriate in this case? How do we know? How does the FBA link to a pragmatic Behavioral Intervention Plan?"). In short, completing a breadth of activities in a rote fashion does not necessarily link to competence. As discussed by Daly et al. (2011), university educators must move from primarily identifying or delineating competencies towards putting them into use in ways that improve graduate preparation and eventual school psychology practice. Developing competence involves increasing critical thinking skills in action and flexibly adapting skills for particular situations (Kaslow, 2004). An individual who is trained to think through *why* and *how* in addition to *what* may develop a more nuanced and less prescriptive understanding of school psychology practice.

Who Knows What Next Year Will Bring?

Gaining a breadth of experiences during the internship is also important because it is unclear where the intern will be practicing next year. Exposure to an array of school psychologist roles and functions as well as a diversity of clients (e.g., differing ages, cultures, disabilities, and economic backgrounds to name a few) during the internship expands the number of positions the intern may be qualified for when entering the field. For instance, an intern who has never worked with students with severe and profound disabilities may not be considered for a position where this is an aspect of the school psychologist's role. If an individual *is* hired to work in a context or with a population they have never worked in before it can be daunting (and potentially unethical, if practicing beyond boundaries of competence), especially if limited or no clinical supervision supports are in place. Even minimal exposure to some activities during the internship may increase an individual's preparedness to enter his or her first year of professional practice.

Why Depth is Important

As trainees progress in their level of knowledge and applied skills through the training sequence, there may be particular areas that are focused on to a greater extent than others. As with breadth, depth should be explicitly linked to the intern's goals for the internship year. In addition to the intern's interests and goals, depth may also stem from (a) opportunities available at the internship site (e.g., an intern who spends a significant portion of time at a therapeutic day school may develop depth in relevant NASP domains and competencies); (b) supervisors' approaches to practice (e.g., a supervisor spends a good deal of time doing group counseling and the intern is involved in planning, implementing, and evaluating group counseling throughout the year); and (c) the foci of the school psychology training program (e.g., a particular program emphasizes coursework and applied experiences in school neuropsychology). Trainees do not always know what area(s) of depth they are interested in pursuing when entering a training program. However, by the time they are applying to internships, trainees should be able to seek a match between their own developing interests and what is offered by the internship site and supervisors.

Linking Depth and Competence

Just like breadth, depth inherently links to competence. Competence develops over time, as does expertise which may only be achieved in a few domains over the course of a school psychologist's career (Ysseldyke et al., 2006). To achieve competence and eventually expertise in a particular domain requires more intensive, supervised training and practice in that area. For example, the expertise literature suggests deliberate practice is required for the development of expertise, which involves intentional, structured, and repeated practice over the course of time in combination with observation, feedback and direct instruction from a knowledgeable other (e.g., a supervisor or mentor; Ericsson & Pool, 2016). A deliberate practice framework can be incorporated during the internship, or even during earlier stages of school psychology training such as during practicum experiences (Justice, Murphy, & Newman, 2018). It is helpful for the intern and supervisors to discuss and prioritize areas of depth as they relate to the intern's goals and internship plan, jointly develop a plan for achieving depth from early on in the year, establish indicators or benchmarks for what it means to be competent in a particular domain, and regularly assess and discuss the intern's progress. The competency documents highlighted in this chapter provide a starting point for making determinations regarding competency development.

Specialization

The concept of depth is expansive. Depth can mean gaining conceptual and applied knowledge with a specific population, in a particular domain of practice (e.g., NASP, 2010a or Fouad et al., 2009), in one or more competencies subsuming a domain (Harrison & Prus, 2008), or an integrated combination of all of these. Depth may be considered analogous to the notion of specialization, or intensive training in a particular area of practice within school psychology (Armistead, 2014).

Reynolds (2011) suggested university educators incorporate specialization into school psychology training programs, given several challenges that make it "increasingly difficult to maintain professional standards and to know all that is required to practice as a school psychologist" (p. 924): the explosion of knowledge in the field; the half-life of knowledge and need for continuing education; advances in scientific methods; challenges in research consumption; and increasing demands for schools as points of service delivery. Through specialization interns begin to master one or more areas with greater intensity than others and school psychologists can become "highly trained professional specialist[s]" rather than "jack of all trades and master of none" (Reynolds, 2011, p. 929). Breadth and depth/specialization may be seen as complementary rather than dichotomous entities. Seeking breadth does not preclude mastering a given domain or domains. One can participate in a number and variety of experiences and simultaneously seek out one or more areas more extensively than others. Further, while some interns may wish to pursue highly specialized positions following training (particularly doctoral-level interns), many others will wish to practice in schools (or other settings) where broad competence, which develops with practice and time, is necessary.

Depth at the Doctoral Level

In Chapter 3, it was suggested that doctoral-level interns may be in a unique position to achieve depth of training compared to non-doctoral trainees, given that they (a) complete more coursework, (b) likely spend more time in field-work including the potential to engage in a number and diversity of experiences within a specific domain, and (c) engage in research, which may connect to an area of depth. Further, the NASP (2010d) *Standards for Graduate Preparation of School Psychologists* specifies that school psychology doctoral programs should offer "greater depth in one or more school psychology competencies. . ." and that while "doctoral programs are typically characterized by advanced competencies in research . . . the program may identify additional competencies. . ." that are emphasized in training (p. 4). In other words, achieving depth is not only a viable option given coursework, fieldwork experiences, and research, it is an expected aspect of doctoral-level school psychology training.

Two additional points about depth deserve mention. First, depth does not equate to the accrual of hours (McCutcheon, 2009), nor is achievement of depth guaranteed by receiving doctoral-level training (Miller et al., 2010). To achieve depth necessitates planning, goal-setting, purposeful intervention, and supervision (Ericsson & Pool, 2016). Second, attaining depth is considered a best practice for trainees at both the doctoral *and* non-doctoral levels (NASP, 2014b); non-doctoral-level interns are expected to achieve depth too. The attainment of depth at the non-doctoral level may look somewhat different than at the doctoral level (e.g., there may not be the same expectation or opportunity for research). However, non-doctoral interns should pursue and achieve depth in at least one area by the internship's conclusion.

Depth and the Hedgehog Concept

In his classic book *Good to Great: Why Some Companies Make the Leap. . . and Others Don't*, author Jim Collins (2001) described the *Hedgehog Concept*, an idea derived from an ancient Greek parable ("The fox knows many things, but the hedgehog knows one big thing"), which was later developed into a well-known essay by Isaiah Berlin. Foxes are quick, clever, and crafty and are seemingly at an advantage in overtaking the ostensibly simple hedgehog. However, the hedgehog does one thing really well – he rolls into a ball with spikes protruding – a method that is consistently successful in diverting even the swiftest of foxes. Collins proposed that "great" businesses were distinguished from "good" businesses based on having a unified and clear vision, a hedgehog of what they can be best at and which can produce long-term success. Three considerations inform the hedgehog: what you can be the best in the world at; what you are deeply passionate about; and what drives your economic engine. The overlap between these three components defines the ideal point of functioning for a business or an individual. Although Collins's book was originally intended for the field of business, the

Hedgehog Concept can also be applied to school psychology interns and the notion of seeking and achieving depth. The Hedgehog Concept as applied to school psychology intern Ellie is illustrated in Figure 8.1.

What Can the Intern Be Best in the World at?

A first consideration in defining an intern's hedgehog is to determine some-thing that he or she might be the best in the world at. Being competent at something is *not* the same thing as potentially being the best in the world in that area. For instance, a doctoral-level intern named Ellie was competent at statis-tics. She successfully completed three statistics courses in graduate school and was able to effectively consume, conduct, and disseminate quantitative research. Nevertheless, she readily acknowledged that she was not born to be a statistician. Statistics was not part of her hedgehog. In contrast, during her school psychol-ogy training Ellie became interested in supervision of psychological services. As an advanced graduate trainee she supervised a few first- and second-year students in her program during their practica and received metasupervision from a course instructor. Ellie also completed a research project investigating supervision prac-tices at her internship school district and presented at a state conference. Ellie would likely acknowledge that although she has a way to go before she is the "best supervisor in the world," her supervision knowledge and skills are a per-sonal strength and will continue to develop over time with training and practice.

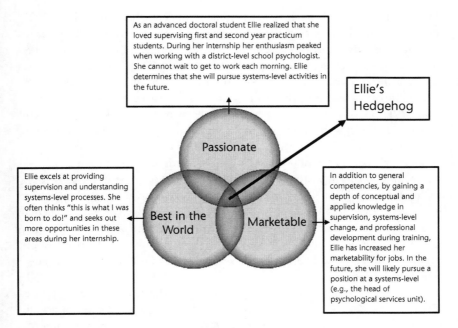

FIGURE 8.1 Doctoral intern Ellie's hedgehog

What is the Intern Deeply Passionate About?

A second consideration is what ignites the intern's passion. When someone is passionate about something, they wake up in the morning and cannot wait to take on that particular task. Passion may arise for numerous reasons, such as believing one's work makes a positive difference and feeling work tasks and expectations are optimally matched with one's skills (Csikszentmihalyi, 1990). Feeling passionate about one's work may be considered antithetical to the experience of burnout as described in Chapter 9. Passion is discovered rather than motivated or manufactured. Supervisors cannot make interns feel passionate about a particular area. However, supervisors can help interns discover what it is about the job that they absolutely love to do. To extend the example of Ellie, one rotation during her internship was completed under the supervision of a school psychology supervisor who worked as a director of special education services. The supervisor's role had a systems-level focus, including coordinating professional learning opportunities for school psychologists and special education staff, providing metasupervision, and introducing systems-level change. Ellie was sparked by observing her supervisor and by working together with the supervisor on various systems-level projects. She realized that she eventually wanted to pursue work at an administrative level.

What Will Make the Intern Marketable?

The final third of the hedgehog was originally conceptualized by Collins (2001) as products or services that can generate significant financial success for an organization. Obviously the "economic engine" element of the hedgehog does not directly apply to the internship in the same manner conceptualized for business. An intern's goal is likely not to make a large financial profit during the internship year and if it is, there is a good chance that he or she will be disappointed. However, interns do want to end the year with skills that make them desirable candidates for future employment. Although breadth is one piece of marketability (i.e., I have gotten a great deal of experiences and would be a good fit for many different positions), gaining depth in a particular area helps an intern stick out from the pack. To continue to build on the example of Ellie, the leadership skills she developed during her school psychology training and internship (e.g., providing supervision, contributing to systems-level change efforts, conducting research, organizing and implementing professional learning sessions) made her highly marketable when applying for school psychologist positions and distinguished her from her peers who did not have such leadership experiences.

To provide another example, gaining a depth of knowledge in a particular area such as Autism Spectrum Disorders (ASDs) and making applied contributions in this area (e.g., participating in a special education evaluation or reevaluation of a student with autism; supporting academic and/or social-emotional interventions for students with autism; providing psychoeducation to staff about ASDs; consulting with parents of students with autism) are opportunities not all interns have and would likely be viewed favorably by potential employers. For some interns (especially those at the doctoral level), seeking an area of depth may also increase qualification to pursue specialty positions such as behavior specialist, response to intervention coordinator, assessment associate, psychologist in a hospital setting, education policy researcher, or school psychology faculty member, among others.

The Hedgehog Concept Beyond the Internship

Collins (2001) pointed out that finding, understanding, and pursuing one's hedgehog is not a simple task. In fact, it took businesses an average of four years to clarify their hedgehog. Finding one's hedgehog is a process that is ongoing for students throughout their school psychology training and during their professional careers. The internship provides a unique opportunity for interns to focus in on their hedgehog, given they are experiencing the day-to-day life of a school psychologist for the first time and are ideally devoting at least some time to discussing professional interests and goals in supervision. The internship is a time for both personal and professional growth. Consistent with the notion that school psychologists are lifelong learners (Armistead, 2014), the hedgehog continues to evolve following internship completion. For example, it seems like a potentially excellent fit for Ellie to pursue work as a coordinator of school psychology services after practicing as a school psychologist for a few years. School psychologists continue to develop pockets of expertise over time (Ysseldyke et al., 2006), a process that can be informed by what they can be best in the world at, what they are passionate about, and what continues to make them professionally relevant and marketable.

Summary

By the end of the internship year it is expected that school psychology interns will achieve both breadth and depth of experiences (NASP, 2014b) and entry-level competencies across all NASP (2010a) domains. Competence refers to the intern's ability to understand and complete tasks as would be expected at a particular developmental benchmark (e.g., beginning the first year of professional practice). Competence includes critical thinking, problem solving, and flexible decision making. Competencies are the atoms of competence that can be developed and evaluated. Four documents assist interns and supervisors to incorporate considerations of competence during the internship –APA's *Competency Benchmarks* (ACBW, 2012a, 2012b; Fouad et al., 2009) and *Competency Assessment Toolkit* (Kaslow et al., 2009), and NASP's *Blueprint III* (Ysseldyke et al., 2006) and

Standards for Graduate Preparation of School Psychologists (2010d). These documents describe foundational and functional competencies and are useful in supporting competency planning and assessment. Interns and supervisors are encouraged to treat competency attainment as an integrated and meaningful process rather than a rote list of technical skills and activities to be completed during the internship year.

Gaining experiential breadth during the internship is important because of the increasingly broad expectations for the school psychologist role, the brevity of school psychology training, and not knowing where the intern will be working next year. Like breadth, depth of experience can increase an intern's marketability. Developing a specialized skill or set of skills may differentiate the intern from other candidates or increase preparedness for specialized positions. Although doctoral students may more easily achieve depth (i.e., they spend more time in coursework and fieldwork; they conduct research; and doctoral programs may offer specialized foci), non-doctoral interns are also expected to seek and achieve depth by the internship's end. Depth can be thought of using the Hedgehog Concept: the ideal alignment of something the intern can be the best in the world at one day, is passionate about doing, which will make him or her professionally marketable. The Hedgehog Concept may be considered applicable to school psychologists throughout their careers.

Critical Thinking Questions and Activities

The following are critical thinking questions for interns, field supervisors, and university supervisors to ponder regarding breadth, depth, and competence.

For Interns:

- What does it mean to be a competent intern? A competent entry-level school psychologist?
- How does internship depth link to prospective job opportunities?
- What is your hedgehog? How do you suppose your hedgehog will evolve during your career?

For Field Supervisors:

- Looking at the overview of assessment approaches from the *Competency Toolkit* (Kaslow et al., 2009), what new approaches may it be beneficial to incorporate into internship evaluation processes?
- In what ways can you encourage interns to think about *how* and *why* instead of *what*?
- Have an explicit conversation with your intern about his or her hedgehog. How can you support the intern to become clearer about his or her hedgehog?

For University Supervisors:

- How is competency assessed at different developmental benchmarks in your training program (e.g., readiness to enter practicum; readiness to begin internship; readiness to enter practice)?
- What areas of depth, if any, are foci in your school psychology training program? Does it matter if areas of depth are implicitly or explicitly identified?
- Realizing that accrual of hours may not link to competence, how can the requirement for interns to document hours be made into a meaningful process?

9

SURVIVAL

It is hard to imagine a helping professional who is not in some way emotionally affected by his or her work. Reactions may range from positive (e.g., pride about helping a client) to negative (e.g., distress). On the negative end of the continuum, work-related stressors have the potential to adversely affect one's ability to deliver services to clients (i.e., problems of professional competence, or PPC; Barnett, 2008; Elman & Forrest, 2007; Forrest & Elman, 2014; Smith & Moss, 2009). For interns, the combination of learning a new role, applying newly learned skills, and having a great number of responsibilities may make the internship an "emotionally hazardous" or highly stressful experience (Solway, 1985, p. 50). Interns who are able to successfully "survive" and thrive during the internship apply effective strategies to cope with stressors, and also receive support from supervisors, peers, and others.

The purposes of this chapter are to (a) illuminate specific stressors faced by school psychology interns and (b) explore potential coping mechanisms, including self-care strategies, as well as a variety of supports from supervisors, peers, and loved ones. The chapter begins with general definitions of stress, distress, burnout and PPC, as well as unique considerations about stress for school psychology interns. Strategies are presented in order to empower interns, supervisors, peers, and loved ones with concrete skills for stress prevention and management. The chapter concludes with critical thinking questions and activities for interns and supervisors.

Stress, Distress, Burnout, and PPC

In literature investigating the impact of stress on psychologists' personal and professional functioning, the terms *stress*, *distress*, *burnout*, and *impairment* are often interchanged (Smith & Moss, 2009). What is more, for a number of reasons, the traditional term "impairment" has been replaced in the professional psychology literature by the term PPC (see Elman & Forrest, 2007; Kaslow et al., 2007). Although these concepts are interrelated, a subtle difference between them is the potential severity with which they may impact one's ability to deliver psychological services, with stress being the least severe and PPC the most.

Stress is a term that is difficult to define with precision. As indicated by the American Institute of Stress (2019), "since stress is such a subjective phenomenon that differs for each of us, there really is no satisfactory definition of stress that all scientists agree on." Broadly speaking, stress is the experience of physical, mental, or emotional strain or tension, or a feeling experienced when demands surpass one's personal and social resources (American Institute of Stress, 2019). Stress experienced by one psychologist as harmful (e.g., leading to PPC) may be a helpful motivator to another psychologist (i.e., eustress), or perhaps not experienced as stress at all by a third. Stress is an experience that likely occurs for all school psychology interns at some point during the internship year. However, as is evident in the description provided, the impact of stress differs per intern and internship context.

Distress is an experience of intense stress that is not easily relieved and that moderately affects one's well-being, including personal or professional functioning (Munsey, 2006). When distress occurs over time and is not adequately addressed it may result in *burnout,* defined as a prolonged response to work-related stress (i.e., a lack of fit between person and job) that includes feelings of exhaustion, cynicism, and inefficacy (Maslach, 2003). Finally, *PPC* is defined broadly as when a psychologist's "performance or behavior does not meet professional and ethical standards" (Jacobs et al., 2011, p. 177).

The experience of stress, distress, burnout, and PPC for a school psychology intern named Lena is illustrated in Figure 9.1. It should be noted that although the terms are visually divided by levels of severity, precisely where each phenomenon ends and the next begins is not rigidly defined (APA, 2006a; Wise & Barnett, 2016; Smith & Moss, 2009). The diagram is intended to convey the slippery slope by which an intern's experience of stress may rapidly progress to a point of PPC that may negatively impact clients.

PPC Are Ethically Problematic

"When distress is not adequately attended to, it can develop into burnout and have a deleterious effect on psychologists' professional functioning and competence," impacting those they serve (Wise & Barnett, 2016, pp. 210–211). Working professionally without attending to PPC violates the overarching aspirational principles that undergird APA's (2017a) and NASP's (2010b) codes of ethics. APA's (2017a) *Ethical Principles of Psychologists and Code of Conduct* calls for psychologists to be self-aware of stress, engage in self-care behaviors, and use appropriate strategies to maintain clinical competence. Principle A of APA's (2017a) Code, Beneficence

The day before an IEP meeting, Lena realized she had not completed the write up of a psychological report that was due. She hastily put together the evaluation that evening. The morning before the meeting, Lena's supervisor noticed several errors in the report, including use of another student's name and incorrect test score reports.

Lena dragged herself out of bed each day to head to her internship. She questioned her choice to become a school psychologist, and whether or not her work made a difference to anyone. Lena emotionally distanced herself from the students and staff at her school as well as her supervisor.

Lena's feelings of stress continued to escalate. She missed several days of her internship due to illness as well as a few university internship seminar meetings. Lena inadvertently neglected some internship responsibilities such as returning phone calls and attending meetings.

At the beginning of the year, intern Lena was surprised by the amount of work required during her internship. She experienced difficulty completing work in a timely manner. Lena began to stay at work late, and to neglect some responsibilities at home. Even though her partner was very supportive, Lena felt awful about the lack of time she spent at home with her three young children.

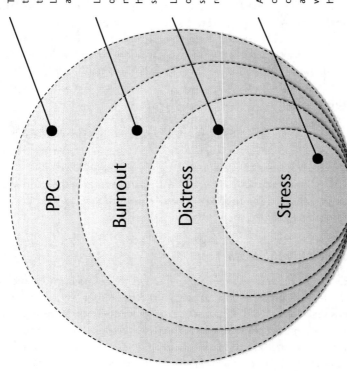

PPC

Burnout

Distress

Stress

FIGURE 9.1 Slippery slope to PPC during the school psychology internship and Nonmaleficence, explicitly calls for psychologists to "strive to be aware of the possible effect of their own physical and mental health on their ability to help those with whom they work" (p. 3).

Beyond guiding principles, specific and enforceable ethical standards from APA (2017a) directly relate to PPC. For example, Standard 2.06, Personal Problems and Conflicts states:

> (a) Psychologists refrain from initiating an activity when they know or should know that there is a substantial likelihood that their professional problems will prevent them from performing their work-related activities in a competent manner.

> (b) When psychologists become aware of personal problems that may interfere with their performing work-related duties adequately, they take appropriate measures, such as obtaining professional consultation or assistance, and determine whether they should limit, suspend, or terminate their work-related duties.

> *(p. 5)*

In short, psychologists should not engage in work activities if their performance is impacted by PPC and if they are already engaged in professional activities when they begin to exhibit PPC, they should seek assistance or perhaps terminate their work (of course, with the client referred to another qualified professional).

Related, Standard 3.04, Avoiding Harm, states: "Psychologists take reasonable steps to avoid harming their clients/patients, students, supervisees, research participants, organizational clients, and others with whom they work, and to minimize harm where it is foreseeable and avoidable" (p. 6). Before stress escalates, it is critical to take action that prevents harm to others. Finally, Standard 2.03, Maintaining Competence, states that "Psychologists undertake ongoing efforts to develop and maintain their competence" (p. 5). Maintaining competent practice includes engaging in self-care and seeking support from supervisors and peers, and therefore such actions may be considered ethical imperatives, both for practicing psychologists and for the psychology trainees (e.g., interns) they supervise.

Stress and Burnout for School Psychology Practitioners and Interns

There is some research on stress and burnout specific to the field of school psychology. Huebner (1993) surveyed a national sample of NASP members looking at symptoms of burnout and the relationship between burnout and job functions. Compared to consulting psychologists' ratings of burnout on a comparable survey, school psychologists experienced higher levels of emotional exhaustion (e.g., feeling overwhelmed by job demands) and depersonalization (e.g., developing cynical, negative attitudes toward clients), and lower levels of personal accomplishment (e.g., feeling incompetent to help clients). When compared to clinical and counseling psychologists, while school psychologists experienced lower levels of depersonalization, they also experienced similar levels of emotional exhaustion and lower levels of personal accomplishment. These data suggest school psychologists may be at a greater risk for burnout than other mental health professionals (Huebner, 1993).

More recently, Schilling et al. (2018) found that in a survey of 122 school psychologists in educational settings in four Southeastern states, 90% reported experiencing burnout during their careers. Having limited support from administrators and role overload were the two biggest contributors to feelings of burnout in their sample. In another recent study, Boccio et al. (2016) found that of 291 school psychologists responding to a survey, nearly one third indicated pressure to practice unethically, including nearly 40% experiencing administrative pressure to make decisions reportedly out of compliance with federal law. Perceived pressures to engage in unethical practice were linked to higher levels of burnout, decreased professional satisfaction in their current position and the field of school psychology, and an increased desire to leave the profession.

Huebner et al. (2002) conceptualized stress and burnout among school psychology practitioners and trainees using three variables: personal risk and resiliency factors, organizational context, and professional roles and functions. Risk and resiliency factors include demographic variables and personality characteristics. For instance, younger, less experienced individuals are more likely to experience symptoms of burnout, as are those with particular personality factors such as introversion and disagreeableness (Huebner et al., 2002). In terms of organizational context, the following factors may relate to burnout: relationships with colleagues, the amount of risk involved in work, being able to work efficiently without barriers, time management, and recognition received for one's work. Role conflict (i.e., divergent roles with competing expectations), role ambiguity (i.e., lack of clarity regarding role expectations), and role overload (i.e., too many demands and too little time) may also influence the experience of stress and burnout. As discussed in Chapter 5, school psychology interns may be particularly vulnerable to these three factors. Finally, job roles and functions may relate to stress and burnout. Work should not be too easy (leading to boredom) or too difficult (leading to anxiety or frustration) but ideally well matched to interns' developing knowledge and skills. In sum, it is critical to assess interns' roles and functions in conjunction with personal factors as well as organizational context in order to more clearly gauge an individual's burnout risk.

Unique Stressors for Interns

Given the unique characteristics of being an intern (see Chapter 5), it is likely that the intern role brings with it some distinctive stressors. Graduate training in psychology is inherently stressful, in general. In a national survey of 387 psychologist trainees, El-Ghoroury, Galper, Sawaqdeh, and Bufka (2012) found that approximately 70% had experienced a personal or professional challenge since the beginning of their training that interfered with their optimal performance as a graduate student. The most prevalently reported stressors (i.e., by more than 50% of participants) included academic responsibilities/pressures, finances/debt, anxiety, and poor work/school-life balance. Although several coping strategies were indicated by participants (e.g., more than 50% found at least some benefit in seeking out friends or family, talking to classmates, exercising regularly, or engaging in hobbies), several barriers impeded these strategies, most commonly lack of time.

Solway (1985) defined three main categories of stressors for psychology interns: clinical, institutional, and personal. *Clinical stress* results from interns' transition from a trainee or student role to now taking on significant professional responsibilities. Examples of clinical stressors include having to prove one's skills in a new context, developing new relationships with supervisors, and learning new techniques. *Institutional stress* relates to the internship training context or environment and includes adjusting to new colleagues, organizational goals, administrative policies and procedures, and accessing administrative resources. Finally, *personal stress* refers to factors indirectly associated with the internship but affecting an individual intern's adjustment. Examples of personal stressors include moving to a geographically new location, developing new friendships, navigating financial matters, and balancing one's personal life with internship demands.

Self-care: Preventing and Remediating Stress, Distress, Burnout, and PPC

With stress during the school psychology internship now more clearly defined, the discussion turns towards a consideration of actions that interns, supervisors, peers, and others can take to prevent and mitigate the potentially negative impact of intern stress.

Intern Self-care

Self-care consists of "routine positive practices and mindful attention to one's physical, emotional, relational, and spiritual selves in the context of one's personal and professional lives" (Wise & Barnett, 2016, p. 210). In short, self-care behaviors are actions interns can take to establish and promote physical and emotional wellness, and to allay stress. It is of little debate that self-care behaviors are critical to professional and personal well-being. However, there is a gap between psychologists' perceptions and practices regarding self-care (APA Advisory Committee on Colleague Assistance, ACCA, 2009).

Barriers to Self-care

Most psychologists readily acknowledge the stressful nature of working in a helping profession as well as the importance of self-care behaviors, yet many continuously overextend themselves and put clients' needs above their own (ACCA, 2009; Norcross & VandenBos, 2018). Barnett and Cooper (2009) suggested several reasons why this may be the case including (a) an illusion of invulnerability (e.g., "I'm knowledgeable about mental health prevention and intervention given my training background, so I'm not at risk"); (b) an increased vulnerability to distress and PPC for those who become helping professionals; and (c) the isolating nature of psychologists' work, which results in an inability to vent, share, or debrief with others. Additionally, a common misperception by psychologists is that engaging in self-care is a selfish behavior (Barnett, 2008; Norcross & VandenBos, 2018). Tamura, Vincent, Bridgeman and Hanbury (2008) identified several additional barriers to engagement in self-care behaviors unique to psychology trainees. For one, many trainees feel they must work non-stop to get ahead in their careers. Processes such as the pressure-filled APPIC internship match (see Chapter 2) may inadvertently encourage such perceptions. Additionally, self-care may not be promoted by training programs as important and faculty or peers may even question the dedication of those who are not workaholics. Further, some trainees may not be aware of the importance of self-care, or how to engage in self-care behaviors.

Self-awareness

Barriers notwithstanding, the reality is that caring for oneself promotes better care for clients served. Barnett (2008) suggested

> that all psychologists see themselves as potentially at risk for distress and impairment. While you need not live in constant fear of this occurring, a state of general vigilance is recommended. Being aware of your vulnerabilities as well as the challenges and demands of your professional and personal lives will help minimize the risk of blind spots, promote prevention activities, and minimize the risk of adverse consequences occurring.
>
> (p. 873)

Stress may have emotional, physical, and social impacts on psychologists, so ongoing monitoring in these areas is critical (Baird, 2016). A checklist of warning signs of distress, burnout, and PPC, adapted from descriptions by Barnett (2008) and Baird (2016), is presented in Table 9.1. The checklist is intended to promote awareness regarding symptoms that may indicate movement beyond typical levels of stress and to encourage a process of ongoing monitoring by both interns and supervisors. The reader should note that the list of items is intended to be representative of typical concerns rather than to be comprehensive and that the three dimensions of concerns considered (i.e., emotional, physical, and social) are interrelated.

TABLE 9.1 Warning Signs of Distress, Burnout, and PPC Identified by Baird (2016) and Barnett (2008)

Emotional Symptoms	Physical Symptoms	Social Symptoms
• Irritable with clients • Less empathy for clients • Presents as bored or disinterested with clients • Not listening to clients or colleagues • Enjoying work less than in the past • Frequent feelings of depression, anxiety, and/or agitation • Attempts to squeeze too much into each day • Frequent cynicism	• Exhaustion/fatigue • Disturbed sleep • Changes in eating patterns (may be related to weight gain or loss) • Frequent headaches, body tension or pain (e.g., back, jaw, neck, shoulders, stomach) • Self-medication (e.g., alcohol, too much caffeine, over the counter or prescription drugs)	• Isolation from friends, family, or significant others • Irritable with friends, family, and/or significant others • Failure to take breaks or time off • Seeking emotional support or nurturance from clients • Enjoying life less than in the past • Feeling like no one understands what you are going through

Self-care Behaviors

Self-care behaviors are ongoing activities that psychologists (inclusive of interns, practitioners, and faculty) engage in to prevent and mitigate stress, thereby promoting their own emotional, physical, and social wellness (Barnett, 2008). There is a burgeoning research base regarding the self-care behaviors that psychologists find most helpful. For instance, Stevanovic and Rupert (2004) surveyed a random sample of licensed psychologists in Illinois and found the most important career-sustaining behaviors to be (1) spending time with partner/family; (2) maintaining a personal-professional life balance; (3) maintaining a sense of humor; (4) maintaining self-awareness; and (5) maintaining professional identity. Of note, the authors also found that psychologists with higher levels of job satisfaction seemed to value career-sustaining behaviors more than individuals with lower levels of job satisfaction and that women in their study engaged in more of these behaviors than men; the latter finding suggests that female psychologists may differ from males with respect to how they approach work-related stressors (Stevanovic & Rupert, 2004).

Turner et al. (2005) investigated self-care strategies used by psychology interns. The most frequently applied strategies were (1) active problem solving; (2) social support from family and friends; (3) exerting control over internship choices; (4) maintaining awareness of internship impact; (5) use of humor; and (6) seeking out other interns for consultation. All of these self-care strategies were rated to be at least somewhat effective. Data from both Stevanovic and Rupert (2004) and Turner et al. (2005) point to both internal (e.g., maintaining a sense of humor, maintaining self-awareness) and external (e.g., spending time with loved ones, seeking peer consultation) strategies as valuable and demonstrate the importance of seeking a personal-professional balance.

Consistent with this research, Huebner et al. (2002) described self-care strategies for school psychology trainees and school psychologist practitioners, including seeking peer consultation and ongoing professional development, maintaining self-awareness of stress and burnout, designing a stress management plan, participating in supervision, and expanding job functions and roles. Various self-care strategies for interns are highlighted in Table 9.2. The strategies are aligned with the categories of stress described earlier in the chapter: clinical, institutional, and personal.

Physical, cognitive, emotional, and financial self-care

Extending the content of Table 9.2, four main categories of personal self-care strategies identified by Baird (2016), physical, cognitive, emotional, and financial, are elaborated in Table 9.3. *Physical self-care* involves actions such as monitoring and responding to stresses that manifest in the body. *Cognitive self-care* involves overcoming unrealistic beliefs or expectations about oneself (e.g., "I am not allowed to make mistakes"), clients and work (e.g., "Theo

TABLE 9.2 Intern Self-Care Strategies to Prevent and Mitigate Stress

Clinical	*Institutional*	*Personal*
• Seek peer consultation.	• Collaborate with other school personnel to try new activities.	• Self-evaluate current levels of stress and burnout.
• Seek clinical supervision.	• Strive for cooperation and support not competition with other interns.	• Develop a stress management plan.
• Engage in a variety of functions and roles.		• Maintain a personal and mental self-care plan.
• Be active in professional organizations.	• Determine when saying "no" to opportunities is okay.	• Maintain a sense of humor.
• Seek professional learning opportunities.	• Seek administrative consultation and supervision.	• Seek personal therapy, if needed.
• Carefully select clinical activities based on time limitations.	• Schedule work breaks.	• Make non-negotiable time to spend with family and friends (e.g., vacations *without* work).
	• Proactively seek clear expectations.	• Attend to physical, cognitive, emotional, and financial needs.

TABLE 9.3 Intern Self-Care Strategies for Physical, Cognitive, Emotional, and
Financial Needs Identified by Baird (2016)

Physical	Cognitive	Emotional	Financial
• Exercise. • Eat a healthy diet. • Monitor stress in the body. • Get a massage.	• Set realistic expectations about self, clients, work, and the world.	• Monitor emotions through a self-check. • Seek therapy, if needed. • Engage in cleansing rituals (e.g., deep breathing between work activities). • Engage in meditation and/or prayer.	• Conduct a cost-benefit analysis of work and health. • Seek expert financial guidance, if needed. • Ask oneself, what does it mean to have enough?

should immediately behave better as a result of our work together"), and the world (e.g., believing a "dysfunctional" school context is typical of all schools or districts). Strategies such as questioning one's own assumptions and expectations, proactively seeking supervisory support regarding cognitive perspectives, and making comparisons across a wide variety of experiences help to promote cognitive self-care. *Emotional self-care* strategies include self-checking one's own emotional state, seeking personal therapy if needed, engaging in rituals such as deep breathing between counseling sessions, meditating, or praying. Finally, *financial self-care* includes assessing one's personal values and goals, and how such values balance with monetary compensation. Ideally, intrinsic rewards received from working in a helping profession (e.g., achieving alignment between personal values and professional practices) counterbalance what may sometimes be considered poor extrinsic incentives.

Supervisor Support

In addition to interns engaging in self-care strategies, supervisors play a critical role in helping prevent and reduce intern stress. Consistent with ecological and strengths-based perspectives articulated within this text (e.g., Chapter 7), addressing stress, distress, burnout, and PPC *must* move outside of the individual trainee to consider the entirety of a "training ecosystem" (Forrest & Elman, 2014). Preventively, supervisors can attempt to ensure adequate training is provided prior to and during the internship so that interns have prerequisite knowledge and skills to effectively meet expectations; being effective at one's job alleviates job stress (Huebner et al., 2002). Related, internship field supervisors can be part of internship interview processes to help determine whether particular candidates will be a good match with the internship site and field supervisors. Supervisors can also promote intern self-care through modeling self-care strategies, providing information about self-care, and accounting for organizational and professional factors that encourage or hinder self-care (Turner et al., 2005).

Learning by Example?

Ironically, while it may seem obvious to readers that the school psychology internship year is in some ways stressful, this is not always recognized via field and university supervisors' actions. For instance, some supervisors may encourage or reinforce interns' workaholic behaviors, or model poor self-care behaviors that are then emulated by interns (Barnett & Goncher, 2014; Tamura et al., 2008). One intern I supervised felt obligated to arrive at her school at 5:30 each morning and not leave until late in the evening because this is what she observed of her field supervisor and thought was expected of her. Another intern who experienced symptoms of burnout tied to a number of accumulated stressors was told by her field supervisor: "Grin and bear it – I am getting you ready for the rigors of school psychology practice."

University supervisors may also be guilty of being poor role models regarding self-care behaviors, stress management, and job enjoyment. In turn, it is possible that the ongoing shortage of school psychology graduate educators (Castillo, Curtis, & Tan, 2014; Clopton & Haselhuhn, 2009; Little & Akin-Little, 2004) at least in part relates to school psychology faculty roles being perceived by students as too demanding or not enjoyable. Given the importance of self-care behaviors throughout the professional lifespan, it is important for field and university supervisors to be cognizant of the type of self-care role modeling they are providing for interns.

Other Supervisor Behaviors

Many processes of supervision described throughout this book are relevant to preventing and mitigating intern stress. Regarding clinical stressors, both field and university supervisors can care for interns by (a) establishing and maintaining a strong supervisory relationship, (b) engaging in open communication, (c) providing explicitly clear expectations, (d) developing and formatively discussing the intern's goals and internship plan, and (e) pushing interns to move outside of comfort zones while simultaneously providing a professional safety net. Supervisors can also help interns navigate institutional stresses such as facilitating the intern's entry into the internship (see Chapter 4), letting the intern know it is acceptable to sometimes say "no" to taking on responsibilities, and encouraging cooperation and collaboration with other professionals.

Supervision Is Not Counseling

Some interns may seek supervisors' guidance regarding personal stresses. At times it is appropriate for supervisors to support intern supervisees regarding personal stress. However, there are also instances when interns' personal stress (and stress reactions) may be more appropriately addressed in personal therapy than supervision. In such instances, it is supervisors' ethical responsibility to direct interns to seek therapy (APA, 2017a). As described by Corey et al. (2010),

> It is the supervisor's responsibility to help trainees identify how their personal dynamics are likely to influence their work with clients, yet it is not the proper role of supervisors to serve as personal counselors for supervisees . . . supervision can be useful in helping supervisees become aware of personal limitations or unresolved problems that intrude into their work with clients. With this awareness, supervisees are then in a position of seeking personal therapy to work through a problem rather than using supervision as a substitute for therapy.
>
> *(p. 168)*

A vignette contrasting two interns, Tisha and Brian, may provide clarification about the sometimes ambiguous boundaries between supervision and therapy.

VIGNETTE 9.1 **TISHA'S AND BRIAN'S PERSONAL STRESS**

Tisha and Brian were interns in the same school psychology training program, working at different school districts in the same state. As interns began to look for jobs, a stagnant economy resulted in only a few positions being available. The twenty students in the school psychology program were applying for the same positions and feelings of competition were rampant. The monthly university seminar, which brought together all twenty interns, seemed to fan the flames of stress. For example, the university supervisor put interns on the spot, asking them individually about their progress in the job hunt in front of all other students. Those interns who had secured positions felt embarrassed to share their good news and those who did not yet have positions felt ashamed.

Tisha felt a great deal of stress and sought out guidance from her field supervisor, Ingrid, with whom she had a strong relationship. Ingrid offered a variety of perspectives to Tisha including encouraging her to be more flexible in her job search and reassuring her that it was acceptable to seek some distance from the competitive interactions happening between peers. Brian also had a strong dynamic with his supervisor, Maria, and sought out her guidance about how to best proceed with finding a job in such a stressful context. In broaching his concerns, Brian also mentioned other personal strains resulting from the

(continued)

(continued)

job-search stress, including not sleeping well, getting in frequent spats with his spouse, and finding himself quickly losing patience with a few high school students he was working with. Maria offered guidance similar to Ingrid's, but also suggested that some of the concerns expressed by Brian may be better addressed through private counseling rather than supervision.

Peer Support

Seeking and receiving support from peers is another way for interns to effectively prevent and mediate stress. Data reported by APA's ACCA (2009) from a survey of 430 psychologists suggested that the most frequent coping response to professional stress was talking to a colleague and 91% of respondents found that strategy to be at least somewhat helpful. Similarly, El-Ghoroury et al. (2012) found that over 70% of psychology graduate trainees in their study found it beneficial to seek out peers for support.

There are multiple additional potential avenues for interns to seek out peer support. In contrast to the vignette about Tisha and Brian, a strong climate of peer support permeates many training programs. Faculty can set the tone for such a climate from students' initial entry into the school psychology program by encouraging positive collaborative interactions among trainees. El-Ghoroury et al. (2012) recommended that training programs consider formalizing peer supports as part of graduate training, for example by matching incoming trainees with more advanced graduate students who can be available to offer guidance, or other supports. When peer support is a training program norm, interns tend to help each other continue to develop clinical skills, navigate program or university requirements, and study for exams such as comprehensive program examinations and state and/or national licensure examinations. Further, in a collaborative climate, interns are more likely to discuss their personal and professional challenges with others engaged in a comparable experience. Fellow interns understand better than anyone the unique challenges faced during the school psychology internship.

Some interns may work in the same school or district as other interns from the same or different training programs. Establishing a community with fellow interns in the district can be supportive in many ways, especially in navigating institutional stressors. Interns from other programs may offer some unique perspectives on practice based on their distinct training experiences. Other individuals in the district may also provide peer support. For example, early career psychologists easily remember what it was like to be an intern, and can provide advice and guidance during the internship. A first-year school psychologist who had graduated from my training program the previous year supported me in many ways during my internship and I think I also supported her as she transitioned from her internship to early career. Peer support may also come from trainees from other disciplines (e.g., a school counseling intern or a student-teacher) or other staff that the intern develops a strong relationship with over the course of the year.

Support from Loved Ones

Family and friends are one of the most frequently accessed and valued sources of support for trainees (El-Ghoroury et al., 2012; Turner et al., 2005). Since loved ones are likely not embedded in the school psychology internship context, they may be able to offer alternative perspectives and insights regarding the intern's experiences. Loved ones also are likely to appreciate hearing about and celebrating the intern's successes throughout the year. Other times it may be frustrating to communicate with family or friends about graduate school or the internship experience because they simply do not understand precisely what the intern is going through. It is difficult to convey the great deal of work involved in internship training, let alone to explain the emotion and stress involved in events like intervening during a crisis, or proposing and defending a dissertation. As a result, interns may feel unsupported or isolated and communicating with loved ones may increase, rather than reduce, stress.

To maximize the value of support from loved ones, maintaining open communication and clear expectations before, during, and following the internship is critical. For example, interns should explicitly address pending realities regarding the internship schedule, workload, and financial compensation (or lack thereof). Such areas can contribute stress to personal relationships throughout the year and discussing them and developing strategies early on is a preventive approach. In addition, Baird (2016) proposed a series of questions to help interns assess the effects of the internship on life and relationships. The following are a few examples of items adapted from Baird that interns may contemplate to continuously monitor the health of their personal relationships:

- When was the last time you did something with just yourself and your significant other?
- When was the last time you did something with just yourself and one or more good friends?
- How often in the past month have you not done something with family or friends due to a work conflict?
- Do you listen to loved ones as well as you would like?
- How does work interact with your personal life?

Interns can think about these items, as well as others, and share thoughts with significant others to evaluate their own personal-professional balance. If the internship is taking a toll on one's personal life, seeking therapy may be appropriate.

A Word from Interns and their Loved Ones

To understand more specifically what supports interns need from their loved ones, I surveyed school psychology graduate students during the writing of the first edition of this text regarding (a) what qualities and actions from loved ones (i.e., significant others, family members, close friends) were most helpful throughout their time in the school psychology program and (b) what advice their loved ones would provide to other loved ones of school psychology graduate students.

TABLE 9.4 Characteristics and Actions of Supportive Loved Ones

Theme	Examples
Understanding the stressful nature of being a graduate student (including time, energy, and other commitments)	• "Flexibility and being available when I actually have time. Understanding that this is very important to me, and though it is not life or death, it's a big deal right now." • "Just being aware and understanding that my time is limited." • "[Loved ones] can be most supportive by expecting a little moodiness or social disconnect. Intermittently reaching out . . . in a caring, non-demanding manner . . . the student will be reminded of their support system yet have the option to get back in touch when they have replenished resources."*
Pragmatic support	• "As a wife and mother of two teenage boys, I most appreciate . . . when they pick up after themselves . . . and when I am given time, guilt-free, to go to the coffee shop." • "As a mother of four children, it was most helpful when my support system would help care for my children so that I can have time to do work . . . it became part [of the] routine when the children would spend time with grandparents, aunt, or dad while I was able to have that time alone." • "Financial support from my parents – welcoming me back home to live with them." • "Help with chores . . . and purchasing chocolate." • "Recording the TV shows I'm missing because I am studying or doing work."
Understanding/ appreciating the field of school psychology	• "Understand that school psychologist does not mean counselor." • "Telling me that the profession I am going into is commendable and all my efforts will be worth it."
Listening	• "Don't try to help, just listen." • "Close friends . . . have been 'sounding boards' allowing me to bounce my ideas off them." • "Reassure the student that [you] are there for support. Let the student know they can always talk to you, don't just assume they will come if they need help."* • "Letting me vent when things aren't going perfectly and listen to my successes as well."

Providing encouragement	• "My husband's continuous belief in me . . . trust that I can make it and the fact that he is there to support me ethically and financially."
	• "Showing encouragement that I can do this. . ."
	• "[Offering] encouragement to continue even when I felt burnt out and stressed."
	• "Above all, hearing encouraging words such as 'you're really going to make a difference in the lives of children.'"
	• "Taking me out to dinner to celebrate the end of the quarter/year or other accomplishments."
Maintaining a long-term focus instead of a short-term focus	• "My parents have said that all the time and hard work will all be worth it in the end when I have a successful and fulfilling career."
	• "I can advise my friend to make sacrifices to complete the program because in the long run the profession will provide her with many rewards."*
	• "Although it may . . . get overwhelming, just know that it is not long term where you may have to carry a bit more of 'the load'."

* Indicates a direct quote from a loved one (e.g., significant others, family members, or close friends). Other quotes are from school psychology graduate students at varying levels of training.

The sample of respondents was one of convenience, consisting of twelve students at various points in the training program who responded to the questions within a one-week period via an online survey. Although not analyzed formally, the responses demonstrate some common themes like those in Table 9.4, along with representative quotes.

Clearly, it can be challenging to be a loved one of a trainee in a school psychology program, especially during the internship year. It is my hope that the themes identified in Table 9.4 are helpful for both interns and loved ones. For interns, the themes may provide a way to talk with their loved ones about what supports might be most helpful during the internship year. In other words, interns can share this list with their parents, children, spouses, boyfriends, girlfriends, and close friends to discuss these themes, as well as other supports perhaps not specified on this list. For loved ones, this list provides an "insider" perspective into the world of being a graduate trainee or intern as well as specific examples of actions they can take to provide support for the ones they love.

Summary

All interns will likely experience stress at some point during the internship year. Ideally, interns will engage in self-care behaviors as well as receive supports from supervisors, peers, and loved ones to prevent and cope with stress. A diagram

STRESSORS

- Clinical Stress
- Institutional Stress
- Personal Stress

PROTECTIVE FACTORS

- Self-Care
- Supervisor Supports
- Peer Supports
- Loved One Supports

FIGURE 9.2   Finding a balance: Stressors and protective mechanisms during the internship

summarizing the balance of stress and support during the internship year is presented in Figure 9.2. Sufficient supports act as supportive mechanisms for interns. When sufficient supports are not in place, stress may escalate into distress (i.e., intense stress not easily relieved), burnout (i.e., prolonged response to stress including exhaustion, cynicism, and inefficacy), or PPC (i.e., professional functioning becoming ineffective). Beyond the obvious negative impact for the intern, PPC are unethical given the potentially detrimental results for clients. Personal factors, organizational factors, and professional roles and functions all contribute to school psychology interns' risk for moving beyond typical levels of stress. Types of stressors for interns include clinical (e.g., new skills, new relationships, new supervisors), institutional (e.g., new context, new colleagues, new goals), and personal (e.g., new friendships, finding a personal-professional balance, dealing with financial matters).

There are several actions interns can take to prevent and respond to stress. First of all, interns should maintain awareness of their emotional, physical, and social well-being and immediately respond to concerns that arise. In addition to self-initiated actions (e.g., exercising, healthy eating, maintaining a sense of humor, engaging in rituals) interns can proactively seek support from supervisors, peers, and loved ones. Supervisors support interns in a number of ways, such as modeling healthy self-care behaviors and making internship expectations explicit and unambiguous. Peers (e.g., other school psychology interns, interns from other disciplines, early career practitioners) may provide invaluable supports to interns, with an "insider" perspective that can be otherwise difficult to find. Finally, loved ones, including significant others, family members, and close friends, provide support to interns during the internship. Supportive behaviors from loved ones include understanding what it means to be a school psychology intern (including time commitments), listening, providing pragmatic assistance, offering encouragement, and maintaining a long-term focus even when the short-term is challenging (e.g., "All the time and hard work will be worth it in the end").

Critical Thinking Questions and Activities

The following are critical thinking questions and activities for interns, field supervisors, and university supervisors to ponder regarding stress and self-care.

For Interns:

- In what ways does your work as an intern affect your emotional well-being? Physical well-being? Social relationships?
- How will you determine if your experience of stress has moved beyond what is typical (e.g., distress, burnout, or PPC)?
- Have a conversation with a loved one about the internship experience (e.g., what you do on a daily basis, what stressors you face, what is rewarding to you) and discuss what supports would be most helpful from that person during the year.
- Set up a group comprised of interns from your university, the interns at your internship site, or other peers with the purpose of providing peer support during the internship year.

For Field Supervisors:

- How would your intern describe your self-care behaviors? Given the intern's perception of your self-care, how valuable do you suppose he or she views self-care to be?
- How can an intern's personal problems be addressed in supervision without a supervision session becoming a therapy session?
- How will you determine if your intern's level of stress has moved beyond what is typical (e.g., distress, burnout, or PPC)?
- What steps will you take if an intern begins to exhibit PPC?

For University Supervisors:

- How is self-care taught and/or modeled in your training program? Based on what is taught and/or modeled, how valuable do you suppose students view self-care to be?

- Assess the nature of peer support in your training program. How might you create or strengthen the quantity and quality of peer support?
- When interns are engaged in the job hunt, it may contribute to a stressful and/or competitive training program climate. How might you support interns (individually and as a collective group) during the search process?

Moving Beyond the Internship

10

THE JOB HUNT

Applications, Interviews, and Employment

The first and second sections of this book (Chapters 1 through 4) focused on orienting interns and supervisors to the internship year and the third section of the book (Chapters 5 through 9) covered the critical relationships that are developed during the internship. The fourth and final section of this book focuses on closing out the internship year and helping the intern transition into a successful first year of professional practice. Thinking about life beyond the internship is a topic that likely produces mixed emotions for interns. Feelings of accomplishment may be paired with disappointment regarding how quickly the year is ending and how much remains to be done. Anxiety about what next year will hold is hopefully accompanied by feelings of anticipation and excitement for new challenges to come.

In this chapter, the processes of searching, applying, and interviewing for jobs are demystified in order to support interns' eventual job procurement. The job process is divided by stages spanning pre-internship through the end of the internship, with each stage subsuming several actions interns can take during the job hunt. Focused attention is given to compiling, shaping, and submitting a professional application; requesting letters of recommendation; and preparing for and completing job interviews. The importance of patience and persistence is emphasized, with the ultimate payoff of landing a job. Actions for supervisors to take during the intern's job hunt process are also included in this chapter. The chapter ends with critical thinking questions and activities for interns and supervisors.

The Job Timeline

A timeline for the job application and interview process is presented in Figure 10.1. This timeline also provides an organizational structure for the chapter, with each part of the process elaborated upon in detail within the ensuing sections.

Although the job timeline is illustrated in a simplified manner to provide an overall sense of what should be happening and when, this schedule is a general one that may differ in some ways per individual circumstances. For instance, some interns may get offered jobs early in the spring (e.g., interns who get offers from their internship districts) while others may not secure a position until August or later. Though there may be some variance in this process, the job timeline offers guidance regarding actions interns can take before their internship even begins through to its end.

Pre-preparation Stage: Pre-internship through October

The process of securing a job can be thought of as beginning long before the intern sends out applications. The *pre-preparation* stage spans pre-internship through early fall of the internship year. The internship application, interview, and hiring process completed the year prior to the internship may be seen as a dress rehearsal for applying and interviewing for jobs. First, internship preparation offers the trainee opportunities to begin compiling and organizing a portfolio of professional materials, including cover letters, a résumé and/or curriculum vitae (CV), work samples, and letters of recommendation. Such materials provide a foundation for materials used during the job application process. Second, internship interviews allow the intern to practice orally representing his or her school psychology knowledge and skills in a manner similar to what will be expected during job interviews. Although internship applications and interviews provide some important preparatory experiences for the eventual job hunt, there are also numerous differences between internship and job processes, as discussed later in this chapter.

During the pre-preparation stage interns also engage in internship planning, goal setting, and ongoing formative evaluation. In so doing, they are gaining skills that should begin to inform where they want to work and how they will present themselves as job applicants. Part of the pre-preparation stage includes self-reflection regarding professional learning, including specific areas of interest that may be a part of future positions. For example, a doctoral-level intern named Cordell had strong assessment and intervention skills but his favorite parts of his doctoral-level training, inclusive of the internship, were completing program evaluations, providing professional learning opportunities for school staff, and working on his doctoral dissertation, including collecting data at his primary internship site. Based on his experiences, as well as discussions with his field and university supervisors, Cordell decided early in the fall of his internship year that he would pursue a post-doctoral research position the following year.

Granted, not all students will have determined a clear job path by the end of the pre-preparation stage. In fact, flexibility is an important characteristic for graduating interns to have throughout the job process. Nevertheless, thinking

Pre-preparation:
Pre-internship to October

- Internship application/interview process serves as a dress rehearsal for job application/interview process
- Determine goals, areas of clinical interest, and desired work settings

Preparation:
November and December

- Begin to gather and update portfolio materials
- Think about goals and interests for next year, and how they match with current experiences
- Request letters of recommendation

Initial Action:
January and February

- Search for openings and decide where to apply
- Send out applications
- Confirm receipt of applications
- Prepare for interviews

Ongoing Action:
March through May

- Continue to search for positions
- Follow up from earlier applications
- Interview for positions
- Gain targeted supervised experiences

Patience, Persistence, and Payoff:
June through August

- Be patient for more opportunities to open
- Be persistent in searching and applying for positions and following up
- Secure a position

FIGURE 10.1 The job process from start to finish.

critically about one's identity as a school psychologist (including professional interests and skills) is beneficial at all stages of training and fall of the internship year may mark an important benchmark for decision-making regarding forthcoming professional pursuits.

Alternatives to School-based Jobs

Although most school psychologists will become school-based practitioners following training, some interns (particularly those at the doctoral level) may determine they want to apply for jobs other than school-based positions. Wasik, Song, and Knotek (2009) offered some questions graduating students can consider when contemplating career options:

- Who do I want to influence?
- What types of professional practice do I want to engage in?
- What kinds of issues affecting children and youth do I want to address?

Depending on the answers to these questions, interns may find themselves interested in practicing at the district, state, or national level; in a research position; at a college or university; in a non-school clinical setting; or pursuing a postdoctoral fellowship.

Leadership and Research Positions

District level practice may include being responsible for a unique program (e.g., director of the preschool intervention team or facilitator of Positive Behavior and Intervention Supports (PBIS) teams in the district), or having administrative responsibilities for a department or unit (e.g., director of psychology services or director of intervention and support). Typically, such positions require a school psychologist with a good deal of prior experience. State or national positions may be options for some graduating interns, including positions in state departments of education or in public or private organizations focusing on education policy decision-making or reform.

Postdoctoral Training

Postdoctoral training may be the right fit for some graduating doctoral-level interns. Postdoctoral positions provide an opportunity for doctoral interns to get another year of the supervised clinical experiences required in most states prior to applying for licensure. Hatcher and Buchtel (2016) provide a helpful overview of postdoctoral training in clinical psychology, including distinguishing between formal (e.g., APA accredited) postdoctoral programs and informal experiences (e.g., developing one's own program, linked with a licensed supervisor).

However, it is challenging to find data about postdoctoral internships (Hatcher & Buchtel, 2016) and specific postdoctoral considerations for doctoral-level school psychologists could not be found during a review of the literature on this topic. School psychologists trained at the doctoral level can assess the alignment of their knowledge, skills, and interests with post-doctoral opportunities and determine if particular positions are well-matched. School psychology specific postdoctoral opportunities can be identified through APPIC's directory which allows users to search by specialty, emphasis/focus area, and other criteria (https://www.appic.org/Postdocs/Universal-Psychology-Postdoctoral-Directory-UPPD).

Research Positions

Some individuals might be interested in pursuing research positions following graduation. Research positions are a viable option for school psychology graduates who are interested in data-based decision making, evaluation, and the application of science and the scientific method. Some positions might be tied to postdoctoral experiences, or funded by training grants, which provide support to senior researchers. Such opportunities could provide an excellent avenue to continue to access research mentoring in the early career. Private companies are also often looking for researchers with strong research and statistical skills. For example, Nebbergall (2011) described her transition from school-based practice to a rewarding educational research position.

Academic Positions

Becoming a school psychology faculty member is another potential avenue for doctoral-level graduates. Indeed, there is currently a shortage of school psychology faculty members in the field (Castillo, Curtis, & Tan, 2014), so job prospects are promising. From my own biased perspective, I believe the faculty role provides an opportunity for school psychologists to do it all: teaching, supervision, research, continued involvement with the profession, and potentially continuing to work in schools via collaborations with other educators.

Academic positions typically involve a combination of research, teaching, and service, with emphases varying per institution and position. For example, Harris and Sullivan (2012) distinguished between *tenure-track positions at research intensive universities* where faculty devote a larger percentage of time to research; *tenure-track positions at teaching-intensive universities* where teaching and supervision are the faculty member's primary responsibilities; *non-tenure track positions*, such as more temporary visiting and adjunct positions and also clinical positions focused on supporting supervision; and finally *nontraditional faculty positions*, such as clinic directors/coordinators. In sum, doctoral-level trainees considering becoming school psychology faculty members can move beyond the question of whether or not to become an academic to consider which type of academic position would be the best fit for them. Interested readers are referred to Harris and Sullivan (2012) and Joyce-Beaulieu and Dixon (2018) for more on the school psychology faculty role.

Non-school Settings

Finally, non-school clinical practice may be a desirable option for some entry-level school psychologists. Non-school positions/settings include community mental health clinics, hospitals, forensic psychology, military bases, prisons, private practice, and many others. Consistent with the content discussed in Chapter 8 regarding depth and specialization, the choice to practice in non-school settings can be linked with professional interests and expertise. Although the majority of school psychology interns will go on to work in schools, and that is the focus of school psychology training, some may choose rewarding alternative career paths.

Preparation Stage: November and December

As fall transitions into winter, interns move into the *preparation* stage, a time during which they update the professional materials in their portfolios, think about their current experiences and how they might be purposefully supplemented, and request letters of recommendation from supervisors and others.

The Professional Portfolio

The professional portfolio is a compilation of several formative and summative documents including the résumé and/or CV, work samples, and letters of reference (Crespi, Fischetti, & Lopez, 1998). During the preparation stage interns begin to edit, sharpen, and update already existing pre-internship materials. Interns should ask themselves: "How have I changed professionally from when I originally created these documents to this point in time?" and "How do I demonstrate my growth of skills so that it is evident to potential employers?" Such questions fit with developmental frameworks and models described at various points within this book.

One way that interns can demonstrate professional growth is by highlighting in their professional materials increases in the breadth and depth of their knowledge, skills, and experiences. Regarding breadth, an intern will want to show potential employers that during the internship he or she has gotten a range of applied experiences and worked with a variety of different students and families. As for depth, graduating interns should be able to demonstrate that they have acquired more experience in certain skills compared to others; these may be considered areas of burgeoning proficiency or expertise.

To illustrate how professional materials may change, a few excerpted bullets from a pre-internship and pre-job CV for a trainee named Joelle are compared in

Figure 10.2. Since Joelle demonstrated extensive involvement in problem solving during her internship, she was able to remove that bullet in her practicum description on her job CV (crossed out on the right side of Figure 10.2). On the other hand, Joelle kept one bullet about PBIS involvement from her practicum CV to demonstrate how she increased her depth in this area during her internship (e.g., she was involved at both the building and district levels) and kept another bullet about play-based assessment because she did not have this experience during her internship year. From the brief excerpt of Joelle's CV, the reader can see that she has taken on several different experiences (breadth) and has increased her level of involvement in the same area (PBIS) from practicum to internship (depth).

Résumés and CVs

Even though they are often thought of as interchangeable, résumés and CVs are not exactly the same. The primary difference is that a résumé tends to be shorter (one or two pages) than a CV (usually more than two pages), which more

CV for Internship Application	Adapting the CV for a Job Application
Joelle W. Lawrence, M.Ed.	**Joelle W. Lawrence, Ed.S.**
SUPERVISED PRACTICUM	SUPERVISED INTERNSHIP
Waukegan School District 60 Fall 2018 – Summer 2019 Waukegan, IL • Participated on a school-based problem solving team • Contributed to school wide PBIS including planning, implementation, and evaluation • Assisted supervisor in completing play-based assessments for preschool students	Waukegan School District 60 Fall 2019 – Summer 2020 Waukegan, IL • Co-facilitated the school-based problem-solving team including creating meeting agendas; collecting, organizing and presenting data; following up on case progress; and providing professional development to team members • Represented our school on the district-level Positive Behavior Intervention and Support (PBIS) team including participating in monthly meetings, and consulting with building principal regarding PBIS implementation SUPERVISED PRACTICUM Waukegan School District 60 Fall 2010 – Summer 2011 Waukegan, IL • ~~Participated on a school-based problem solving team~~ • Contributed to school wide PBIS including planning, implementation, and evaluation • Assisted supervisor in completing play-based assessments for preschool students

FIGURE 10.2 Changes in a CV from internship application to job application.

expansively covers skills and experiences (APA, 2018). The CV, while longer than the résumé, should not be overly wordy or lengthy; redundant or irrelevant information should be avoided. Job notices will usually specify whether they want applicants to submit a résumé or a CV as part of the application.

A sample CV template is featured in Appendix E. The template is intended to provide a helpful example which can be expanded upon or altered. Interns are also encouraged to search online for relevant examples of CVs, especially those that may match their own job aspirations. For instance, when I applied to an academic position in a school psychology program I structured my CV to mirror exemplars I found online of school psychology faculty members. Of note, I had to adapt my CV in some ways to look different from what I included when applying for school-based positions (e.g., I put a greater emphasis on scholarship in my academic CV).

In addition to using template examples, there are several big ideas interns can keep in mind when creating or updating a résumé or CV:

- Every résumé or CV does not need to be identical. Résumés or CVs should demonstrate the unique experiences and skills of the applicant, and match the opportunity to which the intern is applying.
- Instead of listing all experiences in a single section called "Professional Experience," particular areas can be highlighted to demonstrate the applicant's unique skills and experiences (e.g., "Teaching Experience," "Research Experience," or "Leadership Experience").
- Aesthetics and consistency of formatting are important. Sections should be clearly divided by using borders and other formatting tools (e.g., bolding, italicizing, and strategic spacing). Formatting should be consistent throughout the résumé or CV, including fonts used, heading structures, and use of space.
- The résumé or CV should not list "everything but the kitchen sink" (Plante, 1998, p. 509), only the most relevant and current experiences.
- The résumé or CV should be updated as soon as new experiences are completed because it is easy to forget to include relevant activities.
- Honesty is essential. Exaggerations or lies may be questioned during the job interview.

Interns should seek out feedback and assistance when working on their résumés or CVs. Family, peers, field supervisors, and faculty members all can provide valuable input on the résumé or CV, as well as on other job application materials. Some universities also have career or writing centers with staff that can provide support.

Work Samples

Even if they are not required as part of application materials, it may be helpful for graduating interns to include exemplar pieces of their work in their portfolio.

Work samples demonstrate applied competence and professionalism in particular areas of practice. Work samples should be selected based on (a) product quality; (b) what types of work the employer may want to see (i.e., the applicant may wish to provide different work samples for different positions); and (c) what products best demonstrate the applicant's developing skills and professional identity.

A primary type of work sample often included by school psychology job applicants is psychological evaluations (Crespi et al., 1998). Although a psychological evaluation is one piece of data applicants may include in their portfolios, consistent with the broadening roles of school psychologists, it is also important to include other materials. For example, an applicant may incorporate an individual or group counseling summary; a functional behavioral assessment and associated behavior intervention plan; a consultation case write-up and summary; curricula that were written or adapted; or slides from professional learning sessions presented to staff. It is critical that if work samples are included as part of a portfolio, all identifying information is removed. As with the résumé or CV, applicants will not want to include samples of *everything*; materials should be purposefully selected to (a) be representative of the candidate's interests, strengths, and skills and (b) demonstrate the skills the hiring site is looking for in applicants.

Summaries

In addition to work samples, it may be appropriate to include summaries of other relevant information in the portfolio. Such information may act as a supplement or appendix to the résumé or CV. Summaries also save the applicant valuable space on the résumé or CV and make it easier for the hiring committee to see a job applicant's credentials. Examples of information that may be summarized include a list of courses taken during graduate training; professional learning presentations attended; evidence-based interventions implemented; tests administered; or a breakdown of internship hours by particular categories. Job applicants can easily bring summaries to a job interview and ask the committee if it would be helpful to submit such materials.

Transcripts

Academic transcripts are often required as part of the job application process. Interns should order several copies of official transcripts from their undergraduate and graduate institutions and keep those materials on hand to include as part of the portfolio or job application. Following internship completion, interns will want to reorder official graduate transcripts to document successful completion of their degree. Since the degree may not automatically post on the transcript, interns should call the university registrar to ask when it is best to order copies of a finalized, official transcript.

Portfolio Formats

Traditionally, job applicants compile a folder or binder of printed materials to present to potential employers as part of the job application process. More recently, web or disc portfolio formats have become increasingly common (Hill, Kubick, & York, 2011). Job applicants who use such formats may demonstrate to prospective employers their technological competence and innovation. Web-based portfolios have the potential to reach a wide audience, may include a variety of work samples given their large capacity, and are helpful for long-distance interviews. However, they may also make personal information widely available and can be problematic for maintaining confidentiality, and the audience may be unclear or confused about what information they are accessing (Hill et al., 2011). Disc formats (e.g., a CD or flash drive) are easily portable and left with potential employers following an interview and can also store a great deal of information. Applicants can ask hiring sites about format preferences prior to submitting a portfolio.

Supplementary Experiences

As the intern is gathering materials, he or she should (a) continue to think about professional interests and goals, (b) identify any gaps in training that are preventing the intern from meeting those goals, and in turn (c) seek out these experiences if possible. Supervisors should also be cognizant of what activities the intern has or has not had the chance to complete during the year and, to the extent that they can, support interns to close these gaps in training. As has been mentioned previously in this book, interns cannot possibly complete every activity that is expected of professional school psychologists during the internship year. However, if the intern and/or supervisor realize early on in the year that the intern is missing a particular opportunity or skill, the preparation stage is an excellent time to address these gaps.

Letters of Recommendation

During the preparation stage, interns should determine who they will ask for letters of recommendation and proceed with making requests. There are numerous considerations interns and supervisors should keep in mind during the letter request and writing process.

Who to Ask for Letters

First and foremost, the intern should be careful to ask for letters from individuals who have seen them work at their best and that they are fairly certain will write them a positive letter. As expressed by Baird (2016), "Positive letters can be the key to open doors, but negative letters may well lock them shut" (p. 162). The intern should directly talk to the prospective letter writer, be clear about post-internship goals, and ask if the person is able to write a supportive letter on their behalf. When asking for a letter, it is essential for the intern to be sensitive to the potential letter writer's reaction to the request. While enthusiasm likely signals that a positive letter should be expected, hesitancy may be a warning sign that the intern should ask someone else for a letter. Such a reaction warrants a discussion initiated by either party. Although discussing letter writing concerns is a potentially awkward or disconcerting conversation, if approached sensitively it can (a) provide guidance on what the intern can do to improve; (b) prevent the intern from getting a neutral or negative letter and allow the intern to request a letter from an alternative individual; and (c) provide an opportunity to offer the intern alternative options regarding future goals.

It is helpful for interns to have a representative sample of letter writers such as a mix of school psychologist practitioners and faculty members. Having all letters from one source (e.g., only university faculty or field-based practitioners) may raise a red flag to prospective employers that the intern's performance was lacking in some way. There are a number of individuals who may provide letters of recommendation in addition to field or university internship supervisors and university faculty. For example, interns may request letters from co-workers they have collaborated with or who have seen them in action, such as building principals, school counselors, behavior specialists, the school nurse, resource psychologists, teachers, or district-level psychologists, to name a few. In addition to formal letters of recommendation, it may be appropriate to include in a professional portfolio letters received by the intern during the year from students, families, or colleagues (e.g., a thank you note from a mother for the intern's effort and success in providing an academic intervention for her child). Of course, as with all materials, confidentiality should be protected.

When to Ask for Letters

Writers appreciate advance notice from those who are requesting letters of recommendation. Requesting letters at least a month in advance of when they are needed is a general rule of thumb. Since several individuals may be asking the same person for letters at the same time, even more notice may be appropriate. The month of December may be a good time to ask for letters as supervisors or other writers often have some additional time during the winter holidays. As a university supervisor who often writes letters for interns, I find it helpful to establish a deadline for when the intern needs my letter. I also request that the intern follows up with me in person or via email several days before the agreed upon deadline if they have not yet heard from me that the letter was sent out. This acts as a reminder to me and prevents the intern from feeling like a burden for proactively following up.

Other Considerations When Asking for Letters

In addition to being thoughtful about who and when to ask for letters, there are several other considerations for interns requesting letters of recommendation, as pointed out by Baird (2016). First, if there is advanced preparation needed on application materials (e.g., filling out information such as addresses or phone numbers or addressing envelopes), it is helpful for the applicant to complete this work in advance. Second, if there are specific instructions (e.g., District A only wants a letter but District B wants a letter and a specific evaluation tool completed) the intern should make what is needed explicitly clear to the writer. Third, it is helpful for interns to provide a copy of the CV or résumé and a brief summary letter to the writer, including specific characteristics, skills, or activities they wish the writer to include or emphasize. For example, an intern named Patrice requested that I highlight her leadership in the school psychology program's student group as well as a few of the leadership experiences she took on during her internship because she was applying to a newly established charter school seeking candidates with leadership experience. Fourth, interns should keep letter writers posted on job application results. Supervisors and others spend a great deal of time writing letters on behalf of interns because they are invested in their success; it is courteous for interns to stay in touch during the process and let the writer know the outcome. Related, it is also a courtesy to say thank you to the writer either in person, by phone, in an email, or in a handwritten note once the process is complete.

Issues for Supervisors and Other Letter Writers

In theory, letters of recommendation written by supervisors are directly informed by processes of evaluation occurring throughout the internship year. In reality, letters often inflate or exaggerate the skills of applicants and any critical commentary is usually excluded from letters (Kaslow et al., 2007). Stedman, Hatch, and Schoenfeld (2009) found that recommendation letters for pre-doctoral internship applications at medical schools and other settings were not only positively biased but, given their homogeneity, were not contributors to meaningful decision making in the internship selection process. When letter writers *do* include constructive criticism of a candidate, or even weak praise, it may put that individual at a disadvantage when compared to other candidates (Corey et al., 2010). In fact, in a study of criteria in psychology internship selection, Ginkel, Davis, and Michael (2010) found that negative letters of recommendation were one of the top variables used to exclude applicants from further consideration for a position. For these and related reasons, APPIC has begun requiring a Standardized Reference Form (SRF) for internship applications, which highlights anchored competencies rather than objective assessments (see Chapter 2). However, standardized letters are not the norm when applying to professional positions following the internship.

It is therefore critical for letter writers such as field and university supervisors to be thoughtful about what they put into supervisee letters of recommendation. As stated by Corey et al. (2010), "writing objective letters of reference is an ethical obligation of the supervisor as gatekeeper for the profession" but supervisors must "be aware of the implications and consequences of what [they say] about the supervisee" (p. 233). The authors provided several helpful tips for recommendation writers, including:

- Discuss strengths and deficiencies without overstatement or understatement.
- Pay careful attention to what is written in the first and last paragraphs, as readers may focus in on these summaries.
- Ask the requester when the letter is due and complete it in a timely manner.
- Keep a copy of the letter and provide a letter to the supervisee when appropriate.
- Check for accuracy of spelling, grammar, names, and other parts of the letter.
- Be concise.
- Be transparent with the supervisee, if possible, regarding any deficiencies or other negative information that may be included in the letter.
- If describing deficits, do so carefully in an objective way using specific terms. Since negative comments are not common, readers will look carefully at what you write.
- If needed, obtain a release to write the letter.

A sample letter of recommendation is presented in Figure 10.3, written for an intern named JoAnne (who was featured in Vignette 7.1 in Chapter 7). The Figure includes callouts highlighting a few features letter writers may want to include in their letters (e.g., the nature of the relationship with the intern; the candidate's knowledge and skills; breadth and depth of experiences; leadership experiences; and unique or distinguishing applicant interests). In the example provided in Figure 10.3, Jack (the supervisor) felt he was ethically obligated to mention the difficulties JoAnne faced during her internship year. He discussed this with JoAnne before composing the letter and included the information in a way that was honest, maintained confidentiality, and demonstrated JoAnne's professionalism and growth.

Initial Action Stage: January and February

During the *initial action* stage, interns actively begin to apply for jobs. They search for openings and decide where to apply, send out applications, and prepare for interviews.

Narrowing the Search

A helpful action early in the job search process is for interns to narrow down what positions they will search for. School-based positions can be narrowed

Dear Colleague:

I am pleased to write this letter of recommendation on behalf of JoAnne Drew for the position of school psychologist. JoAnne and I have known each other for almost one year. I am currently her primary internship supervisor at Fairview Elementary School in the Thomas County Public Schools. I have been a school psychologist for the past 20 years and an internship supervisor for 15 years. JoAnne is intelligent, an analytical thinker, and a hard worker. I believe she will be an asset to your district as a school psychologist.

> Specify your position, how long you have been in the position, and the nature of your work with the candidate

JoAnne entered the internship with strong conceptual and applied skills that she developed during her school psychology doctoral training, including completing four years of supervised fieldwork. She engaged in activities such as collecting benchmarking and progress monitoring data, completing classroom observations, and contributing to the development of a school wide Positive Behavior Support system. At the preschool level, JoAnne conducted play-based assessments and linked assessments to effective interventions. Given JoAnne's extensive background knowledge and clinical skills, we were eager to hire her as an intern this year.

> Provide information about candidate's background experiences

JoAnne's internship year has added to her breadth and depth of experiences and skills. She has worked across three schools spanning the elementary, middle, and high school levels. At all levels, JoAnne has been involved in special education eligibility decision making and IEP planning. She has worked in self-contained multi-needs classrooms and a self-contained classroom for students with emotional disabilities. Further, JoAnne has been involved at the systems-level by (a) supporting the implementation of a multi-tiered service delivery system for prevention and early intervention, including Response to Intervention and (b) contributing to various school improvement initiatives at all of her sites. In a short year, JoAnne has made a significant impact.

> Highlight breadth and depth of skills, if applicable

> Highlight leadership skills, if applicable

I feel it is important to mention that this year presented several personal challenges for JoAnne and at times she struggled to effectively cope with the stressors she faced. However, JoAnne acknowledged she was having difficulty, sought out supervisory support, and learned new strategies to balance her personal and professional worlds. JoAnne has grown significantly from her experiences this year and she is a resilient individual with strong professional dispositions.

> Recognize challenges or deficits and how they were addressed. Note the candidate's response to the challenging circumstances. Use objective language. Inform the candidate, if possible, of the information you will include in the letter.

To close out this recommendation, I would like to once again highlight JoAnne's strong analytical skills. She has completed several research projects over the past few years and will even be presenting a poster at the upcoming National Association of School Psychologists convention. JoAnne's critical thinking skills have been reflected time and again during her internship, and I am excited for her to share her work on a national stage.

> Highlight unique areas of strength

Should you have any questions, feel free to contact me at jackwrightwood@fes.com or at (987)-654-3210.

Sincerely,

Jack Wrightwood, Ph.D., NCSP
School Psychologist,
Fairview Elementary School
Thomas County Public Schools

FIGURE 10.3 Example of a letter of recommendation, including an identified deficiency

down based on the match between the site and the applicant's specific interests and skills. For instance, during the pre-preparation or preparation stages, an intern may decide to seek out positions at the high school level or work with a specific population of children. Pragmatic factors such as geography may also narrow the job search. One intern I supervised, who had three young children and had recently purchased a new house, determined she would only look for jobs within a fifteen-minute commute. As previously discussed, some interns may wish to seek alternative types of positions, narrowing the search as well. For example, the doctoral intern Cordell, referenced earlier in this chapter, primarily searched for academic and research positions rather than also looking for school-based psychologist positions.

How to Search

A primary method to find out about job openings is by using online resources. Although some positions can be identified with vast national job search engines, it is best for interns to begin with education-, psychology-, or school psychology-specific websites and listservs. For interns seeking local positions, a helpful starting point is state school psychology organizations. Members of these organizations alert colleagues to openings via professional listservs. For those open to relocating, NASP's Career Center (https://nasponline-jobs.careerwebsite.com) is an excellent resource for up-to-date school psychology job postings around the country, including a variety of types of positions (e.g., school-based, academic, and clinical settings). School psychology interns may also find it beneficial to explore education-specific job websites such as http://www.k12jobspot.com. Finally, the website https://www.psyccareers.com hosted by the APA provides information about jobs across a variety of psychology disciplines, providing one means for interns to identify alternatives to school-based positions.

Web-based job searching should be supplemented by networking, as described in previous chapters. Having an ally that is thinking of the intern when a position opens up may be the key to finding out about a position, or securing a job interview. In addition, if there is a particular place an intern may wish to work, it is acceptable to make a cold call to the site or to the office of human resources. Cold calling demonstrates an applicant's proactive qualities and may allow the applicant to access information that is not yet posted elsewhere.

Submitting Applications

Once open positions are identified, the intern should be ready to apply to a few that seem like a good match with his or her interests and skills. Even if an intern is eyeing a particular position, it is advisable to apply for more than one position as most openings will have several applicants. The intern should make sure to pay precise attention to application instructions and deadlines. Violations of either of these put the intern at a disadvantage right out of the starting gate. For electronic submissions, the intern should pay careful attention to issues of formatting and be sure to attach all documents correctly.

Tailoring the Cover Letter and Other Materials

The intern's professional materials are now created, edited, compiled and sharpened. Prospective jobs have been identified and targeted. The only application piece that is missing is a cover letter, a brief document submitted with a job application, tailored to the specific position. An effective cover letter (a) explains the intern's interest in the position, (b) illustrates the intern's unique qualifications for the position, and (c) supplements and/or underscores information offered in the résumé or CV that is most relevant to the specific job. A sample cover letter is provided in Appendix F. Once a cover letter is developed, it is easy for the intern to use this letter as a template that can be personalized when applying to other positions. If possible, the intern should address the letter to a specific person rather than "To Whom it May Concern."

Materials such as the résumé or CV and work samples should also be tailored to fit with where the intern is applying. For example, the intern may wish to change the order of activities listed on his or her résumé or CV, based on what the hiring site is looking for in a candidate, or a new section might be created altogether. Similarly, work samples that may be relevant for one job may be less important to include for another position. Shaping application materials to fit a particular job suggests to the reviewer that the applicant has done his or her homework and is not casting a ubiquitous net while hoping to land any position.

Following Up

Regardless of whether the application was submitted electronically or via "snail mail," the intern should be sure to follow up with a phone call to make sure materials were received (that is, unless the application description specifies that applicants should not call). Following up is important because it is not always clear who collects application materials or how materials get from the point of submission into the hands of reviewers. Of course, it is to the advantage of the applicant to be polite and considerate during follow up even if there were any difficulties with the application process. The person reached on the phone may have some influence in making hiring decisions. Finally, following up is made easier if the intern maintains a spreadsheet record of applications, including contact information of sites and materials submitted and whom he or she has spoken with along the way.

Interview Preparation

As stated by Baird (2016), "the key to an effective interview is what you do *before* the interview, not simply what happens *during* the interview" (emphasis in original, p. 9). Interns can prepare for the interview in terms of *content* and *process*.

Content Preparation

Regarding content, interns should carefully research the site where they are applying and learn about its mission, goals, populations served, challenges and strengths. In addition, the intern can research the individual(s) who will be conducting the interview to learn about their roles and/or approaches to practice. The intern may have done some of this work in advance when preparing application materials but prior to the interview the intern can research pertinent information in greater depth. After learning more about the hiring site, the intern should ask himself or herself, "What can I do as a school psychologist to best support positive outcomes at this site?"

Content preparation also includes being able to demonstrate content knowledge verbally during the interview. The intern should be aware of educational jargon that may arise during the interview, some of which may be site-specific. If applying to out-of-state positions, it will be important for the intern to become familiar with the unique qualities of that state. For instance, the structure of school districts may differ from one state to another, including size, geographical composition, and how school psychologists are assigned. School psychologists' professional practices also can vary between states, for example regarding how students are assessed regarding special education eligibility for particular categories such as specific learning disabilities (e.g., Zirkel, 2017). In addition to site-specific information, applicants may be served well by reviewing broad-based materials, such as chapters from the most recent five volumes of *Best Practices in School Psychology*, edited by Patti Harrison and Alex Thomas, prior to the interview. This is not to cram in last minute knowledge but rather to put pertinent issues in school psychology at the front of one's brain to be able to access them with automaticity during the interview.

Interns should also be prepared to provide examples of content applications from actual cases within the interview. Articulate interviewees convey the work they have done and are doing, how it reflects best practices in the field, what professional lessons they learned doing this work, and how the case resulted in positive outcomes for students and/or teachers. Providing case examples can demonstrate that the intern has applied skills for school psychology practice in addition to well-developed content knowledge. I recommend making a list of the most salient cases and learning experiences during the internship and prior field experiences, noting what knowledge and skill areas are demonstrated by each, and reviewing these prior to the interview so they are easily recalled in the moment.

Process Preparation

Even when an applicant is knowledgeable in relevant content areas, the interview process may make it difficult for the individual to demonstrate all that he or she knows. For example, a supervisor from a hiring school district recently called me for a reference check on a former intern. He was surprised that the applicant appeared nervous and rambled when responding to questions during the interview because this contrasted sharply with how she presented herself in application materials. The supervisor expressed concerns regarding how the intern would present information to parents or school staff. Being nervous is normal when interviewing, and not unexpected by those conducting interviews. However, when nerves drastically affect the applicant's presentation, interviewers may consider it representative of the applicant's dispositions rather than as signifying a stressful situation.

Applicants can alleviate interview anxiety by over-preparing and over-rehearsing for the interview. On the companion website for this book, and currently on YouTube at https://www.youtube.com/watch?v=Ob4do34riZk, is a simulated job interview video with a mock panel of interviewers, intended to help applicants prepare for the job interview process. A transcript of the mock interview is featured in Appendix G, with space provided for interns to write out thoughts regarding each question. The transcript offers numerous specific questions that might be asked during the interview, although of course interviews might include additional questions or activities (e.g., a brief spontaneous writing sample, or demonstration of applied skills). In general, interviewees should be prepared to:

- Tell the interviewer(s) about themselves including training experiences, interests, and skills.
- State clearly why they are interested in this particular position at this particular site.
- Orally work through applied scenarios or case examples using a problem-solving process and/or ethical decision-making model.
- Identify personal strengths they will bring to the position.
- Identify areas they perceive they will continue to need to develop (Note: This is not a trick question asked by potential employers. Ongoing professional learning is essential for school psychologists at *all* levels of training and practice).
- Ask questions about the position and hiring site (Note: The interview process goes both ways; applicants should determine whether the site is a good fit for them).

In addition to practicing interviewing using an online simulation, interns can work with peers to prepare for the interview process, including conducting mock interviews with one another and providing constructive feedback. It may also be helpful for interns to seek out individuals they are not completely familiar with to practice for interviews. For instance, my wife's supervisor (an assistant principal) conducted a mock interview with me prior to me going on job interviews and she provided invaluable feedback.

Job Interviews Versus Internship Interviews

A final point is for interns to realize that job interviews are different from internship interviews. The internship year is supposed to help the intern grow in numerous ways, including content knowledge, ability to apply skills with automaticity, professional identity, and bridging university training with day-to-day practice. Therefore, the answers a prospective intern and a prospective first-year professional provide during an interview, even to the same exact questions, may be qualitatively different. For example, in response to an applied interview question about a crisis response a few key points for prospective interns would be to maintain client safety and welfare, notify and consult with the supervisor, and not intervene beyond boundaries of competence. For the job applicant, although some facets of that answer would hold true, conveying the ability to respond independently and skillfully during the crisis must be conveyed. Interns should think critically about differences between what is expected of interns versus licensed practitioners during the interview and make sure they are able to articulate these differences successfully.

Ongoing Action Stage: March, April, May

During the *ongoing action* stage, the job hunt is in full gear. Interns should continue to search for positions as many new openings are posted during the spring months. In addition, interns should continue to follow up on positions previously applied for. In following up with applications it is appropriate to ask hiring sites about their timeline and process. Some sites may be able to provide firm dates of when they are conducting interviews and others might let the applicant know that their position is already filled. Job interviews are likely taking place with greater frequency during the ongoing action stage.

Interviews

Following the initial action stage, interns should feel adequately prepared to be successful interviewees. However, practice interviews are obviously not exactly the same as in-person interviews. The exact format of the interview (e.g., number of interviewers; number of interviewees; how questions are asked; requirement of an applied activity) varies per hiring site. The level of formality in the interview may also differ from setting to setting. Regardless of precise interview structure, the following are some tips interns can bear in mind:

- Wear professional clothes.
- Leave time for travel. Arriving early may provide an opportunity to meet staff members before beginning the formal interview.
- Remember to bring portfolio materials and copies of materials to give to each member of the interview committee.
- Answer questions directly, succinctly, and clearly.
- Pay attention to non-verbal behaviors, including offering a firm handshake, maintaining eye contact with all interviewers, smiling when appropriate, using a strong voice, and sitting with straight posture.
- Be yourself. Being nervous during an interview is normal but being too nervous or stiff may prevent the intern from showing his or her knowledge, skills, and personality.

Following the Interview

After the interview, interns should send a thank you note to the head of the interviewing committee. A thank you note may include a comment or two about things the intern enjoyed or learned about the hiring site. In addition, it is appropriate to ask any lingering questions about the position. For some positions, a first interview will be followed by subsequent interviews which also may vary in format. Second and/or third round interviews are not uncommon and might take place with individuals not on the initial interview committee, for instance a school superintendent. Later round interviews may also be a time when compensation and benefits for the position are discussed (covered later in this chapter).

Learning from Interviews

Each interview can be seen as an opportunity for the intern to gain practice interviewing. Moreover, when an intern is not hired for a position, some interviewers may provide feedback to the interviewee. Feedback may be unsolicited or may be requested by the interviewee when learning about the decision (e.g., "Is there any feedback you have for me based on the interview?"). Interview feedback can aid interns' performance in future interviews. For instance, one intern was told by an interviewer that the interview committee was impressed with her skills, but they hired a candidate who had more experience with crisis prevention and intervention. In fact, the applicant did have such experiences but realized she did not adequately describe her experiences during the interview.

Getting Targeted Experiences

Even though job interviews are taking place and the intern's thoughts are moving towards next year, the internship year is not yet complete. During the ongoing action stage, the intern is able to seek out particular experiences that best fit with particular jobs or that fill in any existing training gaps. Further, these are supervised training experiences for learning, opportunities that can make the intern a more complete job candidate and professional school psychologist.

VIGNETTE 10.1 **ILEANA'S TARGETED EXPERIENCES**

An intern named Ileana was informed that a school psychologist position in her district was opening in a school working with students with severe and profound disabilities. She had done some related work in a self-contained classroom during her practicum which she excelled at and enjoyed, but still felt inexperienced in this area. With the support of her internship supervisor, Ileana sought out related experiences in the spring, including spending one day a week at the school that would have the opening. During the interview,

Ileana was able to talk about (a) her interests, (b) her proactive behaviors to get more experience, and (c) relevant experiences from her practicum and internship. She was offered and accepted the position.

Patience, Persistence, and Payoff Stage: June, July, August

The final stage in the job process, *patience, persistence, and payoff*, occurs during the tail end of the internship and ends when an intern secures a job. Anecdotally, I have found that as the internship approaches its end, interns get apprehensive if they have not yet secured a position. Naturally, it is scary to close one door when another door is not yet open. However, many excellent positions open up late in the summer due to unplanned situations such as a school psychologist's relocation, retirement, maternity leave or changes in a school district's budget. The need for interns to stay patient cannot be overstated. In addition, ongoing persistence is essential, including continuing to search for positions and following up as needed on applications already in progress.

Accepting a Position

With patience and persistence, the graduating intern will be offered a position – the payoff of the job hunt. Applicants should remember that just because they have an offer, they are not obligated to accept. Further, if, for whatever reason, an intern needs to accept a less than ideal position, it does not mean he or she is obligated to stay in that position forever (Silva, Newman, & Guiney, 2014). Just as an employer may determine the employee was not a good fit, the employee may decide after a year that the position did not work out. On the other hand, a position that may not be the intern's top choice may turn out to be a better fit than anticipated.

Negotiating Salary and Benefits

The ability to negotiate salary and benefits varies from one position to the next. There is often limited salary wiggle room for school psychologist practitioners as many districts have schedules with salary steps based on characteristics such as employees' years of education and experience. Therefore, it is important to research the salary schedule in the district being considered (often publicly available through the district's human resources website) to maximize the entry-level salary step upon which subsequent steps will build. Of note, some districts offer bonuses or additional salary for school psychologists with an NCSP credential. There are also other benefits and general expectations to discuss with prospective employers, such as the availability of funding to access professional learning opportunities, a laptop computer, office space, and other necessary work materials. Also, remember that there are salary differences per region of the country (affected by cost of living, as well as school psychology shortages). This is a relevant consideration for mobile graduates looking to experience a new city or state. Based on data from the most recent NASP member survey in 2014–2015, Walcott and Hyson (2018) reported that the median salary for school psychologist practitioners was $63,000 with the Northeastern region of the US having a median of $70,000 and the Southeast $59,000.

Negotiating salary and benefits for other positions mentioned in this chapter, such as academic positions, is different than for positions in K-12 settings. A full review of these issues is beyond the scope of the chapter. However, readers are referred to the APA's website, which offers several articles about salary negotiations for new psychologists applying to academic and other positions (e.g., Clay, 2015; Winerman, 2014).

Choosing Between Multiple Offers

Sometimes dilemmas arise in the process of making decisions about what position to accept or not to accept. Challenging situations may include having to choose between two or three positions; waiting to hear from a preferred district while sitting on an offer from a less-preferred district; or accepting one position and then getting offered a preferred position a few hours later. Ironically, it is frequently the interns who are the most anxious about whether they will get any offers that end up having to choose from among a few.

When advising interns on challenging circumstances such as these, I always emphasize the importance of interns being professional and transparent. Being professional means not violating any contracts (written or verbal) and not lying to potential employers. Being transparent means letting potential employers know the current circumstances which are being navigated (e.g., "I am very interested in working at your district but I am also expecting to hear from another district later this week. I would like to make a fully informed decision before accepting your offer. Is there any way I could let you know my final decision by Friday afternoon?"). Potential employers appreciate a candidate's honesty and integrity. Further, the intern may have future interactions with individuals in this district or even decide they want to work at that district one day down the road. Acting with a lack of transparency or professionalism may inadvertently damage relationships or burn professional bridges in this small field.

Summary

Obtaining a job is an ongoing process that commences before the internship begins. The pre-preparation stage (pre-internship to early fall) serves as a time for interns to build foundational materials such as a professional portfolio, to engage in preparatory experiences such as internship interviews, and to begin to focus professional goals. Most interns will pursue school-based psychologist positions but others may seek out alternative career options. The preparation stage of the job process involves compiling and editing all materials in the professional portfolio, including cover letters, the résumé or CV, work samples, work summaries, transcripts, and letters of recommendation. Interns should be thoughtful about who, when, and how to ask for letters of recommendation and supervisors should also take care in composing letters for students. Interns should also determine if there are additional supervised experiences that it would be beneficial to complete in order to bridge any gaps in training.

The initial action stage of the job process includes beginning the job search, applying for positions, and preparing for interviews. To effectively search for positions, interns should narrow their search to the extent possible and utilize online resources and professional networks. Prior to submitting applications, materials should be tailored to particular positions. Interns should carefully prepare for interviews and remember that the job interview is not the same thing as the internship interview completed one year earlier. Once initial applications are submitted, interns engage in the ongoing action stage which includes continuing to search and apply for positions, following up on previously submitted applications, and engaging in interviews. Interviews can be intimidating but provide opportunities for learning. During the summer, with adequate patience (e.g., waiting for new positions to open) and persistence (e.g., following up on applications submitted), interns will eventually achieve the payoff of landing a full-time job.

Critical Thinking Questions and Activities

The following are critical thinking questions and activities for interns, field supervisors, and university supervisors to ponder regarding the job application and interview process.

For Interns:

- Using the simulated interview tool provided on the book's companion website, practice job interviewing with a peer. Request specific feedback on what you did well and what you could do better.
- Thinking back to your internship interview, how would you answer some of the questions differently at this point in time?
- Write a list of at least five questions you have for the site(s) where you will be interviewing.

For Field Supervisors:

- How would you respond if an intern who has not performed well during their internship requested a letter of recommendation?

- What are some ways you might support your intern during the job application and interview process?
- Are there additional experiences that the intern should complete before the end of the year to become a better job candidate and a more well-rounded school psychologist?

For University Supervisors:

- What guidance or support, if any, is offered to students from your training program in the job hunt process? If what is currently provided is not sufficient, how might guidance or support be supplemented?
- An intern named Felix accepted a job offer last week but received an offer today from a district where he would much prefer to work. He asks your advice on what to do. How would you respond?
- How does formative and summative evaluation of interns connect to letters of recommendation that are written during the job application process?

11

CONCLUDING THE INTERNSHIP

Over the past several months the intern has entered the internship site; developed and nurtured relationships with supervisors, staff, children, and parents; expanded professional competencies; and applied and interviewed for jobs. Now the time has come for the intern to close out the internship year. Just as there are numerous tasks involved in effective internship entry, successfully concluding the internship year involves several considerations.

To explore these issues, the chapter is organized by the three intern identities described in Chapter 5: trainee, professional, and supervisee. First, completion of trainee responsibilities is addressed including program and university requirements and doctoral dissertation work. Second, closing out professional responsibilities such as terminating with students and staff, and applying for certification as a school psychologist are discussed. Third, concluding supervisee responsibilities is explored including summative evaluations, terminating supervisory relationships, the role of final site visits, and how to pursue supervision and professional learning beyond the internship year. The chapter concludes with critical thinking questions and activities for interns and supervisors.

Closing out Trainee Responsibilities

Interns are nearing the finish line of their graduate training, an accomplishment that is accompanied by a number of tasks to be completed before the year is through. Although much attention is paid to closing out professional responsibilities at the internship site, requirements for interns to complete their training program may not receive adequate consideration.

Completing Program and University Requirements

Before being eligible to graduate, the intern likely has to complete various degree requirements. If the intern is enrolled in a university-based internship seminar, there may be lingering assignments to finish prior to the official end of the course. It is easy for requirements to be neglected when interns are consumed by so many other year end activities, such as closing out cases, saying goodbye to colleagues, applying for state and national licensure, and applying and interviewing for jobs. Aside from specific course assignments that remain, some school psychology programs require students to complete a culminating project such as a portfolio. While faculty may view final assignments as critical for numerous reasons (e.g., helping the intern link theory and practice, providing a summative evaluation, and providing data on training program outcomes), interns may view remaining requirements as time consuming busywork, or final hoops to jump through before moving on to bigger and better things. However, both faculty and interns can contribute to university-based assignments being meaningful learning tools.

Making Assignments Meaningful

Interns and supervisors tend to view program requirements as valuable when they are strategically aligned to meet intern needs such as completing degree and licensure requirements and enhancing professional readiness. Some assignments may even alleviate interns' end of the year stress and prevent frantic last-minute scrambling. For example, in some school psychology program internship seminars, students are required to submit a monthly log and graph of their accumulating internship hours. Monthly logs are easily produced using a program such as Microsoft Excel or Time2Track and (a) demonstrate the ongoing breadth and depth of interns' experiences, (b) document interns' progress towards completing hours required for licensure, and (c) prevent a desperate push to account for time when the year is done.

To provide another example of how assignments may actually be helpful or stress-reducing, some interns are required to complete reflection papers in internship seminars that help them think critically about the work they are doing at their internship sites. Papers can be directly connected to interns' day-to-day work, course big ideas, course readings, and NASP (2010d) training standards, and even aligned to meet a program's end of year portfolio requirements. Papers also provide a way for supervisors to formatively monitor interns' developmental progress during the year (e.g., case conceptualization, problem-solving skills, and work quality) and to provide ongoing feedback.

Interns share with university faculty the responsibility for making assignments valuable. When given a choice, interns should write about or present on topics that are relevant to their interests and their ongoing internship work. For instance, one intern was asked by her field supervisor to provide a professional learning presentation to middle school teachers about managing difficult behaviors in the classroom. She practiced her presentation during an internship seminar and received constructive feedback from peers that helped her restructure a few unclear slides. Another intern was assigned by her field supervisor to complete a special education reevaluation for a student with autism and reflected on this process in an internship seminar paper. In writing the paper, the intern completed a few self-selected readings to help her think through the recommendations to be included in her evaluation.

To summarize, there are likely at least some university-based requirements to be completed prior to the intern's graduation. When developing assignments, university educators should be thoughtful about how requirements align with interns' professional needs. In turn, interns should treat requirements as meaningful opportunities for learning and complete work strategically based on their own professional goals.

Doctoral Dissertation

For doctoral interns, one requirement that may be particularly challenging is completing a dissertation. Research has suggested that approximately 80% of doctoral-level interns have a significant amount of dissertation work remaining upon internship entry and most interns overestimate how much dissertation progress they will make during the year (Krieshok et al., 2000). Not completing the dissertation by the internship's end results in an All but the Dissertation (ABD) status—having completed all doctoral degree requirements and completed licensure but not having completed the dissertation. Some graduates take many years post-internship to complete the dissertation and others do not finish their dissertation work at all, never completing the doctoral degree (Sternberg, 1981).

Perhaps the greatest obstacle to dissertation completion during the internship is finding the time to work on the project in addition to completing full time internship responsibilities and maintaining some semblance of a personal life. This barrier is particularly problematic given the finding that the number of hours put into dissertation work is the single best predictor of dissertation completion during the internship (Krieshok et al., 2000). Other challenges to dissertation completion include poor self-efficacy regarding the ability to complete the dissertation (Krieshok et al., 2000), as well as perfectionism and procrastination (Green, 1997). In addition, Sternberg (1981) suggested that feeling unsupported by faculty; working with unreliable faculty; lacking a supportive graduate student community; and being unprepared to tackle a dissertation are also obstacles to dissertation completion. Given the difficulties of completing a dissertation *at all*, let alone during the hectic internship year, how can interns successfully finish their dissertation work?

Some recommended actions for interns, internship supervisors, and university educators to promote dissertation progress during the internship are summarized in Table 11.1. Perhaps the most salient point is that interns should begin the internship with some dissertation work already completed. Krieshok et al. (2000) found that interns who had not proposed their dissertations prior to the internship only had a 7% chance of defending by the end of the year. In contrast, 78% of those interns who had a formal proposal meeting prior to beginning the internship made at least some dissertation progress. What is more, nearly 50% of interns who began the internship with data collected and 88% of those who began the internship with complete dissertation drafts, successfully completed and defended their research. The message is clear that the more dissertation progress trainees make prior to the internship, the better. In addition to these recommendations, interns may wish to access any of myriad books written to support students in successfully navigating a doctoral dissertation (e.g., Cone & Foster, 2006; Heppner & Heppner, 2004; Rudestam & Newton, 2015; Single, 2009; Sternberg, 1981; White, 2017).

Degree Audits

Interns should not take for granted that all requirements for the degree have been successfully completed or are in the process of being completed. Instead, degree information should be verified through a degree audit. A degree audit is a computer-generated analysis that allows students and advisors to see a student's academic progress up to that point in time, including courses completed and remaining requirements. Audits are often easily processed through the university registrar's office. Even for individuals that are confident they have completed all requirements, it is useful to get a degree audit because there are sometimes errors in administrative documentation. For example, an advisor may have forgotten to sign or submit a particular form at some point during training. It is recommended that the student gets an audit approximately halfway through the internship year which will provide enough time to decipher and correct any existing errors.

Forms, Deadlines, and Other Details

A final facet of successfully closing out the year from the perspective of trainee involves paying careful attention to deadlines, required forms, and other tasks that if accidentally neglected might be disruptive to graduating. Administrative requirements may be from the training program, a college or department within the university, or the university itself. Examples of common administrative requirements are applying for graduation, ordering a diploma, submitting forms regarding the dissertation, and completing evaluations. Students should proactively seek out information, usually available online, on administrative deadlines and requirements early on during their training. In addition, interns should verify with an academic advisor, the training program coordinator, and/or appropriate university personnel that they have completed everything required for graduation.

TABLE 11.1 Actions Interns, Internship Supervisors, and University Faculty Can Take to Support Dissertation Completion during the School Psychology Internship

Who	Actions to Take
Intern	**Pre-internship:** • Select a school psychology program with a strong research culture, where faculty have a record of supporting trainees' successful dissertation progress and completion. • Collaborate with faculty that are actively involved in research. • Select a dissertation chair with a positive track record (i.e., trainees who work with this professor successfully propose and defend) and consider politics in selecting a committee (see Sternberg, 1981, pp. 138–156). • Be a part of a research team and provide and receive research support. • Develop a research project that is doable. • If possible, align the dissertation work to other requirements (e.g., study something already being worked on; use pre-existing data; use course requirements/deadlines as deadlines to complete parts of the dissertation work). • Complete as much dissertation work as possible prior to beginning the internship, including proposing the dissertation (or *at least* set a proposal meeting date). **During the internship:** • Work on the dissertation a bit every day to create and maintain momentum. • Set clear goals and deadlines. • Maintain communication with training program faculty (especially the dissertation advisor) even if the internship site is geographically far away.

(continued)

TABLE 11.1 *(continued)*

Who	*Actions to Take*
Internship Field Supervisors	• Consider requiring students to propose the dissertation prior to beginning the internship. • Provide interns time during the internship to complete research. • Offer support and encouragement for dissertation progress. • Encourage the student to maintain ties with the university during the internship. • Require an end of year research project that can be aligned with dissertation work.
Training Program Faculty	• Consider requiring students to propose the dissertation prior to beginning the internship. • Be engaged in your own research, model the research process, and encourage trainee involvement/collaboration. • Encourage trainees to be involved in research early in their training sequence. • Encourage trainees to be a part of a research team before and during the dissertation. • Maintain ties with trainees during the internship year. • Work with advisees to set goals and deadlines for dissertation work completion.

If any snafus do arise, they are typically correctable. Interns should bear in mind that university faculty and administrators want students to graduate and will by and large provide pragmatic support.

Closing out Professional Roles and Responsibilities

As described in Chapter 5, in addition to being trainees, interns are burgeoning professionals with a variety of responsibilities. The end of the internship year necessitates terminating and transitioning current cases; saying goodbye to students, staff, and families; and completing requirements for state and/or national certification.

Termination

Termination is a term frequently used by mental health professionals to describe the concluding stage of clinical work during which therapeutic relationships with clients come to an end. In my opinion, the word termination inadvertently conveys a haphazard, hasty, or insensitive ending ("Hasta la vista, baby!"). However, when given sufficient planning and preparation from interns and supervisors, and when approached with sensitivity, termination can be a meaningful process of closure that results in growth for clients and interns (Gelman, Fernandez, Hausman, Miller, & Weiner, 2007). An intern's readiness to facilitate the termination process hinges on (a) understanding clients' reactions to termination; (b) understanding one's own reactions to termination; (c) addressing the fact that the internship role is time limited; and (d) acting strategically during termination with the support of supervision.

Student Reactions to Termination

The majority of interns reading this book are likely concluding internships in school-based settings. For termination with students to be successful, it is helpful for interns to be aware of how students might feel about or react to the relationship coming to an end. In helping relationships, common client reactions to termination include anxiety, depression, anger, and reappearance of symptoms (Baird, 2016). Responses vary per individual based on multiple variables such as the age, personality, length and quality of the relationship, and the client's prior experiences with termination or loss (Baird, 2016; Gelman et al., 2007). Although delivering individual or group counseling may only be one part of an intern's role, other direct service activities (e.g., delivering academic or behavioral interventions) may also involve establishing close relationships with students. Therefore, interns and supervisors should determine together which students need a termination process, anticipate potential reactions these students may have to termination, and strategize how to most effectively say goodbye.

Intern Reactions to Termination

Like their students, interns may also have reactions to closing out the relationships developed during the internship year and these reactions may influence the termination process. Some potential intern reactions to termination described by Baird (2016) include feeling guilty about ending a relationship before the work is complete; feeling that no one else sufficiently understands the client(s) to provide the help needed; or worrying that the next individual will be more effective in helping the student than the intern. It is also not uncommon for an intern to feel a sense of relief about terminating with a particular client or clients. Baird additionally points out that interns' reactions to termination may be affected by their own pending transitions. For example, if an intern feels relief or excitement about finishing the year and moving on to a full-time job it may make it hard to understand a student who has difficulty coping with termination. By recognizing and understanding their own emotions, interns may be more effectively prepared to close their work with students as well as others in the school.

Challenges of Forced Termination

Given the time-limited nature of the intern role, termination may feel forced, premature, or artificial. The work is ending due to completion of the intern's placement rather than achievement of a client's goals or consideration of a client's needs (Gelman et al., 2007). Even though the internship placement finishes rapidly, there are several preventive strategies that interns and supervisors can bear in mind regarding termination. First, knowing the intern will only be at the site for one year, supervisors may decide not to assign the intern as primarily responsible for a student with a history of multiple losses (Baird, 2016). Second, especially in the context of therapy, interns should make the time-limited duration of their work transparent to students from early on (Bundy, 2016; Plotts & Lasser, 2013). As the actual termination date approaches, it is important to provide students with sufficient notice (at least a few weeks in advance) to allow time to appropriately close relationships. Third, there are natural transitions during the school year (e.g., vacations) that may provide a preview of student reactions to termination and a chance for the intern to discuss such issues with the student. Such transitions also may help the intern prepare and practice termination (Gelman et al., 2007).

Strategies for Saying Goodbye to Students

Given the complex nature of termination, it is important for interns (with guidance from supervisors) to be strategic in how they approach this process. Following are a few strategies identified by Bundy (2016) to help facilitate termination:

- Encourage the student to share a self-assessment of progress and share observations regarding student progress. It is helpful to describe behaviors in measurable terms to provide evidence that the student changed.
- Anticipate future challenges the student may encounter and talk through how such concerns might be addressed.
- Identify resources the student might access in the future when having difficulties, and discuss a positive vision of the student's future (i.e., how the student can continue a positive path of progress).
- Write a note to say goodbye, including encouragement for the student's continued growth and learning.

In addition to these strategies, the termination process may be connected to various rituals that recognize an ending and/or transition (Baird, 2016). Semrud-Clikeman (1995) analogized termination as a type of graduation for clients, pointing out that the process should be about success rather than loss. Gelman et al. (2007) suggested that creative activities (e.g., composing a memory book) or having a formal celebration may also be contributors to successful termination. The termination of groups may include similar strategies to those previously discussed, such as an ending celebration that includes refreshments; asking group members to assess the progress they made in the group; the intern providing oral feedback to the group as a whole, and individually to each group member; and the intern writing personalized notes to group members (Bundy, 2016).

Strategies for Saying Goodbye to Colleagues

In addition to saying goodbye to students, interns must also terminate relationships with colleagues. Concluding relationships with supervisors is discussed in greater detail later in this chapter; for now, the focus is on the intern saying goodbye to teachers, administrators, and other staff. Similar to when working with students, interns will want to let their colleagues know in advance when they will be finishing the internship. Although the intern or supervisor may assume others know the intern is leaving the school or district, staff may actually not realize the intern is departing. The intern or field supervisor may wish to make a brief public announcement at a staff meeting regarding the intern's status. If appropriate, the announcement may include congratulations regarding a new job the intern will begin the following year. Supervisors may also wish to organize a farewell party (e.g., a breakfast, lunch, happy hour, or ceremony) that gives the intern and staff members a chance to say goodbye in an informal setting.

It is important for interns to note that saying goodbye to colleagues does not mean cutting off relationships. If the intern stays at the school or district following the internship, or works at the site at any point in the future, these will be the intern's professional colleagues. If the intern is at another site, former colleagues are now part of the individual's professional network and may continue to provide emotional and informational support. Making time for personal goodbyes with administrators such as principals and assistant principals is also critical. Interns should be sure to thank administrators for welcoming them into the site and for providing supporting resources (e.g., office space, time for professional development, the supervisor's time that was devoted to supervision). Administrators may wish to ask interns about the overall internship experience and debrief on what they could do better as a site in supporting future school psychology interns.

Writing letters may provide one means for interns to say goodbye to colleagues. Just like sending a letter of introduction to staff at the beginning of the year, interns can send out a universal goodbye note via email, as a letter placed in staff mailboxes, or as a posting in the staff lounge. Interns are also encouraged to write personal thank you notes to any staff they developed special relationships with during the year.

How Supervisors Can Support Interns During Termination

As with other professional tasks during the internship, terminating with students may be a new activity for many interns; having adequate supervisory support during this process is essential. Baird (2016) described several ways field and university supervisors can support interns to smoothly close out the internship year:

- In training programs that require a university seminar, time can be devoted to discussing termination issues in general and with regard to specific concerns interns are facing. Issues of *content* (i.e., what is involved in termination) and *process* (i.e., how to terminate) should be addressed.
- Field supervisors can assist interns in understanding reactions to termination (both from students and the intern) and offer strategies to prevent and respond to such reactions.
- Termination of the supervisor-supervisee relationship can be treated as a model for the termination between the intern and students. Supervisor-supervisee termination discussions may model cognitive (e.g., assessment of strengths, challenges, progress during training, and future directions) and affective (e.g., feelings about one another, the supervision experience, and termination) components that will also be included in intern-student termination.
- Field supervisors and interns should discuss how cases are finishing, if the student will need to work with another individual (e.g., an incoming intern, the supervisor, another staff member), and how best to make such a transition.

In sum, termination is a complex process that requires a great deal of thought and planning. When executed carefully, the termination process can provide opportunities for the intern to say goodbye to students and colleagues, achieve closure on the work they have done together, and celebrate a successful year.

Credentialing

As the year closes out, most interns will apply for state certification or licensure (terminology varies by state but will be referred to here as credential) as a school psychologist in order to legally practice school psychology in public schools. In addition to local credentials, some school psychologists pursue various national credentials and some doctoral-level school psychologists may eventually seek clinical licensure (Rossen, 2014). Given the numerous types of state and national credentials, graduating interns may be unclear about their options. Credentialing processes are briefly described in the sections that follow.

State Credential

Each state delineates its own credentialing requirements for school-based practice as a school psychologist. On NASP's (2019b) website is a recently updated list of school psychology credentialing requirements by state, including step-by-step credentialing procedures, continuing education requirements to maintain credentials, whether the state accepts the Nationally Certified School Psychologist (NCSP) as an alternative route to credentialing, scope of practice in the state, and contact information for the state department of education. This webpage is a helpful starting point in getting ready to apply for local credentialing as a school psychologist.

In addition, school psychology program faculty members as well as field supervisors tend to be knowledgeable about credentialing processes and can provide clarification and support as interns are applying for their credentials. In fact, most have even gone through these processes themselves. Former students who have recently become credentialed are also excellent resources for information. Sometimes hiring districts, through an administrative supervisor or human resources staff, may also provide support to newly hired school psychologists to navigate state credentialing processes. Prior to submitting materials, interns are encouraged to contact the state department of education credentialing office to make sure they have correctly followed all steps towards attaining the local credential.

National Certification

The NASP created the National School Psychology Certification System (NSPCS) to credential school psychologists who meet nationally recognized school psychology qualifications. Graduating trainees from NASP-approved and non-approved programs may be eligible for the NCSP and both NASP members and non-members can apply. Although the NCSP is not required for school psychology practice (i.e., only state certification is needed), according to NASP (2019a) there are several reasons why it may be advantageous to obtain the NCSP degree:

- *Professional recognition.* The NCSP designation signifies the school psychologist has met national standards for training and may enhance the individual's professional recognition, reputation, and credibility.
- *Professional accountability.* The NCSP conveys the school psychologist's commitment to professionalism and ethical school psychology practice.
- *Professional identity and growth.* Continuing professional development is required for maintenance of the NCSP.
- *Professional benefits.* The NCSP is recognized in 33 states as of the publication of this book and is also recognized for reciprocity of credentialing. Therefore, having the NCSP may allow the school psychologist greater ease of mobility if moving to another state. Further, some states and school districts award salary bonuses to NCSPs.

NCSP requirements include (a) completion of sixty graduate semester/ninety quarter hours of study in school psychology (at least fifty-four semester hours/ eighty-one quarter hours of which are exclusive of internship experience) in a school psychology program; (b) completion of a sequence of supervised practicum experiences prior to the internship; (c) successful completion of a 1,200-hour internship in school psychology, with at least 600 hours in a school setting; (d) a passing score (147, as of January, 2019) on the School Psychologist Praxis Test 5402 administered by the Educational Testing Service; and (e) actively engaging in ongoing professional learning. The NCSP must be renewed every three years. The reader is referred to materials available on NASP's website for a full description of the application process and requirements to obtain the NCSP.

Psychologist Licensure

Individuals who are completing a doctoral degree in school psychology may wish to pursue licensure as a psychologist through state Departments of Health Services. Licensure is a prerequisite for independent professional practice as a psychologist and is intended to protect the public and to assure quality service delivery (Association of State and Provincial Psychology Boards, ASPPB, 2019). The ASPPB is an alliance of agencies responsible for the licensure of psychologists in the United States and Canada. According to the ASPPB *PSY|Book* (2019), typical jurisdictional requirements for licensure as a psychologist include: (a) a doctoral degree from a program acceptable to the licensure board (often including APA accreditation); (b) a specified number of hours of supervised experience (usually at least 3,000, with 1,500 being postdoctoral); (c) passing the Examination for Professional Practice in Psychology (EPPP) and, anticipated to launch in January, 2020, the EPPP Part 2; (d) administrative requirements including payment of fees; (e) continuing professional development to maintain licensure; and (f) the expectation that the psychologist will practice within the scope of his or her education and training.

Other Credentials

Crespi (2010) and Rossen (2014) identified and described numerous additional credentials school psychology graduates may pursue. Interested readers are referred to these helpful resources to learn more about credentialing options and procedures for school psychologists. A central issue is that since there are an incredible number of credentialing options, knowing what is available and pursuing these credentials is a daunting task (Crespi, 2010; Hall, Wexelbaum, & Boucher, 2007). As stated by Crespi (2010), "Sometimes more is not better. Sometimes it is only more" (p. 243). It is advisable for students to research and contemplate options prior to even beginning school psychology training or selecting an internship (Hall et al., 2007). If such pre-planning has not occurred, it will be helpful for interns to seek out selected faculty or field mentors to discuss potential professional pursuits and what the intern needs to do to achieve his or her professional goals.

Closing out Supervisee Responsibilities

In addition to concluding trainee and professional responsibilities, the intern must close out the year as a supervisee, including (a) completing and reviewing summative evaluations; (b) terminating supervisor-supervisee relationships; and (c) thinking about supervision and future professional learning.

Summative Evaluations

As discussed in previous chapters of this book, evaluation is a critical component of supervision during the school psychology internship. Summative evaluation occurs at the end of a period of time and is used to make supervisory decisions such as whether or not an intern is ready to enter the field (Harvey & Struzziero, 2008). Summative evaluations may be completed by field supervisors, university supervisors, and interns. As described elsewhere in this text, field and university supervisors will want to evaluate knowledge of content, application of skills, and professionalism. Interns can complete self-assessments as well as assessments of their field and university experiences. Interns and supervisors should complete formative evaluations throughout the year and discuss and address any concerns that arise. Therefore, summative evaluation results should not be surprising for any party.

Nonetheless, providing and accepting critical feedback at the end of the year can be a challenge for interns and supervisors. Interns often hope to hear nothing but praise from supervisors during a final evaluation and supervisors likely want to provide positive reviews of interns' work (Baird, 2016). Although praise is an important part of evaluations, supervisors should also identify areas in which the intern can continue to progress. After all, the intern's career as a school psychologist is just beginning. To help increase interns' receptiveness to feedback, supervisors may ask interns to share a self-evaluation including strengths and areas for continued growth (Baird, 2016). Supervisors can also model receptiveness to feedback by encouraging interns to share evaluations of the internship experience, including internship supervision.

Terminating the Supervisor-Supervisee Relationship

In addition to formally ending relationships with students and colleagues, the intern must conclude relationships developed with supervisors. Depending on the nature of the supervisory relationship, this process may be more or less challenging. As described by Baird (2016):

> The breadth of feelings expressed at termination ranges from bland to profound. I have supervised interns with whom lasting relationships were developed and with whom I still maintain contact. On the other hand, I'm sorry to say that in some cases it seems I have scarcely known my interns, and they have known little about me . . . talking about these issues at termination can help bring a resolution to the supervision relationship that makes it easier for both intern and supervisor to move on.
>
> *(p. 161)*

No matter how the close the dyad, explicitly discussing and concluding the supervisory relationship is an important part of the supervision process. When relationship issues are not addressed, it may prevent interns or supervisors from feeling closure and perhaps even obstruct moving onward to future endeavors (e.g., the supervisor beginning a new supervisory relationship or the intern confidently beginning a new job).

Final Site Visits

At the end of the internship, university supervisors should initiate a final contact with the field supervisor(s) and the intern. The final meeting may occur over the phone, via teleconference, or in person. Topics that may be addressed during a final site visit are consistent with the content of this chapter so far and include (a) termination and closing out or transitioning cases; (b) summative evaluations; and (c) the transition from the internship into professional practice. Relevant questions within each of these areas that can be addressed during the final site visit are listed in Table 11.2. In my own experience, I find the end of the year sneaks up suddenly and interns and supervisors appreciate using site visits as an opportunity to stop, reflect on, and discuss the conclusion of the internship.

TABLE 11.2 Topics to be Addressed During Final Site Visits

Topic	Questions for Consideration
Termination and Closing/ Transitioning Cases	• Has the intern begun to terminate relationships with students and staff? • What termination issues have come up, if any? How have they been addressed? • How will cases the intern worked on be transitioned? • Is there any information that the intern needs to transfer to the field supervisor?
Summative Evaluations	• What progress has the intern made towards goals developed throughout the internship year? • What areas will require continued support as the intern transitions to his or her first year of professional practice? • What constructive feedback does the intern have for the internship supervisor regarding the field-based experience? • What constructive feedback does the intern have for the university supervisor regarding training program support during the internship?
Transition into Professional Practice	• Where is the intern in the job process? What supports are needed from supervisors? • What are common issues in the early career that the intern should bear in mind upon his or her transition (e.g., need for ongoing supervision and professional learning)? • What are some steps the intern can take immediately prior to or upon beginning a new position? • What resources should the intern access from field supervisors prior to ending the internship? • Does the intern have any questions regarding obtaining state or national certification/licensure?

Summary

Concluding the internship year involves the intern closing out responsibilities associated with the roles of trainee, professional, and supervisee. As a trainee, the intern must be sure to complete all school psychology program and university requirements. Faculty can align assignments with other internship requirements and interns can shape assignments to meet individualized needs. For doctoral students, completing the doctoral dissertation during the internship is a challenge. Getting started on the research prior to beginning the internship is a strong predictor of progress. Interns are advised to seek a degree audit prior to graduation to make sure they are ready to graduate and should also pay careful attention to required forms and deadlines.

As burgeoning professionals, interns work with numerous students and staff with whom they must say goodbye. Termination is a complex process that results in mixed feelings from the intern as well as those he or she has worked with. The fact that the internship is time limited means that some relationships may end somewhat abruptly. Interns should give advanced notice and be transparent with others about when they are leaving and plan with supervisors about how to best approach termination. Applying for state and/or national certification or licensure and planning to pursue clinical licensure or other credentialing options are also part of closing out professional responsibilities.

Finally, interns must conclude supervisee responsibilities. Completing and discussing summative evaluations helps serve the gatekeeping function of supervision and allows interns and supervisors to critically reflect on the intern's professional growth in an observable and measurable way. Supervisors and supervisees must close out the supervisory relationship, which may act as a model for other terminations the intern will facilitate. University supervisors should complete a final site visit where a formal discussion about concluding the internship may take place.

Critical Thinking Questions and Activities

The following are critical thinking questions for interns, field supervisors, and university supervisors to ponder as the internship year comes to an end.

For Interns:

- How did your internship goals and internship plan change throughout the year?
- What, if any, issues related to termination covered in this chapter might impact how you close out your internship experience? How will you address these issues?
- Write out three lessons you have learned during the year. Lessons may be learned from negative or positive experiences. How will you apply these lessons in the future?

For Field Supervisors:

- How will you terminate the supervisor-supervisee relationship with your intern?
- How will you support the intern to terminate relationships with students and staff?
- Write out three lessons you have learned during the year. Lessons may be learned from negative or positive experiences. How will you apply these lessons in your future supervision of interns?

For University Supervisors:

- What program or university assignments do interns from your training program have to complete? What is the purpose of these requirements?
- What level of scaffolding is it appropriate to provide for students with regard to completing program and university requirements?
- Write out three lessons you have learned during the year. Lessons may be learned from negative or positive experiences. How will you apply these lessons in your future supervision of interns?

12

THE EARLY CAREER

Déjà Vu and All Things New

The end of the internship is followed in rapid succession by the beginning of the first year of professional practice. The transition will bring familiar feelings (e.g., anxiety, curiosity, anticipation, excitement) and experiences (e.g., entering a new setting, meeting new colleagues, learning the ropes), as well as new challenges and opportunities. This chapter is intended to support the transition from intern to early career practitioner. Distinct characteristics, needs, and challenges associated with the early career stage are described. The importance of supervision and mentoring in promoting a successful transition from trainee to professional is also highlighted. The chapter closes with critical thinking questions and activities for former interns to consider as they become early career school psychologists.

First, Take a Breath

Before diving into what's next, it is important to take stock of the year that was. Acknowledging the professional milestone of completing training should be celebrated with colleagues, family, and friends. Rewarding oneself by taking a well-earned vacation or even a tangible reward recognizing this accomplishment is appropriate (especially given the promise of a forthcoming salary!). Notably, shifting from an intensive experience such as the internship to a more relaxed, quiet period such as the summer following the internship can result in an experience of let-down. A let-down effect might manifest itself in depressed feelings, increased vulnerability to illness (Schoen, 2001), or migraine headaches (Lipton et al., 2014). Therefore, it is advisable to recommit to the kinds of self-care practices described in Chapters 6 and 9 as these may have been neglected when the internship year came to a crescendo. This includes incorporating stress monitoring and stress management techniques such as relaxation and breathing practice

(Lipton et al., 2014) into one's repertoire *before* the internship is complete, *after* it has ended, and *during* the transition to a new role. As was true during the internship, habits of self-care can act as invaluable protective tools during the first year of practice, during the early career, and beyond.

Early Career: A Distinct Professional Stage

Now it is time to enter the early career, considered the first five to ten years of psychologists' professional practice. It is a time that is exhilarating, intimidating, and fraught with several unique challenges. Rønnestad and Skovholt (2013) identified a *novice professional phase* of development for therapists and counselors within their first five years of practice which applies equally well to early career school psychologists. The phase is "highly intense and engaging . . . with many challenges to master and many choices to be made" (Rønnestad & Skovholt, 2013, p. 83). Four key developmental tasks to be navigated by novice professionals such as early career school psychologists are summarized and exemplified in Table 12.1.

In addition to these developmental challenges, novice professionals are confronted with several other issues, which are explored in the sections that follow. Many early career psychologists experience more than one of these challenges at a given time, further compounding the issues. Reviewing common challenges is intended to establish that these are typical or expected, so please do not despair or become overwhelmed. Methods for addressing and overcoming common difficulties are also provided, including an extensive exploration of the important role of supervision and mentoring during the early career.

Imposter Phenomenon

A recent intern graduate might look in the mirror and see a trainee who is not quite ready to tackle independent practice, even when others look and see a competent, professional school psychologist. The *imposter phenomenon* (IP) is

> a subjective experience of phoniness in people who believe that they are not intelligent, capable, or creative despite evidence of high achievement, and who are highly motivated to achieve but live in perpetual fear of being 'found out' or exposed as frauds.
>
> *(Colman, 2015, p. 368)*

IP has been documented as common for individuals entering a new experience, such as graduate trainees transitioning into professional practice (e.g., Hutchins & Rainbolt, 2017), and across several different specific populations such as high-achieving women (e.g., see Clance & Imes, 1978, who coined the term) and individuals from minority backgrounds (e.g., Cokley, McClain, Enciso, & Martinez, 2013).

TABLE 12.1 Rønnestad and Skovholt's (2013) Novice Professional Stage Applied to Early Career School Psychologists

Developmental Task	ESCP Example
Developing a professional identity, including a commitment to the profession.	First-year practitioner Kendra renews her NASP membership even though it is not required as it was by her training program. She also applies for her Nationally Certified School Psychologist (NCSP) credential although she is already certified at the state level.
Moving from dependence to independence.	Harriet, a first-year practitioner, is excited to be free of training program demands. However, she is also nervous and uncertain to be working without the immediate supervisory support she had available last year when she was a school psychologist intern.
Overcoming disillusionment with self, training, and the profession.	Ivan, a second-year practitioner, is feeling inadequate at his job. He is expected to lead a new PBIS initiative in a high school setting but received only limited exposure to PBIS during his school psychology training, which was focused on the primary grades.
Continuing to explore and define professional roles.	Over her first three years of practice, ECSP Dawn realizes she finds her work consulting with teachers to be an effective practice and one she enjoys. She begins to seek out additional opportunities for consultation and limits time spent in less effective, less enjoyable roles.

Note. ECSP = early career school psychologist.

Experiencing IP is linked with psychological distress, life and work dissatisfaction (Sakulku & Alexander, 2011), and negative work outcomes such as avoiding opportunities, procrastinating work, and over-working to compensate for feeling like a fraud (Hutchins & Rainbolt, 2017). Hutchins and Rainbolt (2017) found gender differences in IP coping styles, with women using more active strategies (e.g., seeking instrumental and emotional support; altering misperceptions through external feedback) and men more avoidant strategies (e.g., ignoring IP concerns; working harder). The authors suggested active coping strategies are healthier mechanisms to overcome IP.

Additionally, it can be useful to explicitly label IP when experiencing it and to acknowledge it as a common occurrence. Although they might not be talking about it publicly, many colleagues likely have experienced IP. In fact, approximately 70% of the population experiences IP at some point in time (Gravois, 2007). Even venerated author Maya Angelou was affected by this phenomenon: "I have written 11 books, but each time I think, 'Uh oh, they're going to find out now. I've run a game on everybody, and they're going to find me out'" (Richards, 2015).

In addition to labeling the phenomenon, reframing imposter thoughts and beliefs can be helpful. Author of the popular book *Mindset: The New Psychology of Success*,

Carol Dweck (2016) reminds us that "becoming is better than being" (p. 25). The early career can be conceived as continuing one's professional learning, putting new knowledge and skills into action (ideally with ongoing supervisory support), and building on competence to eventually establish expertise. Acknowledging achievements and owning them (e.g., crediting hard work rather than luck or happenstance for success) is helpful in overcoming IP. So too is "acting as if" – the process of shifting one's self-perception and mindset to that of a competent professional and in turn behaving consistently with this perception. The notion of "acting as if" is different from practicing outside of one's boundaries of competence. The former is a mantra put forth to help new, competent school psychologists align their self-confidence and self-efficacy to be consistent with their actual knowledge and skills. However, if one does not have the prior knowledge or skills to engage in a particular activity, it is an ethical imperative to seek out consultation or supervision, as described elsewhere in this text.

VIGNETTE 12.1 **REGAN'S IMPOSTER PHENOMENON**

First-year school psychologist Regan was asked to provide training on curriculum-based measurement to all teachers in her elementary school. She had extensive background knowledge on the content from her graduate training program and she also had previously supported benchmarking and progress monitoring during her practica and internship training experiences. Although she was confident in her content knowledge, she had only provided a professional training to teachers once before and that was in tandem with her internship supervisor. Although she felt a bit nervous, Regan decided to "act as if" it's no big deal. She requested a presentation template on the topic from her former supervisor, talked to her building principal and teachers about what they were interested in learning from the presentation, and made sure to include the suggested content. She spent some time rehearsing the presentation but did not over-rehearse, especially given how busy she was with learning her new position. The presentation was successful, helped Regan build her confidence, and established her as a valuable resource to her new colleagues.

Financial Challenges

Financial stressors abound in the early career. For example, many new psychologists are faced with high and increasing levels of loan debt (Doran, Kraha, Marks, Ameen, & El-Ghoroury, 2016). Consulting with a financial planner could be a helpful action step at this point in time as debt can be considered in the context of a new salary, living expenses, and overall budget. Further, as explored briefly in Chapter 10, gathering data about expected salaries for prospective positions prior to applying to/accepting a job is an important step. Field and university internship supervisors and other mentors can act as advisors for this process (Green &

Hawley, 2009), including determining what, if any, leeway exists to negotiate salary or benefits.

Additional costs accrue for doctoral-level psychologists interested in independent practice who will complete supervised post-doctoral hours for licensure. Some individuals must pay fees to access supervision. Study materials for licensure exams, as well as the licensure application process itself, can also be expensive (Doran et al., 2016). For tenure-track early career academics, obtaining research funding is considered critical at many institutions; however, most grants are quite competitive. One strategy is to begin by applying for grants specifically targeted to early career professionals (e.g., the Early Career Development and Mentoring Grant through the Institution of Education Sciences' National Center for Special Education Research) or early career school psychologists specifically (e.g., the Society for the Study of School Psychology's Early Career Research Award), which can act as building blocks for future funding.

Challenges for Diverse and Women Early Career Psychologists

The profession of psychology is becoming increasingly diverse (APA, 2017b), as is the field of school psychology (Walcott & Hyson, 2018).[1] Furthermore, data suggest that increasing numbers of women are entering the psychology profession and women outnumber men in psychology (APA, 2017b) and school psychology (Walcott & Hyson, 2018). New professional psychologists from marginalized and traditionally underrepresented groups and women early career psychologists are faced with several unique personal, professional, and workplace issues not experienced in the same way by male colleagues or those from majority backgrounds.

Diversity in the Early Career

Diverse early career psychologists, across psychology specialties, may experience oppression and discrimination in their work, both blatant (e.g., a client not wanting to work with an individual from a minority background; a supervisor denying perceptions of racism in an organization) and subtle (e.g., being considered an expert on diversity whether or not one has this expertise and subsequently being "continually placed in a position of having to direct cultural questions elsewhere, which may lead to a reputation of not being well-informed" [Pedrotti & Burnes, 2016, p. 144]). Less overt (but not less harmful) biased actions are *microaggressions,* or "brief and commonplace daily, verbal, behavioral, and environmental indignities, whether intentional or unintentional, that communicate hostile, derogatory, or negative racial slights and insults to the target person or group" (Sue et al., 2007, p. 271). Whether subtle or flagrant, experiences of oppression and/or marginalization by members of culturally marginalized groups require distinct supports, with mentoring and supervision particularly critical, as discussed later in this chapter.

Pedrotti and Burnes (2016) offered several additional suggestions for supporting diverse early career psychologists, including:

- Senior colleagues of diverse early career psychologists focusing on becoming aware of, acknowledging and shifting existing power differentials in their settings, including being willing to recognize and address bias, discrimination, and microaggressions faced by non-majority colleagues;
- Organizations committing to systems-level changes, such as offering time and space for staff teaching and learning related to cultural responsiveness and competency development; and
- Graduate training programs including more information during preservice level training about diversity, in turn enhancing early career psychologists' awareness of these issues and creating a culture that values and supports diverse professionals.

Although early career psychologists might not have the capacity to directly change or influence each of these features of their work settings, they can seek out professional opportunities in settings where such practices are the norm and avoid those where they are not. Further, it is not only the responsibility of non-majority individuals to advocate about these issues; it is also up to organizational leaders and allied colleagues to provide supports for diverse early career psychologists.

Women Early Career Psychologists

Meanwhile, in professional psychology at large, women psychologists lag behind men in areas such as salary (making 78% as much as men, as of 2010), and continue to be underrepresented in terms of status (e.g., full professor) and leadership roles (e.g., journal editor) in the field (APA, 2017b). A study by O'Shaughnessy and Burnes (2016) found that challenges for women early career psychologists include maintaining a work-life balance while establishing a family and navigating the responsibilities of motherhood. In short, there is evidence of both a glass ceiling and a maternal wall for women psychologists (O'Shaughnessy & Burnes, 2016). APA's (2018) Committee on Early Career Psychologists describes women early career psychologists as engaged in a juggling act requiring focus, practice, and persistence. It is suggested that they evaluate their values and life priorities and recognize that it is simply not possible to do everything at once, and that is okay. For example, despite conventional wisdom that children of working mothers are at a disadvantage compared to peers with one working parent, fifty years of research suggests that infants and toddlers with working moms do not suffer atypical academic or behavioral difficulties (Lucas-Thompson, Goldberg, & Prause, 2010).

Unique Early Career School Psychologist Challenges

In addition to the challenges outlined thus far that are pertinent to all early career psychologists, some distinct challenges arise for early career school psychologists. The school setting is a uniquely complex organizational setting, with school psychologists' roles informed by numerous local and federal educational mandates. School psychologists' roles are also multi-faceted, demanding competency across a wide swath of domains upon entry to practice (NASP, 2010a).

Recent school psychology specific research suggests that challenges of the job, ethical issues in practice, and experiences of burnout are intertwined. In a national survey of school psychologists, Schilling et al. (2018) found 90% of respondents reported feelings of burnout, which were linked with experiencing role overload and a lack of administrative support. Other research has demonstrated that school psychologists perceive pressures to practice unethically, including administrators urging them to make decisions that do not comply with state or federal law (Boccio et al., 2016), and needing to practice outside boundaries of competence due to a lack of supervision access (Silva et al., 2016). In the Boccio et al. study (2016), school psychologists who reported experiencing pressure to practice unethically reported higher levels of burnout, less job satisfaction, and a greater desire to leave their current position and the field of school psychology than those who did not perceive such pressures. Across these three studies, supervision and mentoring are emphasized as potential protective support factors for new psychologists.

Supervision and Mentoring in the Early Career as Key Protective Mechanisms

Supervision is considered to be pivotal for the initial and ongoing professional development of school psychologists (NASP, 2016, 2018). In fact, NASP (2010c) *Standards for the Credentialing of School Psychologists* recommends early career school psychologists engage in a period of induction/professional development upon entering a new setting and participate in supervision or mentoring for at least one hour per week. Further, the first renewal of the NCSP credential now requires a demonstration of one year of post-graduate supervision or mentoring. Yet in a survey of 700 early career school psychologists, less than one third reported receiving clinical supervision and the majority of those individuals for less than one hour per week (Silva et al., 2016). These data stand in contrast with additional results from the same survey, which suggested 68% of early career school psychologists were interested in receiving mentoring or supervision, and 97% viewed engaging in supervision to be somewhat or very important in the early career. There are a number of reasons why supervision is not consistently accessed, such as time, availability, and geographical distance from a supervisor. However, gaps between desired and accessed supervision for those in the early career should be considered problematic.

Mentoring Versus Supervision

Up to this point in the book, processes of supervision have been emphasized that are consistent with the focus on the school psychology internship as part of graduate training. However, mentoring also plays a potentially important role in supporting early career school psychologists. Based on characteristics put forth by APA (2006b) and NASP (2016), *professional mentoring* is defined here as a non-evaluative process by which a mentor or mentors, an individual or individuals with expertise in a particular field, support(s) the career development, professional performance and development of a mentee, or person in the role of learner in the same field, by acting as a role model and support system. This definition is purposefully broad because mentors and mentees can hold a variety of roles and positions relative to each other (e.g., hierarchical vs. peer mentoring) across a variety of settings (e.g., professional settings, organizations, online) and the level of formality can vary from informal to formal. Mentoring is situated in this definition as "professional" in that the relationship is situated within the field of school psychology rather than across disciplines, although sometimes mentoring occurs across professions (e.g., a veteran teacher as a first-year mentor for a school psychologist).

NASP (2016) recently published a document entitled *Guidance for Postgraduate Mentorship and Professional Support* (available via open access on NASP's website), which aims to support new psychologists in structuring effective professional support and mentoring relationships following graduation from school psychology training. The document outlines differences between practicum and internship supervision and postgraduate professional supports; characteristics, roles, and responsibilities of effective mentors and mentees; and process considerations for effective mentoring. In the document, mentoring is also explicitly differentiated from supervision. A supervisor has direct responsibility and vicarious liability for supervisee actions and evaluates the supervisee; that process requires two hours per week (internship) predominately in an individual, face-to-face format. In comparison, a mentor does not have responsibility or liability for the mentee, who is a credentialed professional. Further, mentoring is non-evaluative, is recommended (rather than required) for one hour per week, and permits formats beyond individual, face-to-face meetings (e.g., group, virtual).

Mentoring and supervision are alike in that they both serve a teaching/learning function, provide emotional supports, can lead to enhanced service delivery, and are goal-oriented with goals potentially linked with techniques such as assessment, feedback, and deliberate practice of skills (see Goodyear & Rousmaniere, 2017). Overall, mentoring appears to be more accessible to early career school psychologists than supervision, with 55% of participants in the Silva et al. (2016) sample reporting availability of mentoring (vs. 38% for supervision), and 40% accessing mentoring (vs. 29% for supervision). Given that supervision is an evaluative process, there might be additional accountability built in for all participating parties, perhaps enhancing this process. However, as suggested by NASP (2016), mentoring can also include formal expectations and structures. In sum, if learning is to continue throughout the career, postgraduate professional supports such as supervision and mentoring can both be considered important tools.

Seeking out a Supervisor or Mentor

Accessing supervision or mentoring depends on a variety of factors. Interns can inquire about the potential availability of these supports as they interview for professional positions (see Chapter 10) and for some this information may inform employment decision-making. Examples of professional supports that would be appropriate to ask about during the interview stage include: availability of clinical supervision in addition to administrative supervision; availability of mentoring for new school psychologists, including professional mentoring (e.g., from another school psychologist within the same school district) and other mentoring (e.g., from another staff member in the building); how many other school psychologists are in the school district; and how professional learning is provided within the psychological services unit, including processes by which peer support could be accessed.

Former supervisors, including internship supervisors and faculty members, are often willing and eager to provide ongoing mentoring supports even when the former intern is no longer officially their supervisee. Peer supports also continue to be important, such as staying in touch with former classmates and interns from other universities that worked within the same district; together, a peer mentoring network can be established. It is also possible to access mentoring through professional organizations such as NASP and APA. For example, NASP currently offers a *Find-A-Mentor Program* that connects prospective mentees with volunteer mentors from the field, with the intention of supporting ongoing professional growth. Getting involved in professional special interest groups or organizational leadership opportunities provides additional avenues to access mentoring.

Supervision and Mentoring for Diverse and Women Early Career Psychologists

As previously mentioned, for early career psychologists from diverse backgrounds, as well women early career psychologists, mentoring and supervision opportunities can play as a protective factor in the early career, helping them navigate through a variety of challenges. Green and Hawley (2009) suggested that mentoring can support diverse early career psychologists in reflecting on career trajectory, enhancing professional networks, counseling about financial issues, balancing personal and professional identity, and identifying and securing leadership positions in the profession. Several authors have pointed to the importance of recognizing demographics such as gender, culture, ethnicity, sexuality, and race in mentoring graduate trainees and early career psychologists (e.g., Alvarez, Blume, Cervantes, & Thomas, 2009; Daniel, 2009; Russell & Horne, 2009). The relative ease or difficulty of finding a mentor with a similar background or identity is context dependent, differing by geographical location and professional setting (O'Shaughnessy & Burnes, 2016). Green and Hawley (2009) concluded, based on extant research, that mentor-mentee similarity with respect to demographics is less important for successful mentoring than the mentor's awareness, acknowledgement and appreciation of the mentee's diversity.

Supports from Professional Organizations

A variety of supports geared specifically to early career school psychologists are available through professional organizations such as APA, Division 16 (D16) of the APA, NASP, the SSSP, the Trainers of School Psychologists (TSP), and state psychology and school psychology organizations. Examples of resources from these organizations include early career targeted webinars and convention programming; blog posts; online materials and handouts; funding for attending professional conferences; research funding; and awards to recognize early career contributions. Many of these groups have leadership committees which develop and maintain early career resources and advocate on behalf of early career professionals. Getting involved in a leadership role in one of these groups can act as a resource in and of itself, as it provides opportunities for self-advocacy as well as insights into organizations and the profession. Each organization targets different groups and subgroups of early career school psychologists. For example, NASP generally provides more practitioner-targeted resources while SSSP is more geared toward school psychology academics. Early career school psychologists can benefit from reviewing each organization's website to determine which resources are currently available and how to access them.

Listservs and Social Media

In addition to the aforementioned resources, organizations often offer opportunities to connect via professional listservs and community groups. Several non-affiliated professional groups have also emerged on social media platforms, such as moderated Facebook groups. Listservs and community groups allow for ECSPs to receive immediate feedback and advice from colleagues (including practitioners and academics with a range of expertise and years of experience) on pressing issues, to home in on particular areas of practice interest, and to connect with colleagues with similar interests. NASP currently has approximately forty "Communities" for members to join, including one specifically targeting early career school psychologists. Listservs and social media groups also allow early career school psychologists to learn about what colleagues are doing in different regions in the country, receive information on the latest evidence-based practices in the field, share resources with others, and become active members of the professional community.

Although accessing feedback via listservs or social media can be helpful, several cautions are worth mentioning. Listservs sometimes have a narrow range of respondents who reply to issues and it is possible to not get a response or a receive a response that is less than helpful. Sometimes responses contradict one another and it can be challenging to discriminate facts from opinion or to determine the actual expertise level of respondents. Some school psychology social media groups are dominated by posts focused on venting and commiserating with colleagues. Although such groups are a great source of humorous memes and can help normalize common professional challenges, they also risk becoming a forum for complaining rather than supporting professional learning. Ideally joining a listserv or community group will result in expanded knowledge, resources, efficacy, and effectiveness.

Now that common early career challenges and strategies to overcome them have been discussed, the chapter shifts to focus on a strategy for early career school psychologists to make the most of their first three years.

The First Three Years: Learn the Job, Do the Job, Change the Job

When asked for advice about transitioning from training to practice, a school psychologist supervisor for one of my current University of Cincinnati graduate students put it this way: "First year, learn the job; second year, do the job; third year, change the job." This kernel of wisdom provides a helpful framework for highlighting key strategies as new school psychologists enter and progress in their new roles.

First Year, Learn the Job

Recent school psychology training program graduates come to their new positions with state-of-the-art training focused on contemporary best practices in the field, as well as a passion to make a difference for students. Most early career school psychologists are from the Millennial generation, born between 1980 and 2000, ages twenty-three to thirty-nine as of 2019, a group popularly known for being civic-minded, results-driven and impatient in waiting for change. However, before diving in head first to attempt systems change, it is essential to survey the terrain. Transitioning into a new setting begins with *entry* (see Chapter 4), learning about the school or organizational culture and being accepted into it, a process that ostensibly *precedes* effectively doing the job and making eventual changes in the system (Newman & Rosenfield, 2019).

New school psychologists should reflect upon a number of questions when entering the first year of practice and learning the job; here are some examples that stem from Chapter 4, focused on a similar process of internship entry:

- What is the school or organizational culture?
- What opportunities for collaboration with colleagues are available?
- How is the school psychologist role defined in this setting?
- What are administrators' expectations for my role?
- What are other colleagues' expectations for my role?
- How do others' expectations align with my developing professional identity?
- What are the best ways for me to meet and connect with my new colleagues personally and professionally?
- What questions do I have and who do I ask?
- What professional supports (e.g., mentoring, supervision) will be available to me in this school?

Consistent with internship entry, many of these topics can be addressed before the first year begins. For example, if possible, new school psychologists should schedule time to meet with the building principal(s) at their school(s) during the summer months (most administrators are on twelve-month contracts) to discuss expectations for the year to come. Some individuals are even able to make connections within their hiring districts or schools when they are still interns, meeting with building administrators, heads of psychological service units, or other school psychologists. Of course, such advanced planning is not always possible. Many school psychologists are hired by a district but do not find out their school placements until late in the summer and other individuals might not secure a position until immediately before the school year begins. The point here is that new school psychologists enter settings which possess preexisting, invisible norms and regularities that impact how services will best be delivered. Therefore, it is essential to build relationships and learn the school culture as soon as possible.

In addition to building relationships and learning about the system, first-year school psychologists continue to learn about the profession, as well as the content knowledge and process skills needed to be a successful school psychologist. In some ways the first year of practice is akin to building an airplane while flying it. The year pushes forward, services are delivered to students and caregivers, meetings are held, mistakes are made, and the learning process continues. It is not that the first-year school psychologist is ineffective (although many say that it feels that way!). However, it can be overwhelming to learn the job and do the job simultaneously. By the end of the year, once the ECSP has learned about the school's culture, become an accepted member within the system, and gained some knowledge, skills, and confidence for practice, it is possible to do the job with increased effectiveness.

Second Year, Do the Job

Relationships established during year one can be built upon, as can a track record of effective service delivery, which in turn enhances the acceptability and desirability of services offered. For example, a teacher might recommend the school psychologist's consultation services to another colleague given her own positive experiences as a consultee. A foundation of trust can be built with the building principal and other administrators, which results in becoming a part of a school's leadership team. Relationships with families and students have also begun to be developed, allowing the school psychologist to hit the ground running in year two, for example communicating in advance about intervention services being offered and enhancing the quality of home-school partnerships.

Administrative systems developed during the first year (e.g., an organizational tracking system for initial evaluations and reevaluations) will make task performance more efficient during year two. For example, practitioners frequently comment that report writing time considerably decreases from the internship to the first year to subsequent years. As efficiency increases, more time becomes available for school psychologists to make the position their own. In other words, by the third year of practice it becomes increasingly possible to change the job.

Third Year, Change the Job

New professionals often have a predominately internal, self-conscious focus regarding their work (e.g., "Am I doing this correctly?"). With time, experience, and success the focus shifts outward (e.g., "What are the needs of the client and system?") (McNeill & Stoltenberg, 2016). Therefore, by the third year of practice, ECSPs are better able to evaluate the needs of their school communities and determine if they are meeting them, including the needs of students, parents, and staff. The relationships and credibility established during years one and two of practice can be further expanded upon and cashed in to garner support for systems change efforts through collaborative, systems-level problem solving (see Castillo & Curtis, 2014).

Overcoming Institutional Inertia and Training Washout

For school psychologists to change the job, it is essential that they overcome *institutional inertia*, or the tendency for schools to resist change, and the associated problem of *training washout*, or previous learning fading away rather than being firmed up or expanded upon (Newman & Shinn, 2014). With respect to institutional inertia, ECSPs should remember that just because something has been historically done one way does not mean this is the most effective way or that existing regularities and structures are achieving their intended outcomes (see Chapter 4). Reviewing system-level data in conjunction with conversations with various stakeholders can help identify and verify a school's needs, which can become a focus of systems-level problem solving efforts. Interested readers are referred to Castillo and Curtis (2014) and Morrison and Harms (2018) for more about systems-level consultation, program evaluation, and problem solving.

If the early career school psychologist accepts the way things are as the way they should be, even when the system's current practices do not fit with one's prior training, the status quo will remain the status quo. In such a circumstance, new practitioners might experience disillusionment with training (Rønnestad & Skovholt, 2013), feeling like their graduate programs did not prepare them for the realities of the school-based practice. In turn, what were previously thought of as best practices might be viewed as unrealistic practices and will fade away over time. As a graduate educator, the notion of training washout keeps me up at night worrying about whether or not what I am teaching and supervising will translate into practice.

Among a number of factors, I want to emphasize two that I believe are essential for new school psychologists to overcome institutional inertia. First, it is necessary to possess well developed content knowledge and process skills in problem solving, data-based decision making, consultation, and collaboration. These skills have been relevant for school psychology practice for decades and are pivotal in supporting the delivery of all other aspects of school psychologists' service delivery.

Second, it is essential to be a critical thinker. As described in Chapter 1, this means questioning one's own assumptions and beliefs and being cognizant of how one arrives at well-reasoned decisions and actions (Gambrill, 2012). Critical thinking and evidence-based practice go hand in hand. Reflective, scientist practitioners engage in practices with a high likelihood of success (i.e., they are evidence-based) and adjust as necessary to match practice contexts. No matter how best practices in the field change over time, and they are indeed changing with increasing speed (e.g., Neimeyer, Taylor, Rozensky, & Cox, 2014), collaboration, data-based decision making, problem solving, and critical thinking will *always* provide a compass towards competent practice.

Love the Job

Changing the job can also spark professional engagement, in contrast to experiences of burnout described earlier in this chapter. In other words, changing the job can help an early career school psychologist love the job. After being in a position for a few years, many individuals are able to strategically structure the position to spend more time working in domains that they are passionate about, excel at, and that make a difference for students. For example, a number of school psychologists I have worked with have reported being able to gradually reduce the number of evaluation reports they have written over the years (an aversive task for them), while increasing the amount of teacher consultation they have engaged in, which they have indicated has been more fruitful in supporting students. Others have sought out additional specializations (i.e., depth of knowledge) that have enabled them to take on leadership roles in their schools, or in the district. Examples include early career school psychologists becoming leaders in school- and district-level initiatives related to crisis prevention and intervention, supporting positive behavior supports, and working with English Learning students and their families. Of course, some time will inevitably be spent engaged in administrative work, or other tasks that are not the most stimulating. This is true of virtually any job. However, once an early career school psychologist learns the job and begins to do the job effectively, he or she can change the job in a way that maximizes enjoyment and, most importantly, effectiveness.

Summary and Final Thoughts: Extending the Book's Big Ideas from the Internship to the Early Career

Two purposes of this book identified in the Preface are (1) to provide interns and supervisors with actions to promote a high-quality internship experience and (2) to demystify what tends to be a mysterious and often anxiety-provoking process for school psychology students. I sincerely hope that the book has accomplished its purposes and is a useful and pragmatic resource to support the internship year. Further, I hope interns reading this text can extend the big ideas described in the Preface of this text beyond the internship, into their professional careers. As such, a new big idea of this edition of the book is that *habits of professional learning practiced and established during the internship carry over into the early career.* Accordingly, several habits of professional learning have been discussed, including reflective practice, critical thinking, proactive behavior, stepping out of comfort zones to take risks, and many others. How can these professional habits transition into the early career?

Let's begin by jointly considering the first two big ideas of this book: (1) *The school psychology internship is a dynamic and formative experience, not a static event* and (2) *the development of an intern's professional skills should be treated as an integrated process, not a series of isolated activities.* Following the internship, it may be easiest to shape one's professional work solely based on employer expectations (i.e., this is what the last school psychologist did) and crystallized knowledge and skills developed during the internship year. However, just as the internship is dynamic, formative, and integrated, so are professional practice and professional development.

School psychology is a rapidly changing field. Knowledge attained during graduate training has a half-life, defined by Dubin (1972) as "the time after completion of professional training when, because of new developments, practicing professionals have become roughly half as competent as they were upon graduation to meet the demands of their profession" (p. 487).

The half-life of school psychologists' graduate training is shortened by advances in research and practice, newly developed and changing legislation, shifting characteristics of student populations, and updated legal, ethical, and professional guidelines (Harrison, 2010; Reynolds, 2011). It is estimated that approximately nine and a half years after entering the field, without additional learning, 50% of the knowledge school psychologists developed during training will become obsolete (Neimeyer et al., 2014).

Clearly, school psychologists must stay in touch with changes in the field and adapt. Like when they were interns, school psychologists can (a) engage in ongoing formative assessment of their own strengths and weaknesses (e.g., using NASP's *Self-Assessment for School Psychologists* tool), the needs of clients, and the needs of systems, (b) seek out targeted professional learning opportunities, and (c) make changes in their own professional practices. Remaining static in knowledge and skills is antithetical to the value of lifelong learning instilled during graduate training. Although maintaining a static level of knowledge, skills, and practice may be experienced as *comfortable,* like when they were interns, school psychologists should seek experiences outside of their comfort zones. When crossing from comfort zones into risk zones, school psychologists enter more fertile spots for professional learning – especially when they have immediate access to supervision.

Which brings us to the third big idea underlying this book: *Supervision is a critical component of the internship year but supervision processes need increased clarity . . . to be maximally effective.* Supervision is pivotal not only during the internship year but also throughout school psychologists' careers. Indeed, the NASP (2018) *Position Statement on Supervision in School Psychology* advocates that professional supervision should be available to all practitioners, no matter their level of experience or proficiency. Mentoring is also an important tool for postgraduate professional learning. Having access to a trusted, knowledgeable other who provides assessment-informed feedback that guides deliberate practice of skills is foundational to professional learning.

In addition to being mentored and supervised, school psychologists also go on to act as mentors and supervisors for others, as noted in NASP's (2010b) *Principles for Professional Ethics.* In fact, many early career school psychologists become supervisors of practicum students and by their fourth year (still early career) supervise interns. Practitioners who supervise should seek out ongoing professional development on supervision, including metasupervision (see Chapter 7), as supervision is a distinct competency area (APA, 2015a). Harvey and Struzziero's (2008) text *Professional Development and Supervision of School Psychologists: From Intern to Expert* provides an in-depth consideration of supervision throughout the career, as does Simon and Swerdlik's (2017) text *Supervision in School Psychology: The Developmental, Ecological, Problem Solving Model.* Guiney's (2019) *Supervisor Toolkit* is a handy resource for supervisors at all experience levels. Each of these is an excellent resource for school psychology supervisors' ongoing supervision competency development.

The fourth big idea of this book is that *interns should be active planners, coordinators, and shapers of the internship experience.* Being proactive (as discussed in Chapter 6) is an important behavior during the internship and remains relevant throughout the professional career. As interns complete their internships and enter practice, they are presented with a unique opportunity to shape their own work. Of course, having a "new-hire" status can be challenging, and successful site entry is a prerequisite to making significant systems-level changes. Further, districts likely have particular service needs (which have hopefully been made clear during the job interview). However, recent graduates are also optimistic, enthusiastic, and informed with up-to-date knowledge. During the internship they have developed opinions about what it means to be a school psychologist and what is effective professional practice. These perspectives can be put into action during the early career. The time is ripe to make a difference.

Critical Thinking Questions and Activities

The following critical thinking questions and activities for early career school psychologists are intended to help support the transition from the internship into early career practice.

For Early Career School Psychologists:

- What self-care strategies worked well for you during the internship? How might these translate for you as you move into your early career?
- How will you know if you have successfully entered into your new job?
- If you feel like you have not yet successfully entered into your new job, what actions can you take?
- How will you make sure to access supervision and/or mentoring during your early career?
- Complete NASP's *Self-Assessment for School Psychologists,* and the accompanying *Professional Growth Plan template.* Identify three goals for your first year of practice, and also consider how these goals can be extended in subsequent years.
- Take a tour of professional websites, searching for early career resources. Determine what resources are available and consider how you might benefit from them.
- What habits of professional learning did you learn during your school psychology training, including your internship, that it would be useful to continue during your early career?

Note

1 Despite these recent trends, the diversity of school psychology professionals has not kept up with the diversity of schools (Proctor & Meyers, 2014).

Appendices

Appendix A

SAMPLE APPIC COVER LETTER

October 15, 2019

Dear Dr. Johnson,

I am eager to submit my application for the doctoral psychology internship programs offered through the Clearwater Internship Consortium (CIC). I believe an opportunity within any of the three locations would be beneficial for my learning and future practice. I am interested in the internship program's focus on student success through culturally competent delivery of psychological services with an emphasis on consultation, assessment, and intervention. CIC would provide me with excellent opportunities to expand my professional practice through the numerous training opportunities within the program such as individualized assessment, counseling, crisis intervention, parent training and behavior management consultation with teachers. I appreciate the collaborative efforts between the school and families as I believe this is a critical component to the success of youth academically and behaviorally. My experiences with assessment, consultation, intervention development, data-based decision making, and systems-level initiatives support my interest in your program and make me a great fit.

Currently, I am a fourth-year doctoral student in the School Psychology Program at University of Clearwater, which is APA-accredited and NASP-approved. I have gained experience in providing academic and behavioral assessment and interventions for children and adolescents, conducted functional behavior assessment and analyses in a variety of school settings, and facilitated professional development at alternative schools with an emphasis on data-based decision making. I successfully proposed my dissertation in June 2019 and have started the data collection process. My dissertation seeks to evaluate the effects of a Positive Peer Reporting intervention on the academic engagement and prosocial behaviors of students with emotional and behavioral disorders. Data collection will be completed in December 2019.

My experiences of providing individual, group, and system-wide services in a variety of school settings make me a great fit for an internship within CIC. I have experience in public and alternative school settings where I have consulted with classroom teachers, conducted academic and behavioral assessments, and developed, implemented, and evaluated functionally appropriate interventions, as well as crisis intervention plans. Within these settings, I have worked with individuals with low socio-economic status, low-incidence disabilities and from ethnically diverse backgrounds. Working with individuals from varying backgrounds and experiences is important to me as I continue to develop and improve competency in diversity. Additionally, I have experience working with children and adolescents with EBD, autism spectrum disorder, and other developmental disabilities. As a graduate student, I served as an interventionist on a multi-year project within an urban, public school system. During my first year, I was involved with universal screening of at-risk readers, intervention implementation of a literacy program and evidence-based behavioral strategies, and progress monitoring through the use of curriculum-based measures. This prepared me for my second and third year as a supervisor in which I trained graduate students on behavioral strategies to reduce disruptive behavior and increase engagement during the literacy program so as to improve learning outcomes.

My goals for internship are to increase my experience and knowledge related to culturally competent assessment and intervention that integrate research and practice. I am specifically interested in CIC's focus on collaboration to best meet the needs of students. I have experience collaborating and consulting at the individual, small group, classroom and systems-level and am looking forward to further advance these skills with families and professionals as well as provide culturally responsive services. Additionally, I seek to consistently incorporate the unique differences among individuals and families within my approach to service delivery. I am confident that an internship with CIC will provide these opportunities and allow for me to expand my knowledge and skill set.

Overall, my experiences, interests, and goals are fully aligned with the internship opportunities within CIC and I believe that an opportunity to be part of the CIC team will provide me with a well-rounded internship experience that will best prepare me personally and professionally as a future school psychologist. Thank you for your consideration and time. I look forward to your reply and would welcome an invitation to interview for an internship position for the 2020–2021 year.

Sincerely,
Penny Clark, M.Ed., BCBA
University of Clearwater
Applicant Code #

Appendix B

SAMPLE SCHOOL PSYCHOLOGY INTERNSHIP AGREEMENT

(Adapted from the Illinois State School Psychology Interns Manual, 2014)

Internship Agreement

_____

[Name of School System/Agency]

has agreed to accept

_____

[Name of Intern]

as an intern for the _____ academic year. The internship site and the intern agree to observe the following arrangements in meeting the requirements of the internship:

1. **DURATION:** The internship will begin on _____, and continue through _____. The intern is expected to follow the same daily schedule and yearly calendar as other school psychology staff employed by the local school system/agency. The intern is not required to remain in the employment of the local school system/agency beyond the term of the internship. Furthermore, the intern is not guaranteed employment beyond the term of the internship.

2. **HOURS:** The intern is appointed on a full-time basis for one year. The intern must complete at least _____ hours of supervised experience. As with regularly employed pupil services personnel, the intern demonstrates a commitment to the provision of psychological services not necessarily reflected in hourly schedules.

3. **LOCATION:** The internship will be performed at the following location (s):

    Name of School District: _____

    Address:
    _____

4. **PLAN:** Internship activities shall be determined by a written plan developed jointly by the intern and school district personnel and approved by the University internship supervisor. It is expected the plan will be consistent with the guidelines and objectives as contained in the Internship Handbook and with the internship training standards promulgated by the National Association of School Psychologists (NASP) internship criteria.

5. **COMPENSATION:** The intern is provided a salary commensurate with his or her level of training, experience and period of appointment. The intern will be paid in the amount of $_____ for the term of the internship. Any work related travel necessary to fulfill the requirements of the internship shall be reimbursed in accordance with the policies of the local school system/agency.

6. **CONFERENCES, SEMINARS, AND IN-SERVICE TRAINING:** Ongoing conferences, seminars, and in-service training opportunities available to employed school psychologists should also be available to interns. The intern is encouraged to participate in state, regional, and national level meetings for school psychologists. Expense reimbursement consistent with policies pertaining to agency school psychologists is consistent with policies pertaining to agency school psychologists. Released time for attendance at professional meetings is required. The intern will be expected to attend the following conferences, seminars, and/or in-service training program(s):

    -   Intern/intern supervision workshop
    -   Illinois School Psychologists Association (ISPA) Annual Conference
    -   University Internship Seminars.

7. **WORK ENVIRONMENT:** Consistent with the availability of resources to employed staff, the intern is provided adequate supplies and materials to carry out the functions of the internship. An appropriate work environment should include adequate privacy of office facilities and access to secretarial assistance, telephone services, office equipment, and copying machines.

8. **SUPERVISION:** The cooperating practitioner must hold a valid credential as a school psychologist. Full-time employment at the internship setting for at least one year prior to assuming supervisory responsibilities for an intern is required. Concurrent full-time employment as a school psychologist is required. Cooperating practitioners shall provide at least two hours per week of direct supervision for each intern and be responsible for no more than two

interns at a time. The intern will receive at least two hours of supervision per week directly from:

_____ / _____

(Name of Cooperating Practitioner/Certification Number and State)

The university supervisor (or designate) shall maintain an ongoing relationship with the cooperating practitioner and the intern. The university supervisor (or designate) will make at least one site visit per semester for each intern.

9. **TRAINING COMMITMENT:** The local school system/agency is primarily committed to the internship as a training experience. Employing interns as a means of acquiring less expensive services is unacceptable. Interns are expected to participate in tasks appropriate to the completion of the internship training plan. The intern will not be asked to serve in any capacity other than that for which she or he was appointed.

Signatures for Approval:

_____

Intern   **Date**

_____

Cooperating Practitioner   **Date**

_____

University Supervisor (or Designee)   **Date**

Appendix C
SAMPLE REMEDIATION PLAN TEMPLATE (VERSION 1)[1]

DATE:

Dear Elizabeth:

As you know, you have missed another deadline (i.e., the end of summer 2019) regarding the completion of your master's thesis or doctoral Research Apprenticeship project. Consequently, you are now officially prevented from sitting for the fall semester administration of the doctoral comprehensive examination. The School Psychology Coordinating Committee (SPCC) has met to discuss your failure to meet this deadline. The SPCC, consistent with our Graduate Student Evaluation and Remediation Policies and Procedures, has identified your pattern of behavior as indicative of problematic professional competence in the areas of time management, decision making, and self-evaluation/appraisal.

Our concerns about these problematic behaviors have been shared with you in your annual feedback sessions. Regrettably, the problems have not been ameliorated. Indeed, your performance regarding the research requirement in the PhD program creates the impression you are unresponsive to feedback from faculty in School Psychology. As of this date, the SPCC is no longer willing to accept your unfinished master's thesis as potential credit in lieu of the doctoral Research Apprenticeship.

Even though you have many assets considered important for one entering a helping profession, including strong interpersonal skills and intelligence, the SPCC believes your problematic behaviors have high potential to negatively impact your future professional functioning as a doctoral-level school psychologist. Based upon our identification of competency concerns in the areas specified above, the SPCC has determined that your status in the doctoral program is probationary and remediation is necessary. As such, the SPCC has developed a remedial plan for you.

The plan has the following requirements:

1. You must immediately begin to meet weekly with Dr. Competent, Chair of your doctoral advisory committee, to set goals related to the completion of your Research Apprenticeship project. These weekly meetings must continue until you have officially selected a research mentor to direct your Apprenticeship. This selection must occur no later than October 1, 2019. Once your research mentor is selected, you are required to meet weekly with him/her until the *completion* of your research project, or until your research mentor has determined these weekly meetings are unnecessary. Failure to make and/or keep these weekly appointments will lead the SPCC to conclude that your remediation plan is unsuccessful.

2. You must immediately seek personal therapy (available at no cost from the University Student Counseling Center or at an agency of your choice). Treatment goals must include improved time management, more realistic self-evaluation/assessment of your current functioning and future goals, and improved decision making. You must inform the SPCC of the date of your first therapeutic session. Although the details of your work with the therapist will be confidential you must provide documentation to the SPCC that you are regularly attending these counseling sessions. Failure to *immediately* seek professional therapy and failure to document your regular attendance at these therapeutic sessions, will lead the SPCC to conclude that your remediation plan is unsuccessful.

3. You must have an officially approved Institutional Review Board (IRB) proposal for the Research Apprenticeship project no later January 1, 2020. This deadline requires that you submit your proposal to the IRB in time for its December meeting. Once submitted and approved, you will be required to provide the SPCC the official IRB approval number. If you fail to meet this IRB proposal submission deadline, you will be summarily dismissed from the doctoral program. Most importantly, you must complete *all* requirements for the Research Apprenticeship no later than December 15, 2020. These requirements include, but are not limited to, a colloquium presentation of your project to the Department of Psychology during the fall semester of 2020. If you fail to complete all requirements of the Research Apprenticeship by the stipulated deadline, you will be summarily dismissed from the doctoral program.

If you satisfy *all* requirements specified in the three paragraphs above, you will be restored to full status in the PhD program (i.e., no longer on Probation). Once you are restored to full status, the SPCC will determine when it is appropriate for you to take the doctoral comprehensive examination. If, however, one or more of the above requirements is not satisfied, you will be summarily dismissed from the doctoral program.

If you accept all terms of this remedial plan, please indicate such in writing addressed to the SPCC no later than August 22, 2019. If the Committee does not receive such notice by that date, you will be summarily dismissed from the doctoral program. Consistent with program policies, you may appeal this action by contacting Dr. Merit, Department Chair, within 14 days of receipt of this letter or to the Office of Student Dispute Resolution Services <http://www.linktowebsite.edu/>

Elizabeth, we feel you have numerous strengths. As such, the faculty in School Psychology stands ready to assist you in completing this remedial plan, including your Research Apprenticeship, so you may continue in the doctoral program.

For the School Psychology Coordinating Committee:
Jared Competent, PhD
Coordinator, Graduate Programs in
School Psychology
Professor of Psychology

Note

1 Adapted from "Problematic behaviors: Mediating Differences and Negotiating Change," by T. K. Cruise, & M. E. Swerdlik, 2010, in *Handbook of Education, Training, and Supervision of School Psychologists in School and Community* (Vol. 2, pp. 143–144), by J. Kaufman, T. L. Hughes, & C. A. Riccio (Eds.), New York, NY: Routledge. Copyright 2010 by Taylor & Francis. Reprinted with permission.

Appendix D

SAMPLE REMEDIATION PLAN TEMPLATE (VERSION 2)

Internship Remediation Plan for Mr. Student

Specific concerns were identified with regard to Mr. Student's professional behaviors and field-based competencies as part of the internship midyear evaluation on February 20, 2019. Mr. Student, his field supervisors (Mr. Supervisor 1 and Dr. Supervisor 2), and university internship supervisor (Dr. Newman) developed a plan to support Mr. Student's continued development through the end of the internship. The following items were discussed, and a plan of action identified. We agreed to revisit this plan the week of April 2, 2019.

Item Discussed	Summary and Plan of Action, if Applicable

Mr. Student's strengths	• Several strengths in Mr. Student's work thus far were noted, including:
	
	   o Behavioral problem solving, such as involvement in Functional Behavioral Assessment and Behavior Intervention Plan development
	   o Implementation and monitoring of Social-Emotional Learning interventions across tiers and settings
	   o Leading groups at the high school setting during his internship rotation.

The frequency and structure of supervision	• Mr. Student will pre-schedule 2 hours of weekly, closed-door supervision time with Mr. Supervisor 1 and Dr. Supervisor 2. • Prior to supervision meetings, Mr. Student will develop two or three written questions or priorities to focus on in meetings and share this information at least one day in advance of the meeting with his supervisors.

(continued)

(continued)

Item Discussed	*Summary and Plan of Action, if Applicable*
	• Prior to supervision meetings, Mr. Student will provide his supervisors with any materials (e.g., written reports, structure for presenting information at a meeting, case data) to be discussed in supervision.
	• Prior to supervision meetings, Mr. Student will review any materials to be discussed in supervision (e.g., test manual of an instrument to be administered).
	• Mr. Student has created a calendar including a timeline for completing tasks at each of his schools. He will review his calendar with his supervisors on an ongoing basis.
	• All of Mr. Student's supervisors will provide feedback on his performance using the University Evaluation Tools. Areas of concern during the midyear evaluation can be rated as "Inadequate progress," "Adequate progress," or "More than adequate progress" on a biweekly basis.
	• Peer supervision is available monthly through the university internship seminar beginning in April and individual supervision may be arranged with Dr. Newman, as needed.
Consultation and collaboration	• Mr. Student will identify the process, products, and tools to use in consultation with teachers through advanced preparation for consultation work in the form of a written plan and discussion with scaffolding by his supervisors.
	• Mr. Student will provide evidence of improvement in consultation follow-up including remaining in contact with teachers and following through on intervention planning, implementation, and evaluation through calendar events or case logs.
	• Mr. Student will work with his supervisors to develop written assessment questions and a data collection plan using a RIOT scaffold.
	• Mr. Supervisor 1 and Dr. Supervisor 2 will continue to provide opportunities for Mr. Student to practice consultation skills with teachers and parents.
Assessment and special education decision making	• Mr. Student is currently working on two special education eligibility cases at SCHOOL A. In working through these cases, he will:
	○ Develop written assessment questions and a data collection plan using a RIOT scaffold.
	○ Solicit feedback on the schedule for completing assessment activities.
	○ Discuss progress with Mr. Supervisor 1 during supervision time.

	○ Prepare for testing by accessing/reading through materials such as test manuals in advance and familiarizing himself with computerized scoring processes.
	○ Work with his supervisors to develop a set of sequenced talking points for providing the assessment results at the special education eligibility meetings.
	○ Follow-up on the assessment process to see assessment linked to intervention.
	○ Review state board of education special education guidance documents prior to eligibility meetings in April.
Written communication and products	• Mr. Student will improve in his report writing, including using a template provided by his supervisors to structure written products (e.g., behavioral observation reports, special education evaluations), and will also work towards developing his own style of writing. Dr. Newman has offered to provide written feedback on evaluation reports, as needed.
	• Mr. Supervisor 1 and Dr. Supervisor 2 will continue to provide opportunities for Mr. Student to produce written products and to hone his written communication skills.
	• Mr. Student will keep *all* supervisors in the loop regarding scheduling conflicts, activity planning, or other concerns that necessitate communication across supervisors.

Appendix E

CV TEMPLATE

Benjamin P. Curran, M.Ed.

6 IMAGINARY ROAD, CINCINNATI OH 45242

BENJAMIN.CURRAN@FAKEMAIL.COM | 513-987-6543

Education

University of Cincinnati, Cincinnati, OH   **August 2017 – May 2020**

- Ed.S., School Psychology (Expected August, 2020)
- M.Ed., Behavior Analysis (April, 2018)

The George Washington University, Washington DC   August 2011 – May 2015

- B.A., Psychology, Overall GPA 3.94

Honors And Awards

- University of Cincinnati School Psychology Program Student of the Year (**April, 2019**)
- Presidential Academic Scholarship, The George Washington University (**2011–2015**)
- Summa Cum Laude and Phi Beta Kappa (**May, 2015**)

Supervised Field Experiences

School Psychology Internship

Cincinnati Public Schools, OH   **August 2019 – May 2020**

Fictional Elementary School and Fake High School

- *Consultation.* Developed new teaming system for grade-level and schoolwide problem-solving in collaboration with school psychologist. Provided ongoing case management for teachers and coaching for members of the team managing their first cases. Collaborated with the head of psychological services in facilitating training for all school psychologists in the district on coaching/consultation.
- *Assessment.* Completed comprehensive psychological evaluations to support special education decision-making at the elementary and middle school levels, including assessment of students with diverse cultural, linguistic, and socioeconomic backgrounds. Helped to create instructional matches for students through curriculum-based assessment. Consulted with teachers and parents to utilize assessment data for intervention planning and implementation. Supported response-to-intervention decision making for students suspected of having specific learning disabilities.
- *Direct services.* Provided individual and group interventions (academic, behavioral, and social-emotional) within and outside of classroom, at all tiers within a multitiered system of supports. Planned, co-facilitated, and monitored progress on academic, behavioral, and social skills. Conducted threat and suicide assessments and monitored follow-up services. Served on school- and district-level crisis prevention and intervention teams.

Practica and Field Work Experiences

Cincinnati Public Schools, OH   **August 2018 – May 2019**

Faux Middle School

- Participated in team-based consultation, academic problem-solving, group counseling, and curriculum-based and psychological assessment.
- Co-facilitated consultation team trainings and developed curriculum for ongoing training of team members.
- Supported planning, implementation, and program evaluation of schoolwide positive behavioral intervention and supports, including culturally-relevant intervention adaptations for English Learner students and their families.

University Early Childhood and Family Education Center

- Consulted and collaborated with preschool teachers to support students' academic, behavioral and social-emotional needs
- Co-facilitated a social skills group on emotion regulation for five preschool students
- Provided a parent-education session on managing difficult behaviors in children.

Local High School

- Counseled students in issues of bereavement, trauma, pregnancy, suicide, familial conflict, ethnic identity, and acculturation. Collaborated with students' teachers, families, and other outside service providers in the delivery of services.

Pseudo Elementary School

- Facilitated *Kindergarten Peer-Assisted Learning Strategies* Tier 2 intervention for five kindergartners, including benchmark assessment and progress monitoring using curriculum-based measurement.

Additional Related Experiences (Selected)

University of Cincinnati, Cincinnati, OH   August 2017– May 2019

Graduate Assistant to the Dean

- Provided administrative support to the College of Education, Criminal Justice and Human Services Dean, including coordinating college-level activities and analyzing student satisfaction data.

Unreal Treatment Program, Cleveland OH   August 2015 – July 2017

Residential Counselor and Residential Supervisor

- Provided individual and group therapy to adolescents in a short-term residential setting.
- Supervised and trained on-site staff in the implementation of behavioral support routines for clients.

Publications and Presentations

Curran, B. P., Peer, M., & Buddy, M. (2019). How my school psychology training linked to effective outcomes for students. *NASP Communiqué, 50*(1), 1.

Curran, B. P. (2019, February). *The effect of kindergarten peer-assisted learning strategies at tier two.* Poster presented at the annual convention of the National Association of School Psychologists, Atlanta, GA.

Professional Affiliations

- American Psychological Association
    - Division 16, School Psychology

- National Association of School Psychologists
- Ohio School Psychology Association

References

Dr. Program Coordinator
Professor and Program Coordinator, University of Cincinnati School Psychology Program
513-123-4567 | firstfake.email@uc.edu

Dr. Faculty Member
Assistant Professor, University of Cincinnati School Psychology Program
513-789-9999 | secondfake.email@uc.edu

Ms. Field Supervisor
School Psychologist, Cincinnati Public Schools
513-555-1234 | fakeemail@cpsboe.k12.oh.us

Appendix F
SAMPLE COVER LETTER

February 15, 2019

Dear Dr. Chang,

Please accept my application for a school psychologist position in the Appleton County Schools for the 2019–2020 school year. Enclosed you will find my CV, three letters of recommendation, my official graduate transcript, and two work samples completed during my internship year. I believe my interests and skills match well with the district's mission and the description of the open position. I am currently a school psychology intern working in Morris County Schools. I will complete my internship in the summer of 2019 and obtain the state school psychologist licensure and national certification at that time.

As highlighted on my CV, I have engaged in a breadth of relevant experiences over the past three years, including working at the preschool, elementary, middle, and high school levels with ethnically, linguistically, and economically diverse students and families. In addition to numerous other activities, a primary focus during my internship has been data-based decision making and problem solving. Specifically, I have helped structure a multitiered service delivery system, including Response to Intervention (RtI), at the elementary school level and provided professional learning, including coaching, about RtI for all psychologists in the district. In addition, I have been responsible for collecting psychoeducational assessment data for several students' special education evaluations, implementing academic and behavioral interventions for individuals and groups, and monitoring student outcomes throughout the year. Supporting my school's implementation of positive behavioral interventions and supports has also been an internship highlight. My supervisor and I will present data on the effectiveness of this initiative at the upcoming NASP Convention in Atlanta.

Another interest area for me is social justice advocacy for underserved and marginalized students and families. For example, my school psychology internship supervisor and I are collaborating to change the special education referral process at the elementary level due to an overrepresentation of minority students in special education. Additionally, at my high school, I am working with the school counselor to co-facilitate a group to support lesbian, gay, bisexual, transgender, and questioning (LGBTQ+) students. The data we've gathered thus far suggests students are meeting mutually constructed group goals, including feeling more engaged in the school setting.

In sum, I am eager to begin my career as a school psychologist and I believe my school psychology training and field experiences have provided me the ability to hit the ground running next year. Thank you for considering this application. Should you have any questions, please contact me at (987)-654-3210.

Sincerely,
Fatima Ali, M.Ed.

Appendix G

JOB INTERVIEW VIDEO TRANSCRIPT

Introduction:

The following is a transcript of a school psychology job interview practice video available at https://www.youtube.com/watch?v=Ob4do34riZk. The video provides viewers with an opportunity to practice interviewing skills.

Throughout this video, questions are posed that may come up during an actual school psychology job interview. Please note, actual interviews might look in some ways different than this simulation. For example, the number of interviewers and their roles might vary and the number of questions and their focus might also differ in some ways. However, we believe the items in this simulated interview are representative of the topics you should be prepared to answer during an interview.

After each question, it is recommended that you pause the video and practice providing a response. You may find it useful to record yourself giving these responses using a cell phone, tablet, or other method. By reviewing your video and listening to yourself speak, you can identify areas in which you could improve before entering a real interview situation.

Job Interview Questions:

1. Before we begin with our questions, tell us a little about your background and why you decided to become a school psychologist.
2. Please describe what qualities you believe an effective school psychologist must possess.
3. What particular areas of interest have you developed during your school psychology training?

4. Everyone has unique strengths as well as areas that could use improvement. What are your greatest strengths? Also, what areas are more difficult for you?

5. Now, please tell us about your biggest accomplishment during your internship year.

6. Tell us about a time during practicum or internship when you faced a difficult challenge. How did you approach this challenge? Were you successful in resolving the problem?

7. What experiences have you had working with diverse populations? How should culturally responsive practices be incorporated into the school psychologist's role?

8. How do you suppose working full-time as a school psychologist will differ from your work as an intern?

9. Given the multifaceted nature of the school psychologist role, what do you view to be the most important aspects of the job?

10. School psychologists take on many different roles. What role does consultation have in school psychology service delivery?

11. What assessment tools do you have experience with? What tools do you find most helpful for understanding the student needs?

12. How do you view counseling fitting into the school psychologist role?

13. What is your understanding of Multi-Tiered Systems of Support and Response-to-intervention? Have you been involved with the implementation of MTSS and/or RTI during your practicum or internship?

14. Now describe a time you had too many things on your plate. How did you prioritize your responsibilities?

15. What experiences have you had with crisis prevention or intervention?

16. Describe a time you showed initiative or leadership during your internship.

17. Tell me what you would do if a parent insisted that you test their child when you felt it was either inappropriate or unnecessary.

18. Now describe your understanding of the special education eligibility decision-making process from start to finish.

19. Why are you interested in working at our school district?

20. This position would require you to work in three different school buildings. How would you navigate your position across several schools?

21. If you were hired, you would be asked to work on various teams within the district. Tell us about a time you were a member of a successful team and describe your role in the team's success.

22. As you may know, we have many applicants who would love to join our staff. Is there anything else we should know about you that makes you a unique candidate for this position?

23. Do you have any questions for us about the position or the district?

REFERENCES

Alessi, G. J., Lascurettes-Alessi, K. J., & Leys, W. L. (1981). Internships in school psychology: Supervision issues. *School Psychology Review, 10,* 461–469.

Alvarez, A. N., Blume, A. W., Cervantes, J. M., & Thomas, L. R. (2009). Tapping the wisdom tradition: Essential elements to mentoring students of color. *Professional Psychology: Research and Practice, 40,* 181–188. http://dx.doi.org/10.1037/a0012256

American Institute of Stress (2019). *What is stress?* Retrieved from https://www.stress.org.

American Psychological Association (2006a). *Advancing colleague assistance in professional psychology.* Retrieved from https://www.apa.org/practice/resources/assistance/monograph.pdf.

American Psychological Association (2006b). *Introduction to mentoring: A guide for mentors and mentees.* Retrieved from http://www.apa.org/education/grad/mentoring.aspx.

American Psychological Association. (2015a). Guidelines for clinical supervision in health service psychology. *American Psychologist, 70,* 33–46. doi:10.1037/a0038112.

American Psychology Association (2015b). *Standards of accreditation for health service psychology.* Retrieved from https://www.apa.org/ed/accreditation/about/policies/standards-of-accreditation.pdf.

American Psychology Association (2017a). *Ethical principles of psychologists and code of conduct.* Retrieved from https://www.apa.org/ethics/code/ethics-code-2017.pdf.

American Psychological Association (2017b). *Multicultural guidelines: An ecological approach to context, identity, and intersectionality.* Retrieved from: https://www.apa.org/about/policy/multicultural-guidelines.pdf.

American Psychological Association (2018). *Early career psychologists.* Retrieved from http://www.apa.org/careers/early-career/index.aspx.

American Psychological Association (2019). *Some differences between résumés and CVs.* Retrieved from http://www.apa.org/careers/resources/job-seekers/differences-resumes.aspx.

American Psychological Association Advisory Committee on Colleague Assistance (2009). *Who cares? Barriers, benefits, and resources in colleague assistance and self-care.* Retrieved from https://www.apa.org/practice/resources/assistance/acca-2009-convention.pdf.

Annan, J., & Ryba, K. (2013). Networks of professional supervision. *School Psychology Quarterly, 28*, 170–182. doi:10.1037/spq0000015.

Argyris, C. (1990). *Overcoming organizational defenses: Facilitating organizational learning.* Boston, MA: Allyn & Bacon.

Armistead, L. (2014). Best practices in continuing professional development for school psychologists. In P. L. Harrison, & A. Thomas (Eds.), *Best practices in school psychology: Foundations* (pp. 611–626). Bethesda, MD: National Association of School Psychologists.

Armistead, L., Williams, B. B., & Jacob, S. (2011). *Professional ethics for school psychologists: a problem-solving model casebook* (2nd ed.). Bethesda, MD: National Association of School Psychologists.

Armistead, R. J., & Smallwood, D. L. (2014). The national association of school psychologists model for comprehensive and integrated school psychological services. In P. L. Harrison, & A. Thomas (Eds.), *Best practices in school psychology: Data-based and collaborative decision making* (pp. 9–24). Bethesda, MD: National Association of School Psychologists.

Assessment of Competency Benchmarks Workgroup. (2012a). Benchmarks ratings forms for all levels. Retrieved from www.apa.org/ed/graduate/benchmarks-evaluation-system.aspx.

Assessment of Competency Benchmarks Workgroup. (2012b). Revised competency benchmarks in professional psychology. Retrieved from www.apa.org/ed/graduate/benchmarks-evaluation-system.aspx.

Association of Psychology Postdoctoral and Internship Centers. (2012). AAPI supplemental materials policy. Retrieved from https://www.appic.org/Internships/AAPI/AAPI-Supplemental-Materials-Policy.

Association of Psychology Postdoctoral and Internship Centers. (2016). Frequently asked questions: Internship applicants – preparation and submission of rank order lists. Retrieved from https://www.appic.org/match/faqs/applicants/rank-order-lists.

Association of Psychology Postdoctoral and Internship Centers (2017). APPIC match phase II. Retrieved from https://www.appic.org/Internships/Match/APPIC-Match-Phase-II.

Association of Psychology Postdoctoral and Internship Centers. (2018a). 2018 APPIC match statistics- phase I. Retrieved from https://www.appic.org/Internships/Match/Match-Statistics/Match-Statistics-2018-Phase-I.

Association of Psychology Postdoctoral and Internship Centers. (2018b). AAPI OnLine-APPIC application for psychology internships. Retrieved from: https://www.appic.org/Internships/AAPI.

Association of Psychology Postdoctoral and Internship Centers. (2018c). APPIC membership criteria: doctoral psychology internship programs. Retrieved from : https://www.appic.org/Joining-APPIC/Internship-Membership-Criteria.

Association of Psychology Postdoctoral and Internship Centers. (2018d). Frequently asked questions: Internship applicants- match eligibility and participation. Retrieved from: https://www.appic.org/Match/FAQs/Applicants/Eligibility-and-Participation.

Association of State and Provincial Psychology Boards (2019). ASPPB PSY|Book: Psychology licensing. Retrieved from http://psybook.asppb.org.

Aten, J. D., Strain, J. D., & Gillespie, R. E. (2008). A transtheoretical model of clinical supervision. *Training and Education in Professional Psychology, 2*, 1–9. http://dx.doi.org/10.1037/1931-3918.2.1.1.

Babinski, L. M., Amendum, S. J., Knotek, S. E., Sanchez, M., & Malone, P. (2018). Improving young English learners' language and literacy skills through teacher professional development: A randomized control trial. *American Educational Research Journal, 55*, 117–143. http://dx.doi.org/10.3102/0002831217732335.

Bahr, M. W., Leduc, J. D., Hild, M. A., Davis, S. E., Summers, J. K., & McNeal, B. (2017). Evidence for the expanding role of consultation in the practice of school psychologists. *Psychology in the Schools, 54*, 581–595. https://doi.org/10.1002/pits.22020.

Baird, B. N. (2016). The *internship, practicum, and field placement handbook: A guide for the helping professions* (7th ed.). New York, NY: Routledge.

Barnett, J. E. (2008). Impaired professionals: Distress, professional impairment, self-care, and psychological wellness. In M. Hersen & A. M. Gross (Eds.), *Handbook of clinical psychology* (Vol. 1, pp. 857–884). Hoboken, NJ: Wiley and Sons.

Barnett, J. E., & Cooper, N. (2009). Creating a culture of self-care. *Clinical Psychology: Science and Practice, 16*, 16–20. http://dx.doi.org/10.1111/j.1468-2850.2009.01138.x.

Barnett, J. E., Cornish, J. A. E., Goodyear, R. K., & Lichtenberg, J. W. (2007). Commentaries on the ethical and effective practice of clinical supervision. *Professional Psychology: Research and Practice, 38*, 268–275. http://dx.doi.org/10.1037/0735-7028.38.3.268.

Barnett, J. E., & Goncher, I. D. (2014). Ethics issues in training students and supervisees. In W. B. Johnson & N. J. Kaslow (Eds.) *The Oxford handbook of education and training in professional psychology* (pp. 336–355). New York, NY: Oxford University Press.

Bateman, T. S., & Crant, J. M. (1993). The proactive component of organizational behavior: A measure and correlates. *Journal of Organizational Behavior, 14*, 103–118. http://dx.doi.org/10.1002/job.4030140202.

Bateman, T. S., & Crant, J. M. (1999). Proactive behavior: Meaning, impact, recommendations. *Business Horizons, 42*(3), 63–70.

Belar, C. D. (2009). Advancing the culture of competence. *Training and Education in Professional Psychology, 3*, S63–S65. http://dx.doi.org/10.1037/a0017541.

Benner, P. (1984). *From novice to expert: Excellence and power in clinical nursing practice.* Menlo Park, CA: Addison-Wesley.

Bernard, J. M., & Goodyear, R. K. (2019). *Fundamentals of clinical supervision* (4th ed.). New York, NY: Pearson.

Bindl, U. K., & Parker, S. K. (2011). Proactive work behavior: Forward-thinking and change oriented action in organizations. In S. Zedeck (Ed.), *APA handbook of industrial and organizational psychology* (Vol. 2, pp. 567–598). Washington, DC: American Psychological Association.

Boccio, D. E., Weisz, G., & Lefkowitz, R. (2016). Administrative pressure to practice unethically and burnout within the profession of school psychology. *Psychology in the Schools, 53*, 659–672. https://doi.org/10.1002/pits.21931.

Borders, L. D. (1991). A systemic approach to peer group supervision. *Journal of Counseling and Development, 69*, 248–252.

Brock, S. E., Nickerson, A. B., Reeves, M. L., Connolly, C., Jimerson, S. R., Pesce, R., & Lazzaro, B. (2016). *School crisis prevention and intervention: The PREPaRE model* (2nd ed.). Bethesda, MD: National Association of School Psychologists.

Bundy, M. L. (2016). Transitioning forward: From clinical experiences to a professional school counselor. In J. R. Studer (Ed.), *A guide to practicum and internship for school counselors-in-training* (2nd ed., pp. 259–273). New York, NY: Routledge.

Callahan, J. L., & Watkins, C. E., Jr. (2018). The science of training III: Supervision, competency, and internship training. *Training and Education in Professional Psychology, 12*, 245–261. http://dx.doi.org/10.1037/tep0000208.

Canady, B. E., Rivera, M., Gerdes, J., Ford, A., Johnson, K., & Nayak, N. (2011). Cultural roadmap: Developing cultural learning strategies during internship. *Training and Education in Professional Psychology, 5,* 30–37. http://dx.doi.org/10.1037/a0021856.

Caplan, G. (1970). *The theory and practice of mental health consultation.* New York, NY: Basic Books.

Castillo, J. M., & Curtis, M. J. (2014). Best practices in systems-level change. In P. L. Harrison & A. Thomas (Eds.), *Best practices in school psychology: systems-level services* (pp. 11–28). Bethesda, MD: National Association of School Psychologists.

Castillo, J. M., Curtis, M. J., & Tan, S. Y. (2014). Personnel needs in school psychology: A 10-year follow-up study on predicted personnel shortages. *Psychology in the Schools, 51,* 832–849. https://doi.org/10.1002/pits.21786.

Chafouleas, S. M., Clonan, S. M., & Vanauken, T. L. (2002). A national survey of current supervision and evaluation practices of school psychologists. *Psychology in the Schools, 39,* 317–325. https://doi.org/10.1002/pits.10021.

Clance, P. R., & Imes, S. A. (1978). The imposter phenomenon in high achieving women: Dynamics and therapeutic intervention. *Psychotherapy: Theory, Research and Practice, 15,* 241–247. http://dx.doi.org/10.1037/h0086006

Clay, R. A. (2015). *Your first salary.* Retrieved from https://www.apa.org/monitor/2015/12/first-salary.aspx.

Clopton, K. L., & Haselhuhn, C. W. (2009). School psychology trainer shortage in the USA: Current status and projections for the future. *School Psychology International, 30,* 24–42. https://doi.org/10.1177/0143034308101848.

Cochrane, W. S., Salyers, K., & Ding, Y. (2010). An examination of the preparation, supervisor's theoretical model, and university support for supervisors of school psychology interns. *Trainers' Forum: Journal of the Trainers of School Psychologists, 29*(1), 6–23.

Cokley, K., McClain, S., Enciso, A., & Martinez, M. (2013). An examination of the impact of minority status stress and impostor feelings on the mental health of diverse ethnic minority college students. *Journal of Multicultural Counseling and Development, 41,* 82–95. https://doi.org/10.1002/j.2161-1912.2013.00029.x.

Collins, J. (2001). *Good to great: Why some companies make the leap. . .and others don't.* New York, NY: Harper Collins.

Colman, A. M. (2015). *Oxford dictionary of psychology.* New York, NY: Oxford.

Cone, J. D., & Foster, S. L. (2006). *Dissertation and theses from start to finish* (2nd ed.). Washington, DC: American Psychological Association.

Corey, G., Haynes, R., Moulton, P., & Muratori, M. (2010). *Clinical supervision in the helping professions: A practical guide* (2nd ed.). Alexandria, VA: American Counseling Association.

Council of Directors of School Psychology Programs (2017). 2017 *CDSPP doctoral internship guidelines.* Retrieved from https://docs.google.com/viewer?a=v&pid=sites&srcid=Y2RzcHAubmV0fGhvbWV8Z3g6NTY1OGU3MDQ3NTZhMWJkYQ.

Counselman, E. F., & Weber, R. L. (2004). Organizing and maintaining peer supervision groups. *International Journal of Group Psychotherapy, 54,* 125–143. http://dx.doi.org/10.1521/ijgp.54.2.125.40391.

Crant, J. M., Hu, J., & Jiang, K. (2017). Proactive personality: A twenty-year review. In S. K. Parker & U. K. Bindl (Eds.). *Proactivity at work: Making things happen in organizations* (pp. 193–225). New York, NY: Routledge.

Crespi, T. D. (2010). Certification and licensure for school psychologists: Considerations and implications for education, training, and practice. In J. Kaufman, T. L. Hughes, & C. A. Riccio (Eds.), *Handbook of education, training, and supervision of school psychologists in school and community* (Vol. 2, pp. 229–244). New York, NY: Routledge.

Crespi, T. D., & Dube, J. M. B. (2005). Clinical supervision in school psychology: Challenges, considerations, and ethical and legal issues for clinical supervisors. *The Clinical Supervisor, 24*, 115–135. http://dx.doi.org/10.1300/J001v24n01_06.

Crespi, T. D., Fischetti, B. A., & Lopez, P. G. (1998). Supervision and mentoring for professional employment: Resumes and interviewing for prospective school psychologists. *School Psychology International, 19*, 239–250. https://doi.org/10.1177/0143034398193004.

Crespi, T. D., & Kaufman, J. (Eds.). (2004). Clinical supervision in the schools: Challenges, opportunities, and lost horizons [Special section]. *The Clinical Supervisor, 22*, 59–210.

Cruise, T. K., & Swerdlik, M. E. (2010). Problematic behaviors: Mediating differences and negotiating change. In J. Kaufman, T. L. Hughes, and C. Riccio (Eds.), *Handbook of education, training, and supervision of school psychologists in school and community* (Vol. 2, pp. 129–152). New York, NY: Routledge.

Csikszentmihalyi, M. (1990). *Flow: The psychology of optimal experience.* New York, NY: Harper Collins.

Curtis, M. J., Hunley, S. A., & Grier, J. E. C. (2002). Relationships among the professional practices and demographic characteristics of school psychologists. *School Psychology Review, 31*, 30–42.

Daly, E. J. III, Doll, B., Schulte, A. C., & Fenning, P. (2011). The competencies initiative in American professional psychology: Implications for school psychology preparation. *Psychology in the Schools, 48*, 872–886. https://doi.org/10.1002/pits.20603.

Daniel, J. H. (2009). Next generation: A mentoring program for black female psychologists. *Professional Psychology: Research and Practice, 40*, 299–305. http://dx.doi.org/10.1037/a0013891.

Darling-Hammond, L., Wei, R. C., Andree, A., Richardson, N., & Orphanos, S. (2009). *Professional learning in the learning profession: A status report on teacher development in the United States and abroad.* Dallas, TX: National Staff Development Council.

Deal, T. E., & Peterson, K. D. (2016). *Shaping school culture* (3rd ed.). San Francisco, CA: Jossey-Bass.

Deketelaere, A., Kelchtermans, G., Struyf, E., & De Leyn, P. (2006). Disentangling clinical learning experiences: An exploratory study on the dynamic tensions in internship. *Medical Education, 40*, 908–915. https://doi.org/10.1111/j.1365-2929.2006.02551.x.

Denicola, J. A., & Furze, C. T. (2001). The internship year: The transition from student to new professional. In S. Walfish & A. K. Hess (Eds.) *Succeeding in graduate school: The career guide for psychology students.* Mahwah, NJ: Erlbaum.

Doran, J. M., Kraha, A., Marks, L. R., Ameen, E. J., & El-Ghoroury, N. H. (2016). Graduate debt in psychology. *Training and Education in Professional Psychology, 10*, 3–13. http://dx.doi.org/10.1037/tep0000132.

Dubin, S. S. (1972). Obsolescence or lifelong education: A choice for the professional. *American Psychologist, 27*, 486–498. http://dx.doi.org/10.1037/h0033050.

Dweck, C. S. (2016). *Mindset: The new psychology of success* (Updated edition). New York, NY: Ballantine Books.

Edwards, J. K. (2017). Strengths-based clinical supervision: An examination of how it works. In J. K. Edwards, A. Young, & H. J. Nikels (Eds.). *Handbook of strengths-based clinical practices: Finding common factors* (pp. 253–274). New York, NY: Routledge.

Egodawatte, G., McDougall, D. & Stoilescu, D. (2011). The effects of teacher collaboration in Grade 9 applied mathematics. *Education Research for Policy and Practice, 10*, 189–209. https://doi.org/10.1007/s10671-011-9104-y.

Eklund, K., Aros-O'Malley, M., & Murrieta, I. (2014). Multicultural supervision: What difference does difference make? *Contemporary School Psychology*, *18*, 195–204. http://dx.doi.org/10.1007/s40688-014-0024-8.

El-Ghoroury, N. H., Galper, D. I., Sawaqdeh, A., & Bufka, L. F. (2012). Stress, coping, and barriers to wellness among psychology graduate students. *Training and Education in Professional Psychology*, *6*, 122–134. http://dx.doi.org/10.1037/a0028768.

Elizalde-Utnick, G. (2007). Young selectively mute English language learners: School-based intervention strategies. *Journal of Early Childhood and Infant Psychology*, *3*, 141–161.

Elman, N. S., & Forrest, L. (2007). From trainee impairment to professional competence problems: Seeking new terminology that facilitates effective action. *Professional Psychology: Research and Practice*, *38*, 501–509. doi:10.1037/0735-7028.38.5.501

Erdogan, B., & Bauer, T. N. (2005). Enhancing career benefits of employee proactive personality: The role of fit with jobs and organizations. *Personnel Psychology*, *58*, 859–891. https://doi.org/10.1111/j.1744-6570.2005.00772.x.

Ericsson, A., & Pool, R. (2016). *Peak: Secrets from the new science of expertise*. Boston, MA: Houghton Mifflin Harcourt.

Fagan, T. K. (2010). Putting school psychology training into historical perspective. What's new? What's old? In E. Garcia-Vázquez. T. D. Crespi, & C. A. Riccio (Eds.), *Handbook of education training, and supervision of school psychologists in school and community* (Vol. 1, pp. 13–31). New York, NY: Routledge.

Fagan, T. K., & Wise, P. S. (2007). *School psychology past, present, and future* (3rd ed.). Bethesda, MD: National Association of School Psychologists.

Falender, C. A., Cornish, J. A. E., Goodyear, R., Hatcher, R., Kaslow, N. J., Leventhal, G., . . . Grus, C. (2004). Defining competencies in psychology supervision: A consensus statement. *Journal of Clinical Psychology*, *60*, 771–785. https://doi.org/10.1002/jclp.20013.

Falender, C. A., & Shafranske, E. P. (2004). *Clinical supervision: A competency-based approach*. Washington, DC: American Psychological Association.

Falender, C. A., & Shafranske, E. P. (2017). *Supervision essentials for the practice of competency-based supervision*. Washington, DC: American Psychological Association.

Falender, C. A., Shafranske, E. P., & Falicov, C. J. (2014). *Multiculturalism and diversity in clinical supervision: a competency-based approach*. Washington, DC: American Psychological Association.

Farbman, D. A. (2015). *The case for improving and expanding time in school: A review of key research and practice*. Boston, MA: National Center on Time and Learning.

Fenning, P., Diaz, Y., Valley-Gray, S., Case, R., Spearman, C., Hazel, C. E., . . .Harris, A. (2015). Perceptions of competencies among school psychology trainers and practitioners: What matters? *Psychology in the Schools*, *52*, 1032–1041. https://doi.org/10.1002/pits.21877

Forrest, L., & Elman, N. S. (2014). Trainees with problems of professional competence. In W. B. Johnson, & N. J. Kaslow (Eds.). *The oxford handbook of education and training in professional psychology* (pp. 314–335). New York, NY: Oxford.

Forret, M. (2018). Networking as a job-search behavior and career management strategy. In U-C. Klehe & E. A. J. van Hooft (Eds). *The oxford handbook of job loss and job search* (pp. 275–291). New York, NY: Oxford.

Fouad, N. A., Grus, C. L., Hatcher, R. L., Kaslow, N. J., Hutchings, P. S., Madson, M., . . .Crossman, R. E. (2009). Competency benchmarks: A model for the understanding and measuring of competence in professional psychology across training levels. *Training and Education in Professional Psychology*, *3*, S5–S26. http://dx.doi.org/10.1037/a0015832.

Gambrill, E. (2012). *Critical thinking in clinical practice: Improving the quality of judgments and decisions* (3rd ed.). Hoboken, NJ: John Wiley and Sons.

Gelman, C. R., Fernandez, P., Hausman, N., Miller, S., & Weiner, M. (2007). Challenging endings: First year MSW interns' experiences with forced termination and discussion points for supervisory guidance. *Clinical Social Work Journal, 35*, 79–90. doi:10.1007/s10615-007-0076-6.

Gibson, D. M., Dollarhide, C. T. & Moss, J. M. (2010). Professional identity development: A grounded theory of transformational tasks of new counselors. *Counselor Education and Supervision, 50*, 21–38. http://dx.doi.org/10.1002/j.1556-6978.2010.tb00106.x.

Ginkel, R. W., Davis, S. E., & Michael, P. G. (2010). An examination of inclusion and exclusion criteria in the predoctoral internship selection process. *Training and Education in Professional Psychology, 4*, 213–218. http://dx.doi.org/10.1037/a0019453.

Goodyear, R. K., Borders, L. D., Chang, C. Y., Guiffrida, D. A., Hutman, H., Kemer, G., . . .White, E. (2016). Prioritizing questions and methods for an international and inter-disciplinary supervision research agenda: Suggestions by eight scholars. *The Clinical Supervisor, 35*, 117–154. https://doi.org/10.1080/07325223.2016.1153991.

Goodyear, R. K., & Rousmaniere, T. (2017). Helping therapists to each day become a little better than they were the day before: The expertise-development model of supervision and consultation. In T. Rousmaniere, R. K. Goodyear, S. D. Miller, and B. E. Wampold (Eds.), *The cycle of excellence: using deliberate practice to improve supervision and training* (pp. 67–95). Hoboken, NJ: John Wiley and Sons.

Gravois, J. (2007). You're not fooling anyone. *The Chronicle of Higher Education.* Retrieved from https://www.chronicle.com/article/Youre-Not-Fooling-Anyone/28069

Green, A. G., & Hawley, G. C. (2009). Early career psychologists: Understanding, engaging, and mentoring tomorrow's leaders. *Professional Psychology: Research and Practice, 40*, 206–212. doi:10.1037/a0012504.

Green, K. E. (1997). Psychosocial factors affecting dissertation completion. *New Directions for Higher Education, 99*, 57–64. https://doi.org/10.1002/he.9905.

Griffin, M. L., & Scherr, T. G. (2010). Using critical incident reporting to promote objectivity and self-knowledge in pre-service school psychologists. *School Psychology International, 31*, 3–20. https://doi.org/10.1177/0143034309341609.

Grus, C. L., Falender, C., Fouad, N. A., & Lavelle, A. K. (2016). A culture of competence: A survey of implementation of competency-based education and assessment. *Training and Education in Professional Psychology, 10*, 198–205. http://dx.doi.org/10.1037/tep0000126

Grus, C. L., & Kaslow, N. J. (2014). Professionalism: Professional attitudes and values in psychology. In W. B. Johnson, & N. J. Kaslow (Eds.). *The oxford handbook of education and training in professional psychology* (pp. 491–509). New York, NY: Oxford.

Guiney, M. C. (2018). Addressing problems of professional competence: Collaborating with university training programs to support struggling supervisees. *NASP Communiqué, 46*(6), 6–7.

Guiney, M. C. (2019). *The school psychology supervisor's toolkit.* New York, NY: Routledge.

Gutkin, T. B. (2012). Ecological psychology: Replacing the medical model paradigm for school-based psychological and psychoeducational services. *Journal of Educational and Psychological Consultation, 22*, 1–20. doi: 10.1080/10474412.2011.649652

Haboush, K. L. (2003). Group supervision of school psychologists in training. *School Psychology International, 24*, 232–255. https://doi.org/10.1177/0143034303024002007.

Hall, G. E., & Hord, S. M. (2010). *Implementing change: Patterns, principles, and potholes* (3rd ed.). Boston, MA: Allyn & Bacon.

Hall, J. E., Wexelbaum, S. F., & Boucher, A. P. (2007). Doctoral student awareness of licensure, credentialing, and professional organizations in psychology: The 2005 national register international survey. *Training and Education in Professional Psychology, 1,* 38–48. http://dx.doi.org/10.1037/1931-3918.1.1.38.

Hammer, E. D., & Hammer, E. Y. (2009). Maximizing your graduate training: Issues to think about from the start. In S. F. Davis, P. J. Giordano, & C. A. Licht (Eds.), *Your career in psychology: Putting your graduate degree to work* (pp. 3–12). Malden, MA: Wiley-Blackwell.

Hargreaves, A., & Fullan, M. (2012). *Professional capital: Transforming teaching in every school.* New York, NY: Teachers College Press.

Harris, B., & Sullivan, A. L. (2012). Faculty roles: A primer for students and professionals interested in careers in academia. *NASP Communiqué, 41*(2), 20–21.

Harrison, P. L. (2010). Continuing professional development: A foundation for the future of school psychology, *NASP Communiqué, 38*(5), 2.

Harrison, P. L., & Prus, J. S. (2008). Best practices in integrating *Best Practices V* content with NASP standards. In A. Thomas & J. Grimes (Eds.), *Best practices in school psychology V* (pp. 71–100), Bethesda, MD: National Association of School Psychologists.

Harvey, V. S., Amador, A., Finer, D., Gotthelf, D., Hintze, J., Kruger, L. . . .Wandle, C. (2010). Improving field supervision through collaborative supervision institutes. *NASP Communiqué, 38*(7), 22–24.

Harvey, V. S., & Pearrow, M. (2010). Identifying challenges in supervising school psychologists. *Psychology in the Schools, 47,* 567–581. https://doi.org/10.1002/pits.20491.

Harvey, V. S., & Struzziero, J. A., (2008). *Professional development and supervision of school psychologists: From intern to expert* (2nd ed.). Thousand Oaks, CA: Corwin Press.

Harvey, V. S., Struzziero, J. A., & Desai, S. (2014). Best practices in the supervision and mentoring of school psychologists. In P. L. Harrison & A. Thomas (Eds.). *Best practices in school psychology: Foundations* (pp. 567–580). Bethesda, MD: National Association of School Psychologists.

Hatcher, R. L., & Buchtel, H. A. (2016). Postdoctoral training in clinical psychology. In J. C. Norcross, G. R. VandenBoss, D. K. Freedheim, & Campbell, L. F. (Eds.), *APA Handbook of clinical psychology: Volume 5. Education and profession* (pp. 87–99). Washington, DC: American Psychological Association.

Hatcher, R. L., Fouad, N. A., Grus, C. L., Campbell, L. F., McCutcheon, S. R., & Leahy, K. L. (2013). Competency benchmarks: Practical steps toward a culture of competence. *Training and Education in Professional Psychology, 7,* 84–91. http://dx.doi.org/10.1037/a0029401.

Hebert, G. W. & Patterson, C. (2010). Collaborative supervision of internship experiences. In J. Kaufman, T. L. Hughes, & C. A. Riccio (Eds.), *Handbook of education, training, and supervision of school psychologists in school and community* (Vol. 2, pp. 55–70). New York, NY: Routledge.

Heppner, P. P., & Heppner, M. J. (2004). *Writing and publishing your thesis, dissertation, and research: A guide for students in the helping professions.* Pacific, CA: Brooks/Cole.

Hickey, A. M., Basch, B. J., & Huber, B. J. (in press). *Programming for professionalism in school psychology training.* Trainers' Forum: Journal of the Trainers' of School Psychologists.

Hill, B., Kubick, R., & York, J. (2011). *Getting and keeping your first job as a school psychologist.* Special Event presented at the annual convention of the National Association of School Psychologists, San Francisco, CA.

Hoff, S. (2006, Winter). Internship, a rite of passage. *New York School Psychologist. 24*(1), 10; 31. Retrieved from http://www.nyasp.org/newsletters/news2006winter.pdf.

Holloway, E. L. (1995). *Clinical supervision: a systems approach.* Thousand Oaks, CA: Sage.

Holloway, E. L., & Neufeldt, S. A. (1995). Supervision: Its contributions to treatment efficacy. *Journal of Consulting and Clinical Psychology, 63*, 207–213. doi:10.1037//0022-006X.63.2.207.

Hosp, J. L. & Reschly, D. J. (2002). Regional differences in school psychology practice. *School Psychology Review, 31*, 11–29.

Howard, E. E., Inman, A. G., & Altman, A. N. (2006). Critical incidents among novice counselor trainees. *Counselor Education and Supervision, 46*, 88–102. https://doi.org/10.1002/j.1556-6978.2006.tb00015.x.

Huebner, E. S. (1993). Burnout among school psychologists in the USA: Further data related to its prevalence and correlates, *School Psychology International, 14*, 99–109. https://doi.org/10.1177/0143034393142001.

Huebner, E. S., Gilligan, T. D., & Cobb, H. (2002). Best practices in managing stress and burnout. In A. Thomas & J. Grimes (Eds.), *Best practices in school psychology IV* (pp. 173–182), Bethesda, MD: National Association of School Psychologists.

Hughes, T. L., Kaufman, J., Crespi, T. D., Riccio, C. A., & García-Vázquez, E. (2010). Envisioning the future: Looking into the crystal ball. In J. Kaufman, T. L. Hughes, & C. A. Riccio (Eds.), *Handbook of education, training, and supervision of school psychologists in school and community* (Vol. 2, pp. 321–327). New York, NY: Routledge.

Hughes, T. L., Kaufman, J., & Hoover, S. A. (2010). Creating congruent change: Linking research to practice. In J. Kaufman, T. L. Hughes, & C. A. Riccio (Eds.), *Handbook of education, training, and supervision of school psychologists in school and community* (Vol. 2, pp. 309–319). New York, NY: Routledge.

Hutchins, H. M., & Rainbolt, H. (2017). What triggers imposter phenomenon among academic faculty? A critical incident study exploring antecedents, coping, and development opportunities. *Human Resource Development International, 20*, 194–214. https://doi.org/10.1080/13678868.2016.1248205.

Illinois School Psychology Internship Manual (2014). Retrieved from https://www.ilispa.org/assets/docs/ResourceLibrary/illinois-school-psychology-internship-manual-2014.pdf.

Jacobs, S. C., Huprich, S. K., Grus, L., Cage, E., Elman, N. S., Forrest, L., . . .Kaslow, N. J. (2011). Trainees with competence problems: Preparing trainers for difficult but necessary conversations. *Training and Education in Professional Psychology, 5*, 175–184. doi:10.1037/a0024656

Jimerson, S. R., Burns, M. K., & VanDerHeyden, A. (2016). From response to intervention to multi-tiered systems of support: Advances in the science and practice of assessment and intervention. In S. R. Jimerson, M. K. Burns, and A. M. VanDerHeyden (Eds.), *Handbook of response to intervention: The science and practice of multi-tiered systems of support* (2nd ed.; pp. 1–6). New York, NY: Springer.

Jones, J. M. (2009). *The psychology of multiculturalism in the schools: A primer for practice, training, and research.* Bethesda, MD: National Association of School Psychologists.

Joyce, B. R., & Showers, B. (1980). Improving inservice training: The messages of research. *Educational Leadership, 37*, 379–385.

Joyce, B. R., & Showers, B. (2002). *Student achievement through staff development* (3rd ed.). Alexandria, VA: Association for Supervision and Curriculum Development.

Joyce-Beaulieu, D., & Dixon, A. (2018). Preparing for a career in school psychology. In S. L. Grapin, and J. H. Kranzler (Eds.). *School psychology: Professional issues and practices* (pp. 233–250). New York, NY: Springer.

Justice, N., Murphy, J. M., & Newman, D. S. (2018). A deliberate practice framework for supervision in school psychology. *NASP Communiqué, 47*(2), 8; 10–11.

Kangos, K. A., Ellis, M. V., Berger, L., Corp, D. A., Hutman, H., Gibson, A., & Nicolas, A. I. (2018). American Psychological Association guidelines for clinical supervision: Competency-based implications for supervisees. *The Counseling Psychologist, 46,* 821–845. https://doi.org/10.1177/0011000018807128.

Kaslow, N. J. (2004). Competencies in professional psychology. *American Psychologist, 59,* 774–781. http://dx.doi.org/10.1037/0003-066X.59.8.774.

Kaslow, N. J., Grus, C. L., Campbell, L., Fouad, N. A., Hatcher, R. L., & Rodolfa, E. R. (2009). Competency assessment toolkit for professional psychology. *Training and Education in Professional Psychology, 3,* S27–S45. http://dx.doi.org/10.1037/a0015833.

Kaslow, N. J., & Rice, D. G. (1985). Developmental stresses of psychology internship training: What training staff can do to help. *Professional Psychology: Research and Practice, 16,* 253–261.

Kaslow, N. J., Rubin, N. J., Forrest, L., Elman, N. S., Van Horne, B. A., Jacobs, S. C., . . . Thorn, B. E. (2007). Recognizing, assessing, and intervening with problems of professional competence. *Professional Psychology: Research and Practice, 38,* 479–492. http://dx.doi.org/10.1037/0735-7028.38.5.479.

Kaufman, J. (2010a). Contemporary issues in supervision. In J. Kaufman, T .L. Hughes, & C. A. Riccio (Eds.), *Handbook of education, training, and supervision of school psychologists in school and community* (Vol. 2, pp. 19–35). New York, NY: Routledge.

Kaufman, J. (2010b). Creating a school psychology training program: The horse that became a camel, or what tail wags the dog? In E. Garcia-Vázquez. T. D. Crespi, & C. A. Riccio (Eds.), *Handbook of education training, and supervision of school psychologists in school and community* (Vol. 1, pp. 33–47). New York, NY: Routledge.

Kaufman, J. & Schwartz, T. (2004). Models of supervision: Shaping professional identity. *The Clinical Supervisor, 22,* 143–158. https://doi.org/10.1300/J001v22n01_10.

Kelly, R. M., Cruise, T. K., Swerdlik, M. E., Newman, D. S., & Simon, D. J. (2012). *School psychology intern supervisor training: a state-wide universal system – the Illinois model.* Poster presented at the annual convention of the Trainers of School Psychologists, Philadelphia, PA.

Klose, L. M., Plotts, C., & Lasser, J. (2010). Qualitative evaluation of school psychology consultation experiences. *Trainers' Forum: Journal of the Trainers of School Psychologists, 29,* 24–37.

Knoff, H. M. (1986). Supervision in school psychology: The forgotten or future path to effective services? *School Psychology Review, 15,* 529–545.

Krieshok, T. S., Lopez, S. J., Somberg, D. R., & Cantrell, P. J. (2000). Dissertation while on internship: Obstacles and predictors of progress. *Professional Psychology: Research and Practice, 31,* 327–331.

Ladany, N., & Friedlander, M. L. (1995). The relationship between the supervisory working alliance and trainees' experience of role conflict and role ambiguity. *Counselor Education and Supervision, 34,* 220–231. http://dx.doi.org/10.1002/j.1556-6978.1995.tb00244.x.

Ladany, N., Friedlander, M. L. & Nelson, M. L. (2016). *Supervision essentials for the critical events in psychotherapy supervision model.* Washington, DC: American Psychological Association.

Ladany, N., Hill, C. E., Corbett, M. M., & Nutt, E. A. (1996). Nature, extent, and importance of what psychotherapy trainees do not disclose to their supervisors. *Journal of Counseling Psychology, 43,* 10–24.

Ladany, N., Mori, Y., & Mehr, K. E. (2013). Effective and ineffective supervision. *The Counseling Psychologist, 41*, 28–47. https://doi.org/10.1177/0011000012442648.

Lamb, D. H., & Swerdlik, M. E. (2004). Identifying and responding to problematic school psychology supervisees: The evaluation process and issues of impairment. *The Clinical Supervisor, 22*, 87–110. https://doi.org/10.1300/J001v22n01_07.

Levitov, J. E., & Fall, K. A. (2009). *Translating theory into practice: A student guide to counseling practicum and internship.* Long Grove, IL: Waveland Press.

Lipton, R. B., Buse, D. C., Hall, C. B., Tennen, H., DeFreitas, T. A., Borkowski, T. M., . . . Haut, S. R. (2014). Reduction in perceived stress as a migraine trigger: Testing the "let-down headache" hypothesis. *Neurology, 82*, 1395–1401.

Little, S. G., & Akin-Little, K. A. (2004). Academic school psychologists: Addressing the shortage. *Psychology in the Schools, 41*, 451–459. http://dx.doi.org/10.1002/pits.10188.

Loganbill, C., Hardy, E., & Delworth, U. (1982). Supervision: A conceptual model. *The Counseling Psychologist, 10*, 3–42.

Lopez, E. C., & Rogers, M. R. (2010). Multicultural competence and diversity: University and field collaboration. In J. Kaufman, T. L. Hughes, and C. Riccio (Eds.), *Handbook of education, training, and supervision of school psychologists in school and community* (Vol. 2, pp. 111–128). New York, NY: Routledge.

Lucas-Thompson, R. G., Goldberg, W. A., & Prause, J. (2010). Maternal work early in the lives of children and its distal associations with achievement and behavior problems: A meta-analysis. *Psychological Bulletin, 136*, 915–942. http://dx.doi.org/10.1037/a0020875.

Marks, E. S. (1995). *Entry strategies for school consultation.* New York, NY: Guilford.

Maslach, C. (2003). Job burnout: New directions in research and intervention. *Current Directions in Psychological Science, 12*, 189–192. http://dx.doi.org/10.1111/1467-8721.01258.

Mastoras, S. M., & Andrews, J. J. W. (2011). The supervisee experience of group supervision: Implications for research and practice. *Training and Education in Professional Psychology, 5*, 102–111. http://dx.doi.org/10.1037/a0023567.

McCutcheon, S. R. (2009). Competency benchmarks: Implications for internship training. *Training and Education in Professional Psychology, 3*, S50–S53. http://dx.doi.org/10.1037/a0016966.

McIntosh, D. E., & Phelps, L. (2000). Supervision in school psychology: Where will the future take us? *Psychology in the Schools, 37*, 33–38. https://doi.org/10.1002/(SICI)1520-6807(200001)37:1<33::AID-PITS4>3.0.CO;2-F.

McMahon, C. M., Jenkins, J. E., & Styles, A. N. (2018). National survey of school psychology trainers' perspectives regarding the school psychology internship. *Trainers' Forum: Journal of the Trainers of School Psychologists, 35*(2), 48–59.

McNeill, B. W., & Stoltenberg, C. D. (2016). *Supervision essentials for the integrative developmental model.* Washington, DC: American Psychological Association.

Mehr, K. E., Ladany, N., & Caskie, G. I. L. (2015). Factors influencing trainee willingness to disclose in supervision. *Training and Education in Professional Psychology, 9*, 44–51. http://dx.doi.org/10.1037/tep0000028.

Merrell, K. W., Ervin, R. A., & Peacock, G. G. (2012). *School psychology for the 21st century: Foundations and practices.* New York, NY: Guilford.

Miller, D. C., DeOrnellas, K., & Maricle, D. (2010). What is so special about the specialist degree? In E. García-Vázquez, T. Crespi and C. Riccio (Eds.). *Handbook of education, training and supervision of school psychologists in school and community* (Vol. 1, pp. 49–61). New York, NY: Routledge.

Minke, K. M., & Rossen, E. (2018). Future of school psychology. In S. L. Grapin & J. H. Kranzler (Eds.), *School psychology: Professional issues and practices* (pp. 213–231). New York, NY: Springer Publishing Co.

Miranda, A. H. (2014). Best practices in increasing cross-cultural competency. In P. L. Harrison & A. Thomas (Eds.). *Best practices in school psychology: foundations* (pp. 9–19). Bethesda, MD: National Association of School Psychologists.

Morrison, E. W. (1993a). Longitudinal study of the effects of information seeking on newcomer socialization. *Journal of Applied Psychology, 78,* 173–183. http://dx.doi.org/10.1037/0021-9010.78.2.173.

Morrison, E. W. (1993b). Newcomer information seeking: Exploring types, modes, sources, and outcomes. *Academy of Management Journal, 36,* 557–589. https://doi.org/10.5465/256592.

Morrison, E. W. (1995). Information usefulness and acquisition during organizational encounter. *Management Communication Quarterly, 9,* 131–155. https://doi.org/10.1177/0893318995009002001.

Morrison, J. Q., & Harms, A. L. (2018). *Advancing evidence-based practice through program evaluation.* New York, NY: Oxford University Press.

Moss, J. M., Gibson, D. M., & Dollarhide, C. T. (2014). Professional identity development: A grounded theory of transformational tasks of counselors. *Journal of Counseling and Development, 92,* 3–12. http://dx.doi.org/10.1002/j.1556-6676.2014.00124.x.

Munsey, C. (2006). Helping colleagues to help themselves. *Monitor on Psychology, 37*(7), 35.

National Association of School Psychologists (2010a). *Model for comprehensive and integrated school psychological services.* Bethesda, MD: Author.

National Association of School Psychologists (2010b). *Principles for professional ethics.* Bethesda, MD: Author.

National Association of School Psychologists. (2010c). *Standards for the credentialing of school psychologists.* Bethesda, MD: Author.

National Association of School Psychologists. (2010d). *Standards for the graduate preparation of school psychologists.* Bethesda, MD: Author.

National Association of School Psychologists. (2014a). *Best practices guidelines for school psychology intern field supervision and mentoring.* Bethesda, MD: Author.

National Association of School Psychologists. (2014b). *Best practices guidelines for school psychology internships.* Bethesda, MD: Author.

National Association of School Psychologists. (2016). *Guidance for postgraduate mentorship and professional support.* Bethesda, MD: Author.

National Association of School Psychologists (2018). *Supervision in school psychology* (Position Statement). Bethesda, MD: Author.

National Association of School Psychologists (2019a). *National certification.* Retrieved from http://www.nasponline.org/standards-and-certification/national-certification.

National Association of School Psychologists (2019b). *State school psychology credentialing requirements.* Retrieved from http://www.nasponline.org/standards-and-certification/state-school-psychology-credentialing-requirements.

National School Reform Faculty (n.d.). *National school reform faculty resource book.* Bloomington, IN: Author.

Nebbergall, A. (2011). Alternative careers in school psychology: My experience in the field of education research. *NASP Communiqué, 39*(8), 10.

Neimeyer, G. J., Taylor, J. M., Rozensky, R. H., & Cox, D. R. (2014). The diminishing durability of knowledge in professional psychology: A second look at specializations. *Professional Psychology: Research and Practice, 45*(2), 92–98. http://dx.doi.org/10.1037/a0036176.

Neufeldt, S. A., Karno, M. P., & Nelson, M. L. (1996). A qualitative study of experts' conceptualizations of supervisee reflectivity. *Journal of Counseling Psychology, 43*, 3–9. http://dx.doi.org/10.1037/0022-0167.43.1.3.

Newman, D. S. (2012). A grounded theory of supervision of preservice consultation training. *Journal of Educational and Psychological Consultation, 22*, 247–279. https://doi.org/1 0.1080/10474412.2012.706127

Newman, D. S., Guiney, M., & Silva, A. E. (2017). Strengths-based supervision in school psychology: Accentuate the positive; eliminate the negative. *NASP Communiqué, 46*(1), 1; 21–23.

Newman, D. S., & Rosenfield, S. A. (2019). *Building competence in school consultation: A developmental approach.* New York, NY: Routledge.

Newman, D. S., & Shinn, M. R. (2014, Fall). *EPS 590 School Psychology Internship* [Course syllabus]. Skokie, IL: National Louis University.

Newman, D. S., Simon, D. J., & Swerdlik, M. E. (2019). What we know and do not know about supervision in school psychology: A systematic mapping and review of the literature between 2000 and 2017. *Psychology in the Schools, 56*, 306–334. https:// doi.org/10.1002/pits.22182.

Nichter, M., & Dowda, R. (2017). Strengths-based supervision: Experiences of supervisors and supervisees. In J. K. Edwards, A. Young, & H. J. Nikels (Eds.). *Handbook of strengths-based clinical practices: finding common factors* (pp. 305–322). New York, NY: Routledge.

Norcross, J. C., & VandenBos, G. R. (2018). *Leaving it at the office: A guide to psychotherapist self-care* (2nd ed.). New York, NY: Guilford.

Oberman, A. H., (2016). Understanding the accountability component of the ASCA National model as a school counselor-in-training. In J. R. Studer (Ed.), *A guide to practicum and internship for school counselors-in-training* (pp. 166–182). New York, NY: Routledge.

Olk, M. E., & Friedlander, M. L. (1992). Trainees' experiences of role conflict and role ambiguity in supervisory relationships. *Journal of Counseling Psychology, 39*, 389–397. http://dx.doi.org/10.1037/0022-0167.39.3.389.

O'Shaughnessy, T., & Burnes, T. R. (2016). The career adjustment experiences of women early career psychologists. *The Counseling Psychologist, 44*, 786–814. https:// doi.org/10.1177/0011000016650264.

Parker, S. K., & Bindl, U. K. (2017). Proactivity at work: A big picture perspective on a construct that matters. In S. K. Parker & U. K. Bindl (Eds.). *Proactivity at work: Making things happen in organizations* (pp. 1–20). New York, NY: Routledge.

Pedrotti, J. T., & Burnes, T. R. (2016). The new face of the field: Dilemmas for diverse early-career psychologists. *Training and Education in Professional Psychology, 10*, 141–148. http://dx.doi.org/10.1037/tep0000120.

Phelps, L., & Swerdlik, M. E. (2011). Evolving internship issues in school psychology preparation. *Psychology in the Schools, 48*, 911–921. https://doi.org/10.1002/pits.20602.

Plante, T. G. (1998). How to find a first job in professional psychology: Ten principles for finding employment for psychology interns and postdoctoral fellows. *Professional Psychology: Research and Practice, 33*, 494–498. http://dx.doi.org/10.1037/0735-7028.29.5.508.

Plotts, C. A., & Lasser, J. (2013). *School psychologist as counselor: A practitioner's handbook.* Bethesda, MD: National Association of School Psychologists.

Proctor, S. L., & Meyers, J. (2014). Best practices in primary prevention in diverse schools and communities. In P. Harrison & A. Thomas (Eds.), *Best practices in school psychology: foundations.* (pp. 33–47). Bethesda, MD: National Association of School Psychologists.

Proctor, S. L., & Rogers, M. R. (2013). Making the invisible visible: Understanding social processes within multicultural internship supervision. *School Psychology Forum: Research in Practice, 7*(1), 1–12.

Reynolds, C. R. (2011). Perspectives on specialization in school psychology training and practice. *Psychology in the Schools, 48*, 922–930. http://dx.doi.org/10.1002/pits.20598.

Richards, C. (2015, October 26). Learning to deal with the impostor syndrome. *The New York Times.* Retrieved from https://www.nytimes.com/2015/10/26/your-money/learning-to-deal-with-the-impostor-syndrome.html.

Roberts, M. C., Borden, K. A., Christiansen, M. D., & Lopez, S. J. (2005). Fostering a culture shift: Assessment of competence in the education and careers of professional psychologists. *Professional Psychology: Research and Practice, 36*, 355–361. doi:10.1037/0735-7028.36.4.355.

Romans, J. S. C, Boswell, D. L., Carlozzi, A. F., & Ferguson, D. B. (1995). Training and supervision practices in clinical, counseling, and school psychology programs. *Professional Psychology: Research and Practice, 26*, 407–412.

Rønnestad, M. H. & Skovholt, T. M. (2003). The journey of the counselor and therapist: Research findings and perspectives on professional development. *Journal of Career Development, 30*, 5–44. https://doi.org/10.1177/0894845303030000102.

Rønnestad, M. H. & Skovholt, T. M. (2013). *The developing practitioner: growth and stagnation of therapists and counselors.* New York, NY: Routledge.

Rossen, E. (2014). Best practices in national certification and credentialing in school psychology. In P. L. Harrison & A. Thomas (Eds.), *Best practices in school psychology: foundations* (pp. 541–552). Bethesda, MD: National Association of School Psychologists.

Rossen, E., Politikos, N. N., & Prus, J. S. (2018). Graduate preparation and credentialing. In S. L. Grapin & J. H. Kranzler (Eds.), *School psychology: professional issues and practices* (pp. 43–60). New York, NY: Springer Publishing Co.

Rudestam, K. E., & Newton, R. R. (2015). *Surviving your dissertation: A comprehensive guide to content and process* (4th ed.). Thousand Oaks, CA: Sage.

Russell, G. M., & Horne, S. G. (2009). Finding equilibrium: Mentoring, sexual orientation, and gender identity. *Professional Psychology: Research and Practice, 40*, 194–200. http://dx.doi.org/10.1037/a0011860.

Sakulku, J., & Alexander, J. (2011). The imposter phenomenon. *International Journal of Behavioral Science, 6*, 75–97. https://doi.org/10.14456/ijbs.2011.6.

Sarason, S. (1996). *Revisiting "The culture of the school and the problem of change."* New York, NY: Teachers College Press.

Sarason, S. (2003). The school culture and processes of change. In R. L. Fried (Ed.), *The skeptical visionary* (pp. 79–91). Philadelphia, PA: Temple University Press. (Original work published in 1969).

Schilling, E. J., Randolph, M., & Boan-Lenzo, C. (2018). Job burnout in school psychology: How big is the problem? *Contemporary School Psychology, 22*, 324–331. https://doi.org/10.1007/s40688-017-0138-x.

Schoen, M. (2001). *When relaxation is hazardous to your health.* Calabasas, CA: Mind Body Health Books.

Scott, J., Boylan, J. C., & Jungers, C. M. (2015). *Practicum and internship: textbook and resource guide for counseling and psychotherapy* (5th ed.). New York, NY: Routledge.

Seligman, M. E. P., & Csikszentmihalyi, M. (2000). Positive psychology: An introduction. *American Psychologist, 55*, 5–14. doi:10.1037/0003-066X.55.1.5.

Semrud-Clikeman, M. (1995). *Child and adolescent therapy.* Boston, MA: Allyn & Bacon.

Senge, P. M., Kleiner, A., Roberts, C., Ross, R. B., & Smith, B. J. (1994). *The fifth discipline fieldbook.* New York, NY: Currency-Doubleday.

Sheridan, S. M. & Gutkin, T. B. (2000). The ecology of school psychology: Examining and changing our paradigm for the 21st century. *School Psychology Review, 29,* 485–502.

Shinn, M. R., & Walker, H. M. (Eds.). (2010). *Interventions for achievement and behavior problems in a three-tier model including RTI.* Bethesda, MD: National Association of School Psychologists.

Silva, A., Newman, D. S., & Guiney, M. (2014). Best practices in early career transitions. In P. L. Harrison A. Thomas, & (Eds.), *Best practices in school psychology: Foundations* (pp. 553–566). Bethesda, MD: National Association of School Psychologists.

Silva, A. E., Newman, D. S., Guiney, M. C., Valley-Gray, S., & Barrett, C. A. (2016). Supervision and mentoring for early career school psychologists: Availability, access, structure, and implications. *Psychology in the Schools, 53,* 502–516. https://doi.org/10.1002/pits.21921.

Simon, D. J., Cruise, T. K., Huber, B. J., Swerdlik, M. E., & Newman, D. S. (2014). Supervision in school psychology: The developmental/ecological/problem-solving model. *Psychology in the Schools, 51,* 636–646. https://doi.org/10.1002/pits.21772.

Simon, D. J., & Swerdlik, M. E. (2017). *Supervision in school psychology: The developmental, ecological, problem-solving model.* New York, NY: Routledge.

Simon, D. J., Swerdlik, M. E., Cruise, T. K., & Stein, C. (in press). The ISPA supervisor credentialing program: a statewide training initiative in best practices in supervision. *Trainers' Forum: Journal of the Trainers of School Psychologists.*

Single, P. B. (2009). *Demystifying dissertation writing: a streamlined process from choice of topic to final text.* Sterling, VA: Stylus.

Smith, P. L., & Moss, S. B. (2009). Psychologist impairment: What is it, how can it be prevented, and what can be done to address it? *Clinical Psychology: Science and Practice, 16,* 1–15. https://doi.org/10.1111/j.1468-2850.2009.01137.x.

Solway, K. S. (1985). Transition from graduate school to internship: A potential crisis. *Professional Psychology: Research and Practice, 16,* 50–54. http://dx.doi.org/10.1037/0735-7028.16.1.50.

Sonnetag, S. (2016). Career proactivity. In S. K. Parker & U. K. Bindl (Eds.). *Proactivity at work: Making things happen in organizations* (pp. 49–76). New York, NY: Routledge.

Stedman, J. M., Hatch, J. P., & Schoenfeld, L. S. (2009). Letters of recommendation for the predoctoral internship in medical schools and other settings: Do they enhance decision making in the selection process? *Journal of Clinical Psychology in Medical Settings, 16,* 339–345. https://doi.org/10.1007/s10880-009-9170-y.

Sternberg, D. (1981). *How to complete and survive a doctoral dissertation.* New York, NY: St. Martin's Press.

Stevanovic, P., & Rupert, P. A. (2004). Career-sustaining behaviors, satisfactions, and stresses of professional psychologists. *Psychotherapy: Theory, Research, Practice, Training, 41,* 301–309. http://dx.doi.org/10.1037/0033-3204.41.3.301.

Stoltenberg, C. D. (2005). Enhancing professional competence through developmental approaches to supervision. *American Psychologist, 60,* 857–864. http://dx.doi.org/10.1037/0003-066X.60.8.85.

Stoltenberg, C. D., & Delworth, U. (1987). *Supervising counselors and therapists: A developmental approach.* San Francisco, CA: Jossey-Bass.

Strein, W. (1996). Professional supervision. In T. K. Fagan & P. G. Warden (Eds.), *Historical encyclopedia of school psychology* (pp. 297–298), Westport, CT: Greenwood Press.

Sue, D. W., Capodilupo, C. M., Torino, G. C., Bucceri, J. M., Holder, A. M. B., Nadal, K. L., & Esquilin, M. (2007). Racial microaggressions in everyday life: Implications for clinical practice. *American Psychologist, 62*, 271–286. http://dx.doi.org/10.1037/0003-066X.62.4.271.

Sugai, G., Horner, R. H., & Gresham, F. (2002). Behaviorally effective school environments. In M. R. Shinn, H. M. Walker, & G. Stoner (Eds.), *Interventions for academic and behavior problems II: Preventive and remedial approaches* (pp. 315–350). Bethesda, MD: National Association of School Psychologists.

Sullivan, J. R., & Conoley, J. C. (2008). Best practices in the supervision of interns. In A. Thomas & J. Grimes (Eds.), *Best practices in school psychology V* (pp. 1957–1974), Bethesda, MD: National Association of School Psychologists.

Sullivan, J. R., Svenkerud, N. & Conoley, J. C. (2014). Best practices in the supervision of interns. In P. L. Harrison & A. Thomas (Eds.), *Best practices in school psychology: Foundations* (pp. 527–540). Bethesda, MD: National Association of School Psychologists.

Swalwell, J., & Harvey, V. (2017). Provision of supervision and school psychologists' self-care. In M. Thielking, & M. D. Terjesen (Eds.), *Handbook of Australian school psychology* (pp. 737–755). Cham, Switzerland: Springer International Publishing.

Tamura, L. J., Vincent, W. L., Bridgeman, & Hanbury, R. F. (2008). *Psychologists' pursuit of wellness across the life span: Benefits and barriers to self-care practices.* Retrieved from https://www.apa.org/practice/resources/assistance/acca-2008-convention.pdf.

Tarquin, K. & Truscott, S. (2006). School psychology students' perceptions of their practicum experiences. *Psychology in the Schools, 43*, 727–736. http://dx.doi.org/10.1002/pits.20182.

Thomas, J. P. Whitman, D. S., & Viswesvaran, C. (2010). Employee proactivity in organizations: A comparative meta-analysis of emergent proactive constructs. *Journal of Occupational and Organizational Psychology, 82*, 661–682. doi:10.1348/096317910X502359.

Torki, R. N., & Nese, J. F. (2010). Acronyms in education. *NASP Communiqué, 38*(6), 34.

Turner, J. A., Edwards, L. M., Eicken, I. M., Yokoyama, K., Castro, J. R., Tran, A. N-T., & Haggins, K. L. (2005). Intern self-care: An exploratory study into strategy use and effectiveness. *Professional Psychology: Research and Practice, 36*, 674–680. doi:10.1037/0735-7028.36.6.674.

Wade, J. C., & Jones, J. E. (2015). *Strength-based clinical supervision: A positive psychology approach to clinical training.* New York, NY: Springer.

Walcott, C. M., & Hyson, D. (2018). *Results from the NASP 2015 membership survey, part one: Demographics and employment conditions* [Research report]. Bethesda, MD: National Association of School Psychologists.

Walker, H. M., & Shinn, M. R. (2010). Systemic, evidence-based approaches for promoting positive student outcomes within a multitier framework: Moving from efficacy to effectiveness. In M. R. Shinn & H. M. Walker, (Eds.), *Interventions for achievement and behavior problems in a three-tier model including RTI* (pp. 1–26). Bethesda, MD: National Association of School Psychologists.

Ward, S. B. (2001). Intern supervision in school psychology: Practice and process of field-based and university supervisors. *School Psychology International, 22*, 269–284. https://doi.org/10.1177/0143034301223004.

Wasik, B. H., Song, S., & Knotek, S. (2009). Preparing for careers in school psychology. In S. F. Davis, P. J. Giordano, & C. A. Licht (Eds.), *Your career in psychology: Putting your graduate degree to work* (pp. 231–244). Malden, MA: Wiley-Blackwell.

Watkins, C. E. (2011). Does psychotherapy supervision contribute to patient outcomes? Considering thirty years of research. *The Clinical Supervisor, 30,* 235–256. http://dx.doi.org/10.1080/07325223.2011.619417.

Webb, A. (2000). What makes it difficult for the supervisee to speak? In B. Lawton & C. Feltham (Eds.), *Taking supervision forward: Enquiries and trends in counseling and psychotherapy,* (pp. 60–73). London: Sage.

Wheeler, S., & Richards, K. (2007). The impact of clinical supervision on counsellors and therapists, their practice and their clients. A systematic review of the literature. *Counselling and Psychotherapy Research, 7,* 54–65. https://doi.org/10.1080/14733140601185274.

White, G. E. (2017). *The dissertation warrior: The ultimate guide to being the kind of person who finishes a doctoral dissertation or thesis.* Happy Valley, OR: Triumphant Heart International, Inc.

Wilbur, M. P., & Roberts-Wilbur, J., Hart, G. M., Morris, J. R., & Betz, R. L. (1994). Structured group supervision (SGS): A pilot study. *Counselor Education and Supervision, 33,* 262–279. http://dx.doi.org/10.1002/j.1556-6978.1994.tb00293.x.

Wilbur, M. P., Roberts-Wilbur, J., Morris, J. R., Betz, R. L., & Hart, G. M (1991). Structured group supervision: Theory into practice. *The Journal for Specialists in Group Work, 16*(2), 91–100. https://doi.org/10.1080/01933929108415593.

Williams-Nickelson, C., Prinstein, M. J., & Keilin, W. G. (2018). *Internships in psychology: The APAGS workbook for writing successful applications and finding the right fit* (4th ed.). Washington, DC: American Psychological Association.

Winerman, L. (2014). *Will you earn what you're worth?* Retrieved from https://www.apa.org/gradpsych/2014/04/salary.aspx.

Wise, E. H., & Barnett, J. E. (2016). Self-care for psychologists. In J. C. Norcross, G. R. VandenBos, D. K. Freedheim, & L. F. Campbell (Eds.), *APA handbooks in psychology. APA handbook of clinical psychology: Education and profession* (pp. 209–222). Washington, DC: American Psychological Association. http://dx.doi.org/10.1037/14774-014.

Ysseldyke, J. E., Burns, M. K., Dawson, M., Kelly, B., Morrison, D., Ortiz. . .Telzrow, C. (2006). *School psychology: A blueprint for training and practice III.* Bethesda, MD: National Association of School Psychologists.

Ysseldyke, J., Burns, M. K. & Rosenfield, S. (2009). Blueprints on the future of training and practice in school psychology: What do they say about educational and psychological consultation? *Journal of Educational and Psychological Consultation, 19,* 177–196. https://doi.org/10.1080/10474410903106448.

Ysseldyke, J. E., Dawson, P., Lehr, C., Reschly, D., Reynolds, M., & Telzrow, C. (1997). *School psychology: A blueprint for training and practice II.* Bethesda, MD: National Association of School Psychologists.

Ysseldyke, J. E., & Reschly, D. J. (2014). The evolution of school psychology: Origins, contemporary status, and future directions. In P. L. Harrison, and A. Thomas (Eds.), *Best practices in school psychology data-based and collaborative decision making* (pp. 71–84). Bethesda, MD: National Association of School Psychologists.

Ysseldyke, J. E., Reynolds, M., & Weinberg, R. A. (1984). *School psychology: A blueprint for training and practice.* Minneapolis, MN: University of Minnesota National School Psychology Inservice Training Network.

Zirkel, P. A. (2017). RTI and other approaches to SLD identification under the IDEA: A legal update. *Learning Disability Quarterly, 40,* 165–173. https://doi.org/10.1177/0731948717710778.

INDEX